SOCIAL MOVEMENTS
OF THE 1960s

Searching for Democracy

Doris Wilson gets foot treatment from Dr. June Finer during the
1965 Selma to Montgomery march. © *1978 Matt Herron*

SOCIAL MOVEMENTS OF THE 1960s

Searching for Democracy

Stewart Burns

Twayne Publishers
An Imprint of Simon & Schuster Macmillan
NEW YORK

Prentice Hall International
LONDON MEXICO CITY NEW DELHI SINGAPORE SYDNEY TORONTO

5\96

20560608

SOCIAL MOVEMENTS PAST AND PRESENT

Irwin T. Sanders, Editor

Cover photograph courtesy of Dave McReynolds/WRL.

Langston Hughes, "Harlem." Copyright 1948 by Alfred A. Knopf, Inc. Reprinted from *Selected Poems of Langston Hughes* by permission of Alfred A. Knopf, Inc., and copyright 1948 by Harold Ober Associates Inc., reprinted by permission of Harold Ober Associates Inc.

Poem by Audre Lord from *Sister Outsider*. Reprinted by permission of The Crossing Press.

John Lee Norris, "Just Another Page (September 13–72)," from *Betcha Ain't: Poems from Attica,* edited by Celes Tisdale. Reprinted by permission of Broadside Press.

Social Movements of the 1960s: Searching for Democracy
Stewart Burns

Copyright 1990 by Stewart Burns.
All rights reserved.
Published by Twayne Publishers
An Imprint of Simon & Schuster Macmillan
1633 Broadway, New York, New York 10019-6785
Copyediting supervised by Barbara Sutton.
Book Production by Gabrielle B. McDonald.
Typeset by Compset, Inc., of Beverly, Massachusetts.
Printed on permanent/durable acid-free paper
and bound in the United States of America.

Library of Congress Cataloging-in-Publication Data

Burns, Stewart.
Social movements of the 1960s : searching for democracy / Stewart Burns.
        p.   cm.—(Social movements past and present)
        Includes bibliographical references.
    1. United States—Social conditions—1960–1980.   2. Social
movements—United States—History.   3. Civil rights movements—
United States—History.   4. Radicalism—United States—History.
    5. Feminism—United States—History.   6. Democracy.   I. Title.
        II. Series.
        HN59.B97   1990
    303.48′4′09046—dc20   89-24644
                                                            CIP

ISBN 0-8057-9737-8 (alk. paper).   10 9 8 7 6 5 4 3 2
ISBN 0-8057-9738-6 (pbk.: alk. paper).   10 9 8 7 6
First published 1990

For my parents

Contents

About the Author

Stewart Burns is a social historian who has written widely about American social movements and their impact. His Ph.D. dissertation (University of California at Santa Cruz, 1984) offered a new interpretation of the Populist movement focusing on the interplay of movement-building and electoral politics. He has taught at the University of California at Santa Cruz and Berkeley and at Stanford University. In 1988 he served as scholar-in-residence at Western Gateway Heritage State Park in North Adams, Massachusetts, directing a federally funded, community oral history project on women electrical workers. He is currently assistant editor of the Martin Luther King, Jr., Papers Project at Stanford. A political activist since high school, Burns worked as an antiwar and draft resistance organizer during the Vietnam War and more recently has been active in movements against nuclear power and nuclear weapons.

Preface

During the era called the 1960s several million Americans engaged in making history. They acted beyond the usual bounds of citizenship to change social practices. Many aspired to create a new society. In the process they transformed their own lives. If they did not realize their dreams, they did shape the future—most concretely by abolishing legal segregation, ending the Vietnam War, dislodging racial and sexual discrimination, and altering traditional gender roles. Further changes occurred, especially cultural ones, that were less noticed or harder to measure. This legacy of public activism has inspired many others to make history in less favorable times since.

The meaning of the 1960s is hotly contested. Movement veterans, liberals, and leftists disagree about many aspects of the period but regard the claims of the social movements as fundamentally just. Though going too far in certain ways, or not far enough, the movements bettered American society. Taken as a whole, the movements represented an unprecedented outpouring of genuine democracy. Conservative critics see 1960s activism differently. These crusades for peace and freedom, they say, constituted an "excess of democracy" and a serious crisis for liberal government.[1] The unbridled passion to realize American ideals threatened the survival of democratic institutions. The movements not only generated explosive expectations impossible to fulfill, but precipitated the tragic decline of American global power, with severe long-term consequences. The two sides draw opposing lessons. The left (broadly defined) believes that to solve big problems such as militarism, racism, and sexism, or crises of the economy, environment, and health, democracy needs to be expanded and deepened. The right insists that this only makes things worse; echoing James Madison in the *Federalist Papers,* it argues that democracy must be restrained for the sake of stability.

This volume is a history of the four main social movements of the 1960s and early 1970s. It is also about democracy and its potential. An underlying assumption is that throughout American history two different kinds of democracy have tensely coexisted. Americans are more accustomed to electoral-representative democracy, the politics of elections and interest-group lobbying, of bargaining and compromise. But the alternative tradition of grass-roots democracy, I would argue, has had a greater impact on historical change. This tradition, grounded in principled activism, moral passion, and commitment to substantive purposes, is the characteristic political expression of social movements, radical, liberal, or conservative. The two traditions have sometimes coalesced, but more often, as the Mississippi Freedom Democratic party discovered in 1964, they conflict. During the 1960s more than any other period, perhaps, grass-roots democracy eclipsed its rival.

A map of the contents: Chapter 1 looks at the black freedom movement in the Deep South (mid-1950s to mid-1960s) and touches on the later Black Power movement in Northern cities. Chapter 2 covers two movements that overlapped—the student-oriented New Left and the broader movement it spawned to stop the Vietnam War; a middle section explores the interrelationship of the New Left and the "counterculture." Chapter 3 discusses the feminist movement, from its origins in the black movement and New Left to its full flowering in the mid-1970s. Chapter 4 assesses the effectiveness of these movements in bringing about positive change. Chapter 5 examines a number of issues that help to explain why the movements declined and speculates about alternative paths that might have been pursued.

This study puts social movements—organized, nongovernmental efforts of large numbers of people to attain significant social and personal change—at the center of history. This is particularly appropriate for the 1960s, when presidents, politicians, and the higher leadership circles played lesser roles, responding to and trying to manage change but not initiating it. The book views the historical process more from the bottom up than from the top down. As much as space permits, movement leaders and grass-roots activists speak in their own words. Emphasis is on the linkages between the movements, their common threads, their influences on each other, and above all, the profound impact of the black movement, and black culture, on the New Left, feminism, and the era as a whole. Another theme is the creative tension between the different branches or submovements within each larger movement and how such internal conflicts were played out.

This is a long agenda for a short book. Much has been left out or abbreviated. Close attention is paid to crucial events, developments, and turning points, and to situations deemed typical; some worthy organizations and events, and many individuals, do not get equal time. Matters of less significance are looked at more generally, or summarized. No effort has been made to paint with even brush strokes. A historian, like an activist, has to set priorities and make hard choices. A few further qualifications: First, the term *1960s* is both a historical symbol and a convenient shorthand and should not be taken literally; the era spills out of this decade at both ends. The account begins in 1955 and ends twenty years later. Second, only the major mass movements are covered; others that emerged toward the end of this period, notably for Hispanic and Indian rights, gay liberation, and ecology, call for separate treatment. Third, although these movements took place within a global context of student, youth, and feminist revolt, especially in the West, this study stays within American borders, by and large omitting international connections. Fourth, while informed by sociological theory about social movements, the book does not make explicit reference to it. Theorizing about history is inherently problematic. From Marx onward diverse theories about social movement causation, development, and decline have contributed greatly to understanding this complex subject, using models of class conflict, structural strain, relative deprivation, resource mobilization, and so forth. But they have limitations that give pause to the historian whose capacity to discern patterns and draw analogies is grounded in a respect for contingency and unpredictability. In searching for generality such theories tend to gloss over the particular textures that give movements much of their meaning.

Each of the 1960s' movements had its own specific causes. The black freedom movement arose as a result of economic and demographic changes in the South, especially agricultural displacement and migration to cities; World War II employment and military service that heightened black confidence and expectations; the legal battles of the National Association for the Advancement of Colored People (NAACP), culminating in the 1954 Supreme Court decision banning public school desegregation; the concentration of black youth in (segregated) Southern colleges; and the inspiration of African independence struggles. The New Left and the antiwar movement were catalyzed by the tremendous expansion of the student population during the 1960s, the draft, and the relentless war itself, with its mounting casualties and costs. The "second wave" of feminism gathered force from the rapid growth of female employment that started during World War II, producing new expectations and new grievances; renewed social pressures after the war to keep women at home and to reinvigorate domestic roles and values; and preexisting networks of older female activists in federal and state bureaucracies and younger ones in the Southern freedom movement and the New Left.

These are the trees but not the forest. Broader causative factors influencing the whole era were shared by all the movements and provide a historical context that linked and intensified the more specific factors. Fundamental were the organizing principles of American society as it was reshaped by the Great Depression, global war, and the nation's response to these crises. An implicit postwar "charter," or social contract, came into being: unwritten rules to govern the new social order driven by massive industrial and technological growth, global economic ascendance, and a permanent war economy. The gist of the new social contract was a promise of middle-class prosperity for hard-working white males in the professions and unionized industry in exchange for conformity, for not questioning authority. The majority of citizens were not granted this tacit entitlement—less skilled, nonunion workers, especially in the service sector; blacks and other racial minorities; and women, many of whom benefited indirectly as housewives but paid a big price in self-worth. As a result of the "deepening sense of exclusion, constraint, and disillusionment" experienced by these overlapping groups, Richard Flacks concludes that "by the sixties structural and cultural frameworks designed to establish social stability instead set the stage for new forms of upheaval, protest, and conflict."[2] Thus the limitations of the postwar charter helped to generate large-scale movements that eventually nullified it.

Ever since the crusade to abolish slavery, a recurring impetus behind social movements in the United States has been the clash between the values of the "American creed" that furnishes a national identity for Americans—liberty, individualism, democracy, constitutionalism, and equality—and social realities, such as oppression of black people and women, that trampled on these ideals.[3] Partly because of movement efforts, the founding values not only have been kept alive for two centuries but have been redefined and expanded by new generations. In the 1960s the glaring contrast between textbook ideals of freedom and equal opportunity on the one hand and unabated racial and sexual subjugation on the other, along with conscription and an unjust war, impelled many blacks, women, and youth to close the gap between ideal and reality. Adding fuel to the fire, the postwar charter and the "affluent society" molded by it nourished the dream of unfettered self-expression and self-fulfillment embedded in the American creed, whose realization was more possible, for more people, than ever before. Such aspirations, reinforced by the consumption needs of advanced capitalism, collided with older capitalist values—the "Protestant ethic" of hard work, thrift, and deferred gratification—as well as with the increasing bureaucratization of American life. These "cultural contradictions" were probably the most decisive cause of the movements of the 1960s.[4]

Deserving mention is one other factor that had little to do with the origins of these movements but much to do with their growth and decline: the power of the mass media, especially network television. These were the first movements to enjoy the mixed blessing of the age of video. The media "framed," distorted, and often trivialized their political messages, but also transmitted them to a vast nationwide (and international) audience that comprised a majority of the American public. They became mass movements in some measure because of the mass constituency they thus gained access to. But when the media lost interest and turned off the lights, their decline was all the more precipitous.

I wish to express gratitude to a number of people who aided and abetted the making of this book. First, I want to thank Irwin Sanders, the series editor, and Twayne editor Athenaide Dallett, for their support and thoughtful suggestions. Over the past decade John H. Schaar and Barbara Epstein, both of the University of California at Santa Cruz, have deepened my thinking about American social movements. Clayborne Carson of Stanford University has taught me important things about African-American history and made available key source materials on the black freedom movement. Deborah Burns offered helpful editorial advice. Richard Flacks of the University of California at Santa Barbara, Larry Casalino, and Randy Schutt made trenchant criticisms of the manuscript that enabled me to see things in new ways. For many years Flacks has been my most valued guide in studying the dynamics of recent movements. James MacGregor Burns of Williams College has taught me a great deal about writing history and afforded me unusual opportunities to practice the craft. Jane Benson's insights about radical feminism, creative counsel, and keen judgment made a substantial contribution. All the errors, of course, are mine. Finally, I want to acknowledge all the veterans of these movements, living or dead, whose courage and commitment give us hope.

Stewart Burns

Chapter One

We Shall All Be Free

My Soul Is Rested

In August 1955 a fourteen-year-old black youth from Chicago visited relatives near Greenwood, Mississippi, gateway to the flat, fertile, cotton-rich Delta. Emmett Till had once had polio and had a speech defect as a result. After buying some candy at a rural store in Money, the high-spirited boy allegedly said "Bye, baby" to the white female proprietor. Hardly a more serious crime existed in the canons of Jim Crow justice. Three days later, after midnight, her husband and brother dragged him from the cabin where he was staying to a barn at a nearby plantation, where they found a photo of a white girl in his wallet. Unfamiliar with Southern etiquette, he told them she was his girlfriend. The men beat him savagely, shot him through the head, cut off his testicles, and dumped him in the Tallahatchie River with a heavy cotton gin fan wired to his neck. Till's mutilated body somehow bobbed to the surface and was discovered by a white teenager fishing. The killers, who later confessed, were acquitted. The case drew a surprising degree of national publicity. Why all this fuss over a dead nigger in the Tallahatchie? asked a white Mississippian. "That river's full of niggers."[1] It was a particularly barbaric example of a "normal" practice of white repression by which at least 4,000 black people had been lynched since Reconstruction. Lynching was the core of a violent system of social control that sanctioned beatings, bombings, and other terrorism to make black people afraid to assert their rights.

Legal slavery had been abolished by the Thirteenth Amendment at the close of the Civil War, but in the century that followed white Southerners had fought to preserve its psychological, social, and economic foundations by other means. After the plantation economy collapsed—in part because "freed" blacks refused to continue laboring under slavery-like conditions—Southern oligarchs imposed a new system of official segregation to restore their control. The Fourteenth Amendment, which ostensibly guaranteed black people "equal protection of the laws," was used by the Supreme Court in 1896 to put a national stamp of approval on mandatory segregation as long as it was "separate but equal." The *Plessy v. Ferguson* ruling signified the expiration of the "first cycle" of black struggles for civil rights, which had reached its zenith during the Reconstruction era.

Just when Southern whites succeeded in reconsolidating their hold over the black population, the worldwide demand for the South's agriculture, especially cotton, plummeted and it became increasingly mechanized. These changes pushed many black sharecroppers and farm laborers off the land into Southern cities. The expansion of Northern industry fueled by World War I generated a mass migration of several million black people to the North by the end of the next world war—one of the largest migrations in human history. "In the course of a few decades," write Frances Fox Piven and Richard Cloward, "a depressed southern rural peasantry had been transformed into a depressed urban proletariat" in both the North and the South.[2] Whatever small economic strides blacks made during the 1920s were reversed by the Great Depression, and New Deal relief and job programs did not help much. Those black families who had stayed on the land in the South were hurt by federal farm policies favoring big growers. War production and military service helped many blacks escape from poverty. (President Roosevelt instituted fair hiring rules in the defense industry after black labor leader A. Philip Randolph threatened a march on Washington in 1941.) As peace broke out and black veterans returned with new self-esteem, expectations rose for greater advances in the postwar era. Two new circumstances made black freedom more auspicious: the diminished need of dominant economic interests to preserve the Jim Crow system, since blacks had become somewhat marginal to Southern agriculture; and the difficulty faced by the federal government in winning the allegiance of Third World nations, especially in Africa, while graphic racial subjugation still existed in the United States. The main barrier was no longer economic forces but entrenched racism itself—and the white power structures, state and local, that depended on it.

Southern black people never ceased fighting for their rights, despite the stranglehold of institutionalized "white supremacy" tacitly supported by Northern elites. But protests were sporadic, small-scale, and generally unnoticed beyond the locality. As before, "legal" and extralegal violence, or threats of it, hounded those who did not fully obey the rigid code of conduct.

The National Association for the Advancement of Colored People (NAACP), founded in 1909 by path-breaking black scholar W. E. B. Du Bois and others (replacing the unsuccessful National Afro-American League), resolved to focus on fulfilling the constitutional promise of the Fourteenth and Fifteenth amendments by taking a juridical approach aimed at civil and political (but not economic) rights for African-Americans; this approach created the framework for the later freedom movement. It distanced itself from the then-popular philosophy of Booker T. Washington, which stressed moral and economic uplift rather than legal rights. The NAACP devoted the next half-century to fighting within the federal courts for freedom, in particular by doggedly pursuing test cases that challenged segregation in education. In the 1930s and 1940s the other main organizational support for black rights came from the Communist party; consequently, a number of leading black reformers like Du Bois, actor/singer Paul Robeson, and novelist Richard Wright gravitated toward it.

The NAACP's ultimate triumph was the unanimous Supreme Court decision in May 1954, *Brown v. Board of Education of Topeka, Kansas,* which nullified *Plessy v. Ferguson* and declared public school segregation unconstitutional (and, by implication, *all* segregation). It is probable that the ruling would not have been reached, and certainly not with unanimity, had it not been followed by an order to integrate schools gradually—"with all deliberate speed"—which was in fact what happened. Still, the historic decision triggered "massive resistance" to ending Jim Crow by state and local politicians and the newly formed White Citizens Councils, all of whom employed legal maneuvers, economic reprisals, and outright defiance. The resurgent Ku Klux Klan and its kin resorted to covert terror.

The same month that Emmett Till was killed, Rosa Parks, a forty-two-year-old black woman from Alabama, took part in a workshop on racial integration at the Highlander Folk School in the Appalachian Mountains of Tennessee. Long active in civil rights work, she had served for years as an officer of the Montgomery chapter of the NAACP, had organized the local NAACP Youth Council (whose members had tried to desegregate city buses), and had been secretary of the Alabama NAACP. Highlander had been started in the depth of the Depression by an indomitable, witty white man named Myles Horton, born and bred in the poverty of Appalachia, who burned with desire to help poor people gain power to improve their lives. Highlander became a key training center for Southern community activists and labor organizers. Like a modern-day Socrates, Horton would fire one question after another at workshop participants to enable them to find answers to social problems from their own experience, then would teach them how to use this method to develop grass-roots leadership and activism.

Parks was deeply affected by her visit to the mountain retreat, which at that time was mainly devoted to supporting civil rights agitation. She experienced Highlander as a microcosm of a racially integrated society: "I found out for the first time in my adult life that this could be a unified society, that there was such a thing as people of differing races and backgrounds meeting together in workshops and living together in peace and harmony. . . . I gained there strength to persevere in my work for freedom."[3]

Four months later, in the early evening of 1 December 1955, Rosa Parks climbed on a city bus after working hard all day at her tailoring job in a big Montgomery department store next to historic Court Square, once a center of slave auctions and the first capitol of the Confederacy. The square sparkled with Christmas lights, and a bright banner declared, "Peace on Earth, Goodwill to Men." She sat down in a row between the "white only" section and the rear seats reserved for "colored"; custom was that blacks could sit in the midsection if the back was filled. Soon a white man got on the crowded bus and the driver—who a decade before had ejected Parks for refusing to enter through the back door—ordered her and three other black passengers to stand so that the white man could sit alone. The others reluctantly got up but Parks did not budge; she was put off by the driver's command, since she believed she was not violating the law. He called the police, but she felt no fear. She was taken to jail and convicted of breaking the segregation code. Parks had not planned her quiet protest but had prepared well for it. "I had almost a life history of being rebellious against being mistreated because of my color," she recalled. On this occasion more than others, "I felt that I was not being treated right and that I had a right to retain the seat that I had taken. . . . The time had just come when I had been pushed as far as I could stand to be pushed. . . . I had decided that I would have to know once and for all what rights I had as a human being and a citizen."[4]

Parks was bailed out by E. D. Nixon, an older activist who had been president of both the local and state NAACP, worked as a Pullman porter on the train to Chicago, and served as a regional officer of the Brotherhood of Sleeping Car Porters founded by A. Philip Randolph. Considered by associates the "most militant man in town," he was the backbone of civil rights activity in Montgomery. Parks had worked closely with him for years; it was he who had arranged for her to do the Highlander workshop.[5] Nixon had been waiting for just such a test case to challenge the constitutionality of the bus segregation law that had inflicted so much daily injustice on most of Montgomery's black population. Two women had been arrested for similar "crimes" in the past year, including a fifteen-year-old high school student, but those cases did not seem promising. Parks was ideal—no one had more respect in the black community. "If ever there was a woman who was dedicated to the cause," Nixon recalled, "it was Rosa Parks."[6]

Word of her arrest spread quickly to members of the Women's Political Council, a superbly organized civil rights group of black professional women led by Jo Ann Robinson, a dynamic English professor at the black Alabama State College. Daughter of a poor Georgia farmer, she herself had been mistreated by a white bus driver six years before; with her humiliation turned to anger, she had been challenging the bus law through "proper channels" ever since, to no avail. The council had been planning a bus boycott for months and decided the time had come. Members stayed up all night after Parks's arrest mimeographing thousands of leaflets at Robinson's office and with the help of her students handed them out all over town. The women contacted Nixon, who agreed to spearhead the effort. He came home, took a sheet of paper, and drew a rough sketch of the city, measuring distances with a slide rule. "I discovered nowhere in Montgomery at that time a man couldn't walk to work if he wanted to." He said to his wife: "We can beat this thing."[7]

Nixon knew that to have any chance of success the boycott had to get the united support of black ministers, the traditional leaders of black communities. He called them one by one, starting with Ralph Abernathy, the passionate young pastor of the First Baptist Church who had an earthy sense of humor and a "gift of laughing people into positive action." Abernathy thought the boycott was a great idea.[8] Third on the list was twenty-six-year-old Dr. Martin Luther King, Jr., the new minister of the reputable Dexter Avenue Baptist Church who had lived in Montgomery for only a year. "Brother Nixon," he replied, "let me think about it awhile, and call me back." When Nixon did so, King was enthusiastic. "I'm glad you agreed," Nixon said, "because I already set the meeting up to meet at your church."[9]

King had grown up in Atlanta, the son of a prosperous minister of one of the largest Baptist congregations in the country. Despite his prominent position among Atlanta's blacks and his influence with the white power structure, "Daddy" King was incensed by segregation and led efforts against it in the 1930s, including a voting rights march to City Hall. He ruled his home "like a fierce Old Testament patriarch," frequently whipping his kids, but Martin Jr. admired him, declaring him to have been "a real father to me."[10] Second child and first son, Martin was a gifted boy with a quick mind who excelled at everything—schoolwork, sports (especially wrestling), dancing, debating, oratory. From age six he soloed hymns at church services and conventions, and by his early teens his voice had matured into a rich, deep baritone that awed his listeners in song or speech.

Wounded by the barbs of segregation yet motivated by his mother's constant counsel to believe he was "somebody," he resolved to improve the lives of black people—but how? In adolescence he rebelled against Daddy King's demand that he also become a minister but eventually changed his mind and, fully trained at eighteen, was installed as assistant pastor of his father's church. After graduating from Atlanta's Morehouse College a year later, he attended Crozer Seminary in Pennsylvania and earned his doctorate at Boston University, where he scrutinized the whole gamut of Western philosophy and theology and searched for ways to translate the ideas that inspired him, from Social Gospel to Reinhold Niebuhr, into an effective method of social change. Hired to take over the middle-class Montgomery church, he moved there with his wife Coretta Scott King, a talented singer who had given up a musical career to marry him. By the time of Nixon's call, King had dabbled in civil rights work and had considered running for president of the local NAACP.

The 2 December meeting of black leaders at King's church decided unanimously to organize a bus boycott. By meticulous organizing, the joined networks of the Women's Political Council and the black ministers spread the message to virtually all of Montgomery's 50,000 black citizens that weekend, especially at Sunday services. On Monday morning, 5 December, barely a dozen black people got on the buses. Thousands rode cut-rate cabs, horse-drawn wagons, and mules, or walked. Day one was successful beyond anyone's expectations. A community meeting had been called at the Holt Street Baptist Church, the city's largest, that night, and the boycott leaders gathered beforehand to plan. They created an organization to coordinate the protest—Abernathy named it the Montgomery Improvement Association—and King was elected president unopposed. This was partly because he was new to the community and free from involvement in divisive conflicts that had weakened local leadership, and partly because his oratorical gifts were already respected by his colleagues. The parley left it to the mass meeting to decide whether the boycott would continue.

When King got home he had twenty minutes to prepare what he thought would be "the most decisive speech of my life," one that had to not only fire up his audience but blend militance with moderation.[11] Feeling paralyzed, overcome by anxiety and inadequacy, he prayed; then he hurriedly sketched an outline and tore off to the church, which was overflowing long before starting time. As the meeting opened with "Onward, Christian Soldiers" and other spirituals, 5,000 black people patiently stood outside in the cold night listening to the meeting through loudspeakers. "I've never heard singing like that," said a reporter. "They were on fire for freedom."[12]

After prayers and scripture readings King walked to the pulpit, gazed out at the television cameras, put aside his scribbled notes, and gave an electrifying speech that retold the story of Parks and all others who had been abused on the buses, exhorted the boycotters to use persuasion and not coercion, and ended by proclaiming: "If you will protest courageously, and yet with dignity and Christian love, when the history books are written in future generations, the historians will have to pause and say, 'There lived a great people—a black people—who injected new meaning and dignity into the veins of civilization.' This is our challenge and our overwhelming responsibility."[13] His words were greeted with long, loud applause, which erupted again when Parks was introduced and everyone acclaimed their hero. Abernathy read the boycott demands, and with ecstatic spirit all stood up to affirm that they would not ride the buses until the demands were met. Wild cheering echoed from inside and out. King wrote that the real victory had already been won in this first great meeting of the freedom movement, "where thousands of black people stood revealed with a new sense of dignity and destiny."[14]

When the city prohibited the black-run taxis from lowering their fares, the Women's Political Council constructed a remarkably efficient car pool system—modeled on one used in a successful Baton Rouge boycott three years before—that became the critical tool to sustain the protest. The small army of drivers included ministers, businesspeople, teachers, laborers, students, and homemakers. Private cars, pickup trucks, and a fleet of shiny, brand-new, church-owned station wagons collected passengers at forty-eight dispatch stations—many of which were churches, where passengers could stay warm at dawn—and brought them back to the stations after work. Hymns wafted out the car windows as these "rolling churches" criss-crossed the city with what the arch-segregationist White Citizens Council admitted was "military precision."[15] Some preferred to walk, as far as twelve miles a day, to underline their determination and hope. "I'm not walking for myself," said an elderly woman turning down a ride. "I'm walking for my children and my grandchildren." Another woman, Mother Pollard, vowed to King that she would walk until it was over. "But aren't your feet tired?" he asked. "Yes," she said, "my feets is tired, but my soul is rested."[16]

Mass meetings were held twice weekly, rotating between churches, and along with prayers and passionate singing of spirituals, the ministers took turns giving rousing "pep talks" to inform and fortify the participants. As King put it, "Christ furnished the spirit and motivation, while Gandhi furnished the method."[17] King had been attracted to nonviolent doctrines since he had first read Thoreau's essay on civil disobedience as a college student at Morehouse, and he had learned about Gandhi at Crozer; but it was all intellectual until Rosa Parks made it real for him. Tutored by Bayard Rustin and Glenn Smiley, experienced Gandhian activists from the Fellowship of Reconciliation, and later by James Lawson, King got a quick education in the theory and practice of *satyagraha,* or truth force (literally translated, "clinging to the truth").[18] He and his colleagues turned the church meetings into schools of nonviolent resistance, explaining it as "Christianity in action," and ran workshops to train people in direct action techniques. As sociologist Aldon Morris points out, the "religious doctrines of the black church provided the ideological framework" within which the nonviolent philosophy was communicated.[19] Though King came to accept nonviolence as an entire worldview and way of life, most participants in the freedom movement then and later, having been subjected to years of personal and institutionalized violence, had to make a leap of faith to go along with it even as a tactic. Moments arose during the year-long boycott in Montgomery when participants' commitment to tactical nonviolence was sorely tested by the white bombings of ten homes and churches.

The public demands of the boycott for fairer treatment were moderate and could have been implemented without even changing the segregation law, but the intransigent mayor and commissioners tried every trick to preserve the precarious status quo—ploys to divide the leaders from each other and their followers, concocting a bogus settlement, and mass prosecution of King and ninety others. Yet the black citizenry persevered month after month and their solidarity kept growing. On the same day in

November 1956 that the city won an injunction to shut down the car pools, the boycott's circulatory system, the U.S. Supreme Court upheld a June ruling of the federal court in Montgomery that the state and city bus laws were unconstitutional. A legal order came a month later. At two giant meetings four days before Christmas, 8,000 souls voted triumphantly to end the boycott, the largest and longest organized protest by black people in the nation's history up to then. Despite more violence by white extremists, desegregation of the buses moved fairly smoothly. Other bus boycotts were organized in Birmingham, Mobile, and Tallahassee. Martin Luther King, Jr., emerged from the victorious crusade the most celebrated black leader since Booker T. Washington. The freedom movement had taken off.

Through every twist and turn of the movement during the next decade, the black church—Baptist churches mainly, but also African Methodist (AME)—would be its driving force and institutional base, at once spiritual, moral, cultural, political, organizational, and financial. The black church was "born in protest" in the early days of slavery, and the "invisible institution" had served the dual purpose of helping blacks to survive while motivating them to improve their conditions.[20] Nat Turner was not the only preacher to lead a slave revolt, and black churches North and South played a vital role in the abolitionist movement. After Reconstruction, however, many Southern churches lost their combative spirit and accommodated to Jim Crow. Ministers gained influence and prestige as brokers between white elites and black folk. E. Franklin Frazier writes that as "a result of the elimination of Negroes from the political life of the American community, the Negro Church became the arena of their political activities . . . the arena in which the struggle for power and the thirst for power could be satisfied."[21]

Though the Southern black church had grown into a formidable and quite visible institution, its deep involvement in the freedom movement harked back to its role in resisting slavery. The resources it provided included skillful, charismatic leaders insulated from white society; a large, tightly organized constituency; a communications network; an independent financial base; relatively safe meeting places in which to plan tactics and generate commitment; and most critical, the "common church culture"—grounded in a rich heritage of empowering prayers, oratory, and spirituals—that could be directly applied to political goals.[22] Ever since slavery the male preacher had been the acknowledged leader of the black community, closely attuned to the needs and aspirations of his followers.

Oratorical wizards like King now had ready opportunity to reshape the cultural content of black religion into a weapon of protest—for example, by reinterpreting Biblical stories and portraying Jesus and Moses as revolutionaries. The dynamic relationship between the charismatic clergy and the common church culture created a mighty engine of grass-roots social power.

Since in Montgomery King had supremely demonstrated the leadership style of the black preacher, there was never any doubt that his fellow ministers would choose him to head a new regional federation intended to link up the church-based movements that were sprouting in several Southern cities. The genius of the Southern Christian Leadership Conference (SCLC) and its affiliates was its "ability to unite community leaders by bringing them directly into leadership positions while simultaneously organizing the black masses"; indeed, the mass base of the church was "built into" the SCLC structure.[23]

King took the reins of SCLC in the fashion that the activist ministers who formed it were accustomed to: he was to them as each was to his own congregation, the unquestioned authority and center of attention. Yet King nurtured a remarkable cadre of second-level leaders, both in the Atlanta headquarters and in the affiliates: gifted and courageous organizers like Fred Shuttlesworth, Hosea Williams, James Bevel, Andrew Young, and Ralph Abernathy, his closest confidant. He encouraged exhaustive debate among these leaders before making the final decisions. Journalist Lerone Bennett commented that King, like Franklin D. Roosevelt, showed "a rare talent for attracting and using the skills and ideas of brilliant aides and administrators."[24] As its name implied, SCLC was run by strong collective leadership, but King's dominant role made it seem more like a typical organizational hierarchy. Unlike in a hierarchy, however, the source of King's power was his ability "to get more warm bodies in the street at one time than anybody else" in American history.[25]

How would they use this power to effect change after the victory in Montgomery? As it solidified itself institutionally and financially, SCLC floundered in charting a strategy and direction for the budding movement. It tried to mount a South-wide voter registration campaign with little success, organized a "Prayer Pilgrimage" to Washington for voting rights, and built solidarity among activists in isolated communities, but the momentum of the freedom movement slowed to a crawl. Was Montgomery just an aberration?

The Students and "De Lawd"

Late Monday afternoon, 1 February 1960, four well-dressed young men, first-year students at the mainly black North Carolina A&T College in Greensboro, bought some school supplies at Woolworth's, then sat down at the lunch counter and ordered coffee. "I'm sorry," the waitress said, "we don't serve you here."[26] Showing their purchases, the students asked why they could be served at one counter and not at another. She called the manager, who tried to reason with them, and a cop paced back and forth behind them, holding his club but not sure what to do. The students refused to move until the store, crowded with onlookers, closed for the day. The four close friends planned this protest the night before; it was the culmination of weeks of "bull sessions" about the injustice of segregation and how it violated the country's democratic ideals. Franklin McCain later recalled that, though influenced most by Gandhi, what precipitated their action was the "courage that each of us instilled within each other."[27] They quickly organized their college and others nearby and returned to the lunch counter every day that week in growing numbers until by week's end hundreds had joined the "sit-in." Soon, more than 90 percent of the area's black college students were sitting in, picketing, or boycotting segregated eating places.

By wire service and student grapevine, news of the sudden protest flashed across North Carolina and the nation. Though a few experimental sit-ins had been tried in Nashville and elsewhere, the idea now spread "like a fever."[28] The next week students staged lunch counter sit-ins in Winston-Salem, Durham, and other North Carolina communities. By February's end protests had erupted in over thirty cities in seven states, and by April sit-in protests pervaded the entire South. Local movements were particularly strong in Nashville, Atlanta, and Orangeburg, South Carolina. Almost without exception the young women and men stayed calm and resolute when catsup and other food was flung at them, and when they were jabbed with lighted cigarettes and sometimes badly beaten—with little police interference. As the actions grew larger and better organized and moved further south, white violence increased, and so did arrests. Historian Clayborne Carson notes that "never again during the decade would the proportion of students active in protest equal the level reached at southern black colleges" during this period.[29]

By the end of 1960 hundreds of lunch counters and restaurants had been opened to all. Why did this spectacular wave of protest surge forth at the dawn of the new decade? The answer lies in a combination of factors: favorable media attention, a carefully built protest infrastructure revolving around SCLC, a concentration of students in Southern black colleges, and the gripping example of African liberation movements.

When Ella Baker, executive director of SCLC, first heard about the sit-ins, she called her long list of contacts at Southern colleges. "What are you all going to do?" she asked in the deep, resonant voice that made her a powerful speaker. "It is time to move."[30] In her mid-fifties, Baker had acquired enormous wisdom in three decades as an organizer. As a young child growing up in a small North Carolina town, she heard stories from her ninety-year-old grandmother about slave revolts—and about how she had been flogged for refusing to marry the man chosen by her owner; instead, she married a rebellious slave preacher. Valedictorian of her class at Raleigh's Shaw University, Baker moved to Harlem just before the Depression. During the 1930s she traveled the country setting up black consumer cooperatives. In 1940 she began a long association with the NAACP, recruiting members and organizing chapters and Youth Councils throughout the South, later serving as director of branches and head of the New York office. She had an extraordinary ability to inspire people of all ages, especially young people, and to give them a deeper perspective on social change. A founder of SCLC, she rose to the challenge of directing its Atlanta headquarters. Because she was a woman, Baker was never accepted as an equal by King and his associates, despite her genius as an organizer. They did not take seriously her bold suggestions to improve SCLC and its voting rights campaign. She grew more and more critical of its centralized, charismatic leadership and resigned in the summer of 1960. Her successor, Rev. Wyatt Walker, commented that she "could not fit into the mold of a preacher organization. It just went against the grain of the kind of person she is and was."[31]

Baker realized that the new student movement would not last unless a structure was created to provide communication and coordination between local groups. Borrowing funds from SCLC, she organized a conference of student activists from over fifty colleges and high schools in twelve Southern states, at Shaw University during Easter weekend of 1960. King spoke to the 200 fervent activists, but Baker fought an attempt by SCLC to capture the student groups as its youth wing. As did most of the students, she believed they needed an autonomous organization "with the right to direct their own affairs and even make their own mistakes."[32] She hoped that they would be less cautious and more radical than the organization she was leaving. The young activists set up the loosely structured Student Nonviolent Coordinating Committee (SNCC), with delegates from every Southern state, and adopted a statement of purpose that affirmed its commitment to nonviolence as "the foundation of our purpose, the presupposition of our belief, and the manner of our action." Baker donated a small office in the Atlanta SCLC headquarters, and during the rest of 1960 she and Jane Stembridge, a white seminary student, breathed life into the organization. SNCC (pronounced "snick") aimed at ending all forms of racial domination and building a "redemptive community."[33] But as the sit-in movement slowed, the new body shifted from being the coordinating arm of a mass movement into a cadre of ex-students committed to long-term organizing, mainly in rural Southern communities.

Inspired by Ella Baker, SNCC came to embody an idea and style of leadership that would clash with the leadership model of SCLC. Opposed to the centrality of one or a few charismatic leaders able to attract big crowds, big media, and big money but who do not stay around for follow-through and tend to get co-opted, SNCC stood for what Baker called "group-centered leadership." She believed that what grass-roots movements needed was "the development of people who are interested not in being leaders as much as in developing leadership among other people."[34] It boiled down to the question of how change comes about. SNCC activists asserted that deep and lasting change can only come from empowering people at the grass roots, and that this takes commitment to local people over time—not to ephemeral media stars. Here was no abstract position: it grew out of the understanding that if racial subjugation were to be overcome, especially in the rural South, black people would have to rely on themselves, not on outside leaders. Because most SNCC activists believed that they and their organization had to exemplify their values, prefiguring the redemptive society they sought to create, and because they shared a common risk of death, they were reluctant to recognize leaders among themselves, or claimed that "we are all leaders."[35] This antileadership ethos—actually a vision of an alternative kind of leadership, decentralized and participatory—and the emphasis on the process of change, expressed by its slogan "Let the people decide," became SNCC's hallmark in the next few years, and the closest it came to an ideology. SNCC represented not a coherent set of ideas as much as an intangible mood and spirit, a way of life.

SNCC's identity and reputation for fearless militancy were established by the legendary "freedom rides" of 1961 to desegregate bus terminals in the heart of the Deep South. This bold tactic was conceived and organized by the Congress of Racial Equality (CORE), founded by James Farmer and others, which had pioneered the use of nonviolent direct action to integrate restaurants in Chicago in the early 1940s. In 1947 CORE had joined the Fellowship of Reconciliation in a freedom ride through the Upper South. Since the Supreme Court had earlier in 1961 declared segregated terminals unconstitutional, Farmer and other CORE leaders hoped that "putting the movement on wheels," and refusing to bail out of jail, would generate massive publicity and force federal intervention to carry out the law.[36]

A dozen CORE activists, half black and half white, boarded two buses and left the nation's capital in early May 1961, intending to traverse every Deep South state and reach New Orleans ten days later. They eluded violence until Rock Hill, South Carolina, where Nashville seminary student and SNCC organizer John Lewis and Albert Bigelow,.a white World War II Navy commander turned pacifist, were assaulted by white toughs when they entered the waiting rooms of the bus terminal. The journey continued through Georgia, and then, across the Alabama border, a brutal mob armed with iron bars attacked the Greyhound bus in Anniston, smashed its windows, slashed its tires, and forced it to make an unscheduled stop outside of town. A fire bomb thrown inside ignited a blazing inferno, and the choking protesters barely escaped before the bus exploded. When the second bus pulled into Anniston an hour later, eight men jumped on, tore into the freedom riders, and nearly killed a retired white professor. Demanding that black and white sit apart, they accompanied the riders to Birmingham, where the Ku Klux Klan awaited them.

Long-time CORE activist Jim Peck, a white, told what happened when he and a black youth named Charles Person tried to integrate the terminal there: "As we entered the white waiting room and approached the lunch counter, we were grabbed bodily and pushed toward the alleyway leading to the loading platform. . . . Six of them started swinging at me with fists and pipes. Five others attacked Person a few feet ahead. . . . When I regained consciousness, the alleyway was empty. Blood was flowing down my face. I tried to stop the flow with a handkerchief but it soon became soaked."[37] Rev. Fred Shuttlesworth, Birmingham SCLC chief, called an ambulance. After shaking hands with Person, whose face was badly swollen, Peck was taken to the hospital, where he lay for hours in surgery and left with fifty-three stitches in his head. Having faced enough danger for the moment, the CORE activists decided to halt their ride for freedom.

It was SNCC's turn. Diane Nash and other leaders of the Nashville student movement resolved that the ride must continue at all cost. Ten students, mostly black, took a bus to Birmingham. "These people faced the probability of their own deaths before they ever left Nashville," Nash remembered. "Several made out wills. A few more gave me sealed letters to be mailed if they were killed. Some told me frankly that they were afraid, but they knew this was something that they must do because freedom was worth it."[38] They were arrested at the Birmingham bus station, held in jail, and then driven by Police Commissioner Eugene "Bull" Connor over a hundred miles to the Tennessee border, where he dropped them off on a deserted highway just before dawn. Fiercely determined to complete their mission, they had Nash send a car to return them to Birmingham.

Joined by a few comrades at the terminal, among them eighteen-year-old Spelman College student Ruby Doris Smith, the SNCC activists had trouble finding a bus driver brave enough to take them to Montgomery. "I have only one life to give," one exclaimed, "and I'm not going to give it to NAACP or CORE!"[39] After a night fortifying themselves with "freedom songs," the group finally got to the Alabama capital on a bus protected by police cars and helicopters; the new attorney general of the United States, Robert Kennedy, had intervened on their behalf. But when they pulled in to the bus station, the police had disappeared and the riders were attacked by a vicious mob. John Lewis was beaten until blood gushed from his head, and Justice Department official John Siegenthaler, President Kennedy's personal emissary, was knocked out cold when he came to someone's aid. Two riders were nearly beaten to death; one of them was badly maimed. The president issued a public statement expressing his concern and calling for peace. This was the city where a longer battle over buses had been fought and won five years before.

A mass meeting was held the next night at Ralph Abernathy's church, and King flew in to speak in support of the freedom riders. He had already been on the phone with Attorney General Kennedy. Before the meeting King conferred in the church basement with James Farmer, Diane Nash, and Abernathy about what to do. The phone rang. Kennedy was calling again to ask King to stop the freedom ride to allow a cooling-off period. Nash shook her head. "The Nashville Student Movement wants to go on," she said firmly. Farmer asked King, who was ambivalent, to "tell the attorney general that we have been cooling off for 350 years." "I understand," he responded, and turned down Kennedy's request.[40]

As the meeting took place upstairs, several hundred white rioters besieged the church, throwing rocks through its stained-glass windows. Those inside, showered with glass, emboldened themselves for hours with spirited singing. The mob was about to break down the doors when a battalion of U.S. marshals, sent by the attorney general, dispersed them with tear gas. Kennedy recalled a later phone call with King, who feared for his life. "I said that our people were down there. And that as long as he was in church, he might say a prayer for us. He didn't think that was very humorous. He rather berated me for what was happening to him at the time. And I said to him that I didn't think that he'd be alive if it wasn't for us, and that we were going to keep him alive, and that the marshals would keep the church from burning down."[41] The marshals were reinforced later that night by National Guard troops reluctantly activated by the Alabama governor, John Patterson, a JFK ally who nevertheless had been evading phone calls from the president.

Three days later two busloads of freedom riders, National Guard, and reporters left for Jackson, Mississippi, escorted by legions of police in cars and aircraft. It was like a military operation, Farmer remembered. The young riders were angered when King refused to come with them, saying he was on probation. "We're all on probation," one told him. "That doesn't stop us. We're in a war."[42] Onlookers in Jackson witnessed the amusing spectacle of protesters being led into the terminal by National Guardsmen, with police opening doors for them, then promptly being arrested. They served almost two months in county jails and at the tough Parchman state pen, where defiant singing of freedom songs got them through. The training ground of prison steeled their commitment to an uncertain future of struggle. Freedom rides continued over the summer. Hundreds of SNCC activists descended upon the Jackson bus station and joined their sisters and brothers in jail. In September 1961 the Interstate Commerce Commission (ICC) banned segregation in interstate terminals. The freedom rides not only "led to desegregation of southern transportation facilities," Carson concludes, they also "contributed to the development of a self-consciously radical southern student movement prepared to direct its militancy toward other concerns."[43]

An important turning point in the freedom movement was the frustrating, year-long campaign against segregation in Albany, the hub of rural southwest Georgia; it was to be the first full mobilization of a black community since Montgomery, the first serious interorganizational conflict, and the first defeat. Youthful SNCC organizers Charles Sherrod,

Cordell Reagon, and Charles Jones moved to the city of 60,000 (almost half black) in fall 1961. Initially rebuffed by older black leaders and the local NAACP, they concentrated on mobilizing students at the all-black high school and at Albany State. Some of their recruits were active in the NAACP Youth Council and had recently held a rally against white harassment of black women at the college. Discovering that the bus and train terminals had not complied with the ICC ruling, the SNCC trio and the Youth Council launched mass protests to enforce desegregation of these and other public places, including schools, libraries, and parks. Not wanting to be overshadowed, the more moderate local leaders formed a coalition with SNCC called the Albany Movement, made up of most active black organizations. The NAACP elders kept at arm's length, however; they were at loggerheads with SNCC's nonviolent militance and sought to discredit it.

When in December the campaign sagged and the local leaders invited King to help revive it, his jailing for leading a peaceful march in Albany sparked huge turnouts and national publicity. But SNCC people resented King, whom they derisively called "De Lawd," for his cautious style and willingness to "settle for half a loaf"—especially after an oral "agreement" negotiated by moderate blacks with city officials turned out to be a hoax.[44] And they accused SCLC and executive director Wyatt Walker of trying to monopolize the movement they had pulled together. Civil disobedience continued into the spring and summer coupled with effective boycotts of white-owned stores and segregated city buses (forcing the bus company out of business). Yet the Albany Movement proved no match for ingenious Police Chief Laurie Pritchett, who had studied earlier protests and had even read King's book on Montgomery. His officers arrested thousands without violence, impressing Northern reporters, and he found plenty of jail space in nearby towns. The chief and the uncompromising city commissioners maneuvered deftly through the movement's divisions and held fast to Jim Crow. Albany had nothing comparable to the vivid brutality brought on by the freedom rides to force federal intervention. Pritchett's "efficient police state" took the heat off the Kennedy administration, which preferred "order over justice."[45] Activists felt betrayed by the new president. By late summer 1962 the local crusade seemed a lost cause. King and SCLC left town, but SNCC activists, entrenched in the community, dug in for a few more years of diligent organizing.

Though defeated in its immediate goals, the "singing movement" of Albany was triumphant on another level—as an unprecedented expression of black cultural and spiritual power, rooted in a shared heritage of oppression and resistance. In church, on the street, and in jail, protesters of all ages poured out their souls in freedom songs. At mass meetings there was more singing than speaking. Some of the songs were traditional to the south Georgia black belt. Others were shaped by participants in the heat of battle, with words about the latest crisis—"Ain't gonna let Chief Pritchett turn me 'round"—fused with old spirituals that had been sung by slaves. Bernice Johnson Reagon, an Albany State student activist, daughter of a local Baptist preacher, and soon one of the traveling SNCC Freedom Singers, commented that after singing, "the difference among us would not be as great. Somehow, making a song required an expression of that which was common to us all." Singing was the main language of protest, especially for the illiterate, and the vital tool to build solidarity, sustain morale, instill courage, and deepen commitment. "A transformation took place inside of the people," Reagon recalled. "The singing was just the echo of that."[46]

One song she led, with "a force and power within myself I had never heard before," was called "We Shall Overcome." Striking South Carolina tobacco workers had adapted it from a slave spiritual and brought it to Highlander Folk School, a spawning ground of freedom songs, and a place where organizers learned them; at Highlander Zilphia Horton and Pete Seeger wrote new lyrics for it. By 1961 "We Shall Overcome" was already a favorite of the freedom movement, but Reagon and other Albany song leaders molded it into the movement's anthem, its battle hymn, sung at the end of every big meeting—all standing, crossing arms and holding hands, gently swaying back and forth—and at almost every protest. Its power was indescribable. When they rose to sing it, Charles Sherrod remembered, "nobody knew what kept the top of the church on its four walls. It was as if everyone had been lifted up on high."[47] This magnificent singing spirit and the songs that sprung from it were the rich harvest of Albany's black community and part of its legacy to future struggles.

Six years had passed since SCLC's only decisive victory over Jim Crow, in Montgomery. SCLC leaders learned from the Albany experience that an effective citywide movement must focus on a single target and a clear-cut goal; have a definite strategy and careful planning; be unified, and controlled by SCLC leaders; and get help from a police chief who, unlike Albany's Pritchett, was willing to use brutal tactics and expose the ugliness of racism for the nation to witness. With these lessons in mind, SCLC decided to wage an all-out, systematic campaign of direct action in Birmingham (population 350,000, 40 percent black), the industrial center of the South and reputed to be the most segregated city in the country, an American Johannesburg. White terrorists had blown up so many buildings that locals called it "Bombingham." SCLC had an impressive affiliate there, led by Fred Shuttlesworth, that had prepared the soil with boycotts and community organizing. The immediate goal would be to desegregate lunch counters and hiring at the downtown department stores. The strategy was for SCLC to throw its resources into mass demonstrations and a boycott of the stores, aiming to split the business elite from the political elite. They sought a morale-lifting victory that would "set the pace" for the South and spur the federal government to enact sweeping legislation outlawing segregation.[48]

SCLC leaders saw the campaign as a drama, building up "step by step, until it reached a crisis point, where the opposition would be forced to yield." The top command divided up responsibilities and methodically planned every detail of this "tremendous organizational operation," down to counting the chairs, stools, and tables in each store.[49] King met with many local black leaders to overcome their initial opposition. Workshops trained thousands in nonviolent combat, and mass meetings in churches were held every night for over two months, fueled by passionate speeches and the freedom songs that King called "the soul of the movement."[50]

SCLC postponed the start until after the mayoral election in March 1963 between Police Commissioner Bull Connor and a more moderate segregationist. With the electoral outcome in dispute, Birmingham had two city governments, in effect, until the courts ruled against Connor a few weeks later. Not willing to wait, SCLC took to the streets. After several small skirmishes Connor won a state court injunction barring King and his colleagues from leading more protests. King declared at a spirited mass meeting that he would violate the order, even though the movement had run out of funds and he was needed to raise bail money. On Good Friday, King and Abernathy, both in blue jeans, and fifty others marched downtown in a glare of publicity. The two walked up to the burly Connor, then knelt in prayer. Several police grabbed them by the backs of their shirts and threw them into paddy wagons, the others joining them in jail. King was held incommunicado in a dark cell with no mattress or blanket until, at Coretta King's request, President Kennedy interceded.

When conditions suddenly improved, he spent his week behind bars scribbling a long letter in the margins of a newspaper and on scraps of paper, responding to a statement in a Birmingham daily by white Alabama clergy condemning his tactics and timing. "Letter from Birmingham Jail," published widely, was the most cogent justification of civil disobedience since the essay by Thoreau that he had read years before. King offered an American reinterpretation, not of quiet pacifism, but of Gandhi's militant method of *satyagraha*. He had been well schooled since the day of Rosa Parks's arrest.

"You are quite right in calling for negotiation," he wrote the white ministers.

Indeed, this is the very purpose of direct action. Nonviolent direct action seeks to create such a crisis and foster such a tension that a community which has constantly refused to negotiate is forced to confront the issue. It seeks so to dramatize the issue that it can no longer be ignored. . . . I have earnestly opposed violent tension, but there is a type of constructive, nonviolent tension which is necessary for growth. . . . I submit that an individual who breaks a law that conscience tells him is unjust, and who willingly accepts the penalty of imprisonment in order to arouse the conscience of the community over its injustice, is in reality expressing the highest respect for law.[51]

When King and Abernathy were set free, the crusade moved into full swing. While the boycott disrupted downtown business, wave after wave of men and women marching to City Hall were mauled by police dogs and hurled against walls and pavement by ferocious, machine gun–like fire hoses. Connor's jails had no more room for them. In early May the leaders decided to unleash their secret weapon, an army of children as young as six, carefully trained by James Bevel, an organizing genius who, said SCLC associate Hosea Williams, "could do more with young people than any human being on the face of the earth."[52] In the following days thousands of jubilant youngsters, braving dogs and fire hoses with songs and shouts of "We want freedom!" rode off to jail in school buses.

One Sunday afternoon in May an uncanny event interrupted the daily routine of brutality and augured victory. Rev. Charles Billups, a local preacher, led hundreds of black people on a prayer pilgrimage to the city jail, singing "I Want Jesus to Walk with Me" and other spirituals. At the border of white Birmingham they were blocked by Bull Connor's men and an armored car. The police commissioner ordered them to turn around, but instead they prayed. "Turn on your water, turn loose your dogs," Billups replied. "We will stand here till we die." "Dammit," Connor yelled to his men, "turn on the hoses."[53] The police and fire fighters, "their deadly hoses poised for action, stood facing the marchers," King recalled. The latter, "many of them on their knees, stared back, unafraid and unmoving. Slowly the Negroes stood up and began to advance. Connor's men, as though hypnotized, fell back, their hoses sagging uselessly in their hands while several hundred Negroes marched past," despite Connor's screams to stop them.[54] A few fire fighters cried. "You would have to say that the hand of God moved in that demonstration," said one participant.[55] If not by God, they were surely empowered by their shared movement culture.

The forces of "public safety" were not as restrained the next week, and young blacks on the sidelines responded with rocks and bottles, hinting at the possibility of a violent uprising. The Kennedys pressured major steel corporations with Birmingham branches to use their influence and sent an assistant attorney general to negotiate the boycott demands with white business leaders. When King agreed to a temporary halt in the protests, Shuttlesworth—hospitalized from a serious fire hose injury—was furious, and reminded King that they had resolved to fight until victory. Shuttlesworth threatened to go on regardless. "That's what people are saying," he scolded his superior. "You go to a point and then you stop. You won't be stopping here."[56]

Fortunately for the unity of SCLC and the movement, the business elite, hurting badly from the boycott and negative publicity and realizing the city had been paralyzed, agreed to most of the demands, which were still opposed by intransigent city officials. Despite the bombing of the home of King's brother a few days later and other white retaliation, King and SCLC had won a crucial though limited victory. The campaign would show, David Garrow suggests, that "even small tangible gains could represent extraordinary symbolic victories, even if those people closest to the struggle could not appreciate it at the time."[57] The electrifying drama of Birmingham, conveyed by unprecedented television coverage, sparked protests throughout the spring and summer in hundreds of cities across the South, a contagious phenomenon that King called a revolution.

Of the major civil rights organizations, only the NAACP (especially its state and local chapters) had given primary attention to the campaign to desegregate public education, partly because this arena was more amenable to a legalistic approach. Yet the pace was slower than even the Supreme Court had desired, and a decade after the historic decision little more than cosmetic changes had come to pass. De jure and de facto tactics of delay and evasion proved so effective that by 1963 only about one percent of Southern black children attended school with whites. Washington acted decisively only as a last resort when unyielding Southern governors brazenly flouted federal commands. A reluctant President Eisenhower, who had not publicly backed the Brown ruling, sent 1,000 paratroopers to Little Rock, Arkansas, in 1957 after a vicious mob, encouraged by the defiance of Governor Orval Faubus, tried to prevent nine black students from entering Central High School. Five years later President Kennedy ordered the Army and National Guard to enforce the admission of James Meredith to the lily-white University of Mississippi. Two days of fierce street battles between the troops and a few thousand incensed whites left two dead and hundreds injured. Governor Ross Barnett finally gave in. Then in June 1963, shortly after Birmingham, Alabama's new governor, George Wallace, won lasting fame, and a few elections, by "standing in the schoolhouse door" of his state's university to block Vivian Malone and James Hood from enrolling. At the last minute he stepped aside to avoid arrest by U.S. marshals. Many smaller confrontations with less visibility integrated other schools and colleges from Virginia to Texas.

The more established civil rights leaders, like Roy Wilkins and Whitney Young, and their white liberal allies, worried that the revolution might get out of hand, and thought that it should be managed from above. Thus, in spring 1963 multimillionaire philanthropist Stephen Currier of the Taconic Foundation formed the Council on United Civil Rights Leadership (CUCRL), a coalition of the "Big Six" organizations represented by Wilkins (NAACP), Young (Urban League), King (SCLC), James Farmer of CORE, SNCC executive secretary James Forman (rotating with chair John Lewis), and Dorothy Height of the National Council of Negro Women. Farmer discovered that "civil rights generalship was one-fourth leadership, one-fourth showmanship, one-fourth one-upsmanship, and one-fourth partnership."[58] Though Forman considered it mainly a "fundraising gimmick" and much of the discussion had to do with how money would be divided (with SNCC at the losing end), CUCRL did provide a forum to try to resolve interorganizational grievances and to think about broader strategy.[59] The elite council was often polarized between the bureaucratic inertia of Wilkins and Young and Forman's impatient militancy. Caught in the middle, King's thoughtful, low-key presence served as a reconciling force between opposites.

At one of CUCRL's first meetings revered labor leader A. Philip Randolph proposed that the Big Six organize a massive march on Washington to pressure Congress to pass a comprehensive civil rights bill; after all, Randolph's mere threat to invade the capital in 1941 had forced FDR to ban discrimination in war industry. The leaders seized on the "march for jobs and freedom" as also a way to unify the movement at this cross-roads—in King's words, "to unite in one luminous action all of the forces along the far-flung front" and to provide an appropriate climax to the "thundering events of the summer."[60] Randolph asked his protégé Bayard Rustin to be the architect of the delicate supercoalition (including white religious and labor leaders) required to pull off this endeavor. In late June CUCRL leaders met with President Kennedy, who tried to talk them out of it, fearing violence that would damage the civil rights bill Birmingham had put on his front burner. Randolph's eloquence persuaded him to give it equivocal support.

August 28, 1963—the day after pioneering black leader W. E. B. Du Bois died at ninety-five—a quarter of a million people, black and white together, surged forth in the summer heat from the Washington Monument to the Lincoln Memorial. They had come on buses and trains from all over but especially from the Deep South, and large contingents represented white religious faiths and, despite lack of support by the AFL-CIO, many labor unions. Haunting freedom songs—including "Oh, Freedom!" by Odetta and "We Shall Overcome" by Joan Baez—blended with speeches by the civil rights generals. Though forced by the more moderate leaders to soften his words, SNCC's John Lewis pierced the optimistic mood with a candid speech that criticized conventional liberalism and expressed "great reservations" about Kennedy's legislation, since it would do nothing about police brutality or voting rights.[61]

At the end of the long afternoon Martin Luther King, Jr. stood beneath the anguished chiseled face of Abraham Lincoln and, inspired more than ever by the sea of listeners, left his carefully crafted text and in powerful rippling cadences painted in rich colors his vibrant dream of racial justice. It would be acclaimed as one of the greatest speeches in national history, equalled perhaps only by the Civil War address at Gettysburg given 100 years before by the man in stone gazing out over King's shoulder. None were more uplifted by the dream and the day's drama than the thousands of poor black people whom SNCC had bussed from the Deep South. "It helped them believe that they were not alone," a SNCC activist remarked, "that there really were people in the nation who cared what happened to them."[62] Yet some Southern organizers had a hard time sharing De Lawd's dream. Sitting on the grass, young black activist Anne Moody of CORE told herself that back in Mississippi, "we never had time to sleep, much less dream."[63]

On a Sunday morning two weeks afterward King's dream was shattered, at least for the moment, when a dynamite bomb exploded in Birmingham's Sixteenth Street Baptist Church—a center of the spring crusade—killing four black girls as they were putting on their choir robes. Later in the fall John F. Kennedy died in Dallas. Congress passed the Civil Rights Act the next spring.

The Salt of the Earth

In late August 1962, one year before the March on Washington, a tired, strong-willed woman with a great smile and shining eyes strode into a meeting at her church in Ruleville, a Mississippi Delta town not far from where Emmett Till had been bludgeoned to death. "Until then I'd never heard of no mass meeting and I didn't know that a Negro could register and vote," Fannie Lou Hamer recalled.

Bob Moses, Reggie Robinson, Jim Bevel and James Forman were some of the SNCC workers who ran that meeting. When they asked for those to raise their hands who'd go down to the courthouse the next day, I raised mine. Had it up high as I could get it. I guess if I'd had any sense I'd a-been a little scared, but what was the point of being scared. The only thing they could do to me was kill me and it seemed like they'd been trying to do that a little bit at a time ever since I could remember.[64]

Forty-four years old, Hamer was the youngest of twenty children of sharecropper parents. She had picked cotton all her life, for the previous eighteen years with her husband on a nearby plantation. She had always known poverty and injustice. When she was a young girl, a white farmer had poisoned their mules just when her family was getting a little ahead. For a long time she had wanted to help her kind. "Just listenin' at 'em, I could just see myself votin' people outa office that I know was wrong and didn't do nothin' to help the poor. I said, you know, that's sumpin' I really wanna be involved in."[65] Chief among those who did not care about poor people, in her opinion, was powerful Senator James Eastland, owner of a huge cotton plantation in Hamer's county. He ruled the county like a feudal baron.

Hamer rode with seventeen others on a SNCC-chartered bus to the county seat of Indianola, birthplace of the White Citizens Councils, where the registrar "brought a big old book out there, and he gave me the sixteenth section of the Constitution of Mississippi, and that was dealing with de facto laws, and I didn't know nothin' about no de facto laws." Unable to interpret it to his satisfaction, she "flunked out" along with the

Fannie Lou Hamer pickets at SNCC voter registration protest, Hattiesburg, Mississippi, Courthouse, 1963. © *1978 Matt Herron*

others. Driving home they were all arrested because the bus was "too yellow." The plantation owner kicked her off her land—"I didn't have no other choice because for one time I wanted things to be different"—and the house where she stayed in town was shot up by vigilantes. It was one hell of a winter. "Pap couldn't get a job nowhere 'cause everybody knew he was my husband. We made it on through, though, and since then I just been trying to work and get our people organized."[66] Soon she joined SNCC, its oldest field organizer.

Why was she drawn to this brash young outfit?

Nobody never come out into the country and talked to real farmers and things. . . . Because this is the next thing this country has done: it divided us into classes, and if you hadn't arrived at a certain level, you wasn't treated no better by the blacks than you was by the whites. And it was these kids what broke a lot of this down. They treated us like we were special and we loved 'em. . . . We didn't feel uneasy about our language might not be right or something. We just felt like we could talk to 'em. We trusted 'em, and I can tell the world those kids done their share in Mississippi.[67]

SNCC had been struggling for a year to register black voters in the "closed society" of Mississippi, the most white-supremacist state of the South, where rural blacks were still treated much like slaves. Blacks were almost half the population but only 5 percent were registered—in some counties none at all—owing to intimidation and reprisals in general, and the literacy test and poll tax in particular. An alternative to King's strategy of dramatic appeals to the liberal conscience to effect federal action, the Mississippi campaign was the outcome of a conflict within SNCC between those who favored more civil disobedience to force de-segregation and others who argued that racism would not be overcome until blacks had political power, and that it made practical sense to concentrate on rural areas that were disproportionately represented in legislatures and Congress. Wary of co-optation, some were suspicious of a voter registration strategy because it was urged by the Kennedy administration, which would obviously benefit from an enlarged black electorate. The attorney general had proffered the carrots of foundation money and tax exemption if the movement would abandon direct action and had helped set up the Voter Education Project to disperse funds. At a SNCC conference at Highlander, Ella Baker broke the logjam with a proposal to have two wings in SNCC, one for direct action and another for voter registration. But voter registration won out as SNCC discovered that no

Citizenship education leader Septima Clark teaches literacy for voter registration,
Southern Voter Education Project, Camden, Alabama, 1965. *Bob Fitch*

action was riskier, more militant, even more revolutionary, than organizing blacks to vote in Mississippi, whose reputation for terrorism had kept
it off-limits to SCLC and the rest of the movement.

Bob Moses, the driving force behind the voting campaign, moved to
McComb, a small city in southern Mississippi, where he set up the first
of a string of registration "schools." In his mid-twenties, the quiet and
contemplative Moses had grown up in Harlem, had been a Harvard graduate student in philosophy and a fan of Camus, and was teaching high
school when he heard about the North Carolina sit-ins and abruptly vol-
unteered for duty at the makeshift SNCC office in Atlanta. On a visit to
Mississippi that summer he was persuaded by a local NAACP leader,
Amzie Moore, that enfranchising black people should be SNCC's main
mission. Moses would become a legend in SNCC not only for courage
but for his ability to motivate participation and leadership in others, symbolized by his habit of sitting in the back of the room at meetings and
saying little. "Organizers raise certain questions," he once said. "People
develop answers."[68] With Moses as guide, SNCC activists learned "how
to find potential leadership, how to groom it," Lawrence Guyot recalled,

"and the most painful lesson for some of us was how to let it go once you've set it into motion."[69]

McComb tested the mettle of Moses and his small cadre and set the tone for further campaigns. They were routinely beaten and arrested—more than once in a town called Liberty—when they accompanied local blacks to the county courthouse. Herbert Lee, one of the brave farmers who supported them and a father of nine, was gunned down by a state legislator, who was never prosecuted. After a march to protest the cold-blooded murder, Moses and his associates were jailed for two months. Routed for the moment, they left McComb in December 1961, recruited people from the grass roots, and fanned out into several other counties, centering their efforts in the flat Delta country.

Risk and repression became a way of life. Diane Nash, married to James Bevel and pregnant at that time, was sent to prison for teaching nonviolence to young people. Refusing bail, she declared that "since my child will be a black child, born in Mississippi, whether I am in jail or not he will be born in prison."[70] SNCC people were fired at in their cars—twenty-year-old Jimmy Travis barely survived a bullet in his spine—and SNCC offices were invaded by mobs. When Leflore County supervisors cut off federal food aid to poor blacks as punishment, SNCC went all out to mobilize food caravans from the North, helped by comedian Dick Gregory. This action greatly boosted the registration campaign, since activists could easily draw the connection between children going hungry and lack of political power. In several county seats SNCC organized "Freedom Days," which culminated in courthouse marches to register en masse.

An incident in June 1963 typified SNCC's battle for democracy in Mississippi. Returning from a voter registration workshop in South Carolina, Fannie Lou Hamer and a few coworkers got off the bus for a rest stop in the small Delta town of Winona. When they tried to use the white-only cafe, they were arrested and taken to county jail. Hamer heard SCLC's Annelle Ponder screaming, and praying to God to have mercy on her captors. She heard more screams from another direction, and sixteen-year-old June Johnson passed by her cell, face bloodied. Then they came for her. "You, bitch, you," they yelled. "We gon' make you wish you was dead."

The memory burned into her soul:

The State Highway patrolman came and carried me out of the cell into another cell where there were two Negro prisoners. The patrolman gave the first Negro a long blackjack that was heavy. It was loaded with something and they had me to lay down on the bunk with my face down, and I was beat. I was beat by the first Negro until he gave out. Then the patrolman ordered the other man to take the blackjack and he began to beat. That's when I started screaming and working my feet 'cause I couldn't help it. The patrolman told the first Negro that had beat me to sit on my feet. I had to hug around the mattress to keep the sound from coming out.[71]

The merciless beating left her permanently injured, but more deter-mined than ever to fight for human rights. While she was in jail, state NAACP leader Medgar Evers was assassinated at his home in Jackson.

That fall the Council of Federated Organizations (COFO), set up to coordinate the registration work of all civil rights groups in Mississippi but staffed mainly by SNCC, decided to conduct an alternative election in November to demonstrate blacks' desire to vote. COFO nominated for governor black pharmacist Aaron Henry, the new head of the state NAACP, and for lieutenant governor, white Tougaloo College chaplain Ed King, who had been badly beaten in a Jackson sit-in. Reinforced by white students from the North, COFO workers canvassed the state and over 80,000 black people cast "freedom ballots" in churches, homes, gro-cery stores, and on the street—four times the number officially allowed to register. The success of the bold venture, making COFO a statewide force, persuaded Moses and other SNCC organizers that Mississippi blacks could build an electoral vehicle independent of the state Demo-cratic party.

In early 1964 SNCC initiated a campaign to sign up voters for the Mississippi Freedom Democratic party (MFDP), founded at a Jackson rally in April. Its immediate purpose was to challenge white Democrats for recognition as the legitimate Mississippi delegation at the Democratic National Convention in August. Intended to be a truly participatory po-litical organization that might someday supplant its rival, the MFDP was also seen as the "best means of physically organizing the Negroes of Mississippi, of finding indigenous leadership."[72] When as expected MFDP workers were systematically excluded from the segregated party's pre-cinct and county meetings, they set up their own, meticulously adhering to legal procedures. Four MFDP nominees qualified for the June Dem-ocratic primary, among them Hattiesburg activist Victoria Gray to op-pose Senator John Stennis, and Fannie Lou Hamer as a candidate for Congress. Unsuccessful, they ran as independents in the fall.

Meanwhile, COFO launched the Mississippi Summer Project, a grandiose plan to import hundreds of white college students to help in a climactic registration campaign parallel to the MFDP effort. They needed white students to create a crisis that would force meaningful federal intervention to protect activists and voting rights. (South-based FBI agents did nothing except take notes and mingle with local cops.) COFO staff calculated that if white students were beaten or killed, it would grab the attention of the nation, which had ignored the black victims of Mississippi's reign of terror—sixty deaths since 1961. Many in SNCC were very concerned, however, that the more articulate and highly educated whites would overshadow the indigenous organizers, worsen the deference and powerlessness of poor blacks, and take over leadership roles.

In mid-June, while volunteers learned the ropes in a marathon training workshop at an Ohio college—Hamer lifting them to the heavens with her singing and Moses preparing them for possible death—three civil rights activists disappeared in Neshoba County after a traffic arrest. Two were white—CORE organizer Michael Schwerner, and Andrew Goodman, fresh from the first Ohio training session; one was black, eighteen-year-old James Chaney from Meridian, Mississippi. As usual, the FBI was slow to respond. COFO demanded that the Justice Department send marshals to protect the movement, but Robert Kennedy and aides replied that they had no authority. Six weeks later the bodies of the three men were found buried in an earthen dam. They had been beaten and shot, Chaney horribly mutilated. The deputy sheriff who arrested them had turned them over to the Klan. The lynching fastened the eyes of the nation on Mississippi Freedom Summer.

By late June 1964 upwards of a thousand mostly white Northern students were settling into dozens of communities all over the state. The young women and men stayed with black families who generously made room for them, or slept on cots and mattresses in ramshackle "freedom houses." In 100-degree heat they trudged along dusty dirt roads in their straw hats and blue denim and nervously talked with people on cabin porches about their right to vote. The students escorted the few who dared register to the courthouse, where most often they failed the rigged exam. Rejected for the ninth time, one old man looked down as he walked out and said wistfully, "I want my freedom all right. I do mighty bad, I'll tell you that."[73]

Over the summer more black people were killed for aspiring to be citizens, and dozens of church headquarters were burned or bombed. Volunteers helped organize marches to protest brutality by police and the Klan, and many were jailed. At times even SNCC had trouble keeping up with the feisty militance of local black teenagers bent on integrating restaurants and movie theaters. "The kids were moving, with or without us."[74]

Many college students taught in the forty "freedom schools," directed by Yale historian Staughton Lynd. These schools were set up to provide an alternative to inferior public schools, to teach literacy and other skills, and to build the foundation for a statewide youth movement. Gathering under trees or on church steps, black high school students—2,000 altogether—learned not just the three R's but literature, foreign languages, black history and culture, how social problems might be solved, and the meaning of democracy. It was not what they learned but how that mattered most: by role-playing, by talking and writing stories and poems about their lives, by feeling equal with and teaching their teachers. In August freedom school students assembled for a convention in Meridian, where they articulated their grievances in an impressive, wide-ranging platform.

Having made but modest gains, the nonpartisan registration crusade lost steam as attention shifted to the Freedom Democratic party. "Have you freedom-registered?" was asked everywhere, in churches, on backwoods roads, and long before sunup riding plantation buses with cotton pickers. Party conventions in each county chose delegates to the five congressional district conventions, which in turn would send delegates to the state convention in Jackson. At one district convention Hamer stood at the front of the church, warmly greeting, hugging, and laughing with delegates, participant Sally Belfrage reported. "Volunteers who had never seen her before met her now and were instantly cowed with admiration. . . . People straight out of tarpaper shacks, many illiterate, some wearing a (borrowed) suit for the first time, disenfranchised for three generations, without a living memory of political power, yet caught on with some extraordinary inner sense to how the process worked, down to its smallest nuance and finagle. And yet when all the wheeling and dealing was done, they had chosen the four best people among them."[75] The Freedom Democratic party's skillfully organized, singing state gathering was "probably as close to a grass roots political convention as this country has ever seen," in historian Howard Zinn's judgment.[76] Most of the 800 delegates were black, most were poor, and many were women. Ella Baker gave a passionate keynote address, and sixty-eight men and women were elected to fight for the party at the national convention in Atlantic City, New Jersey. The MFDP had suddenly sprouted into a serious threat to the Democratic power structure of Mississippi—and of the nation.

The balloons, bright lights, and glitter of Atlantic City—its ocean air smelling of "popcorn and seaweed"—felt like another world to the MFDP delegates.[77] Not that they left Mississippi behind; 1,000 of their constituents followed them to the resort town, all wearing their Sunday best. The delegates and supporters had two tasks: to vigorously lobby every delegate they could get their hands on to back the MFDP challenge, and to sustain a round-the-clock vigil on the famed boardwalk in front of the convention hall. James Forman was surprised to see SNCC organizers Ivanhoe Donaldson and Charles Cobb, "the blue jean twins of Mississippi . . . all dressed up now in Ivy League outfits," pressing the flesh as if their lives depended on it.[78] With nine state delegations already lined up, and a thorough legal brief submitted by prominent Democratic broker Joseph Rauh, counsel for the United Auto Workers, the MFDP strategy was to garner enough votes in the credentials committee to force a roll-call vote on the floor to decide on recognition. Their trump card was that their state's all-white delegation was unwilling to declare loyalty to the national party and its nominees. King, James Farmer, and other notables testified on the MFDP's behalf at a nationally televised hearing, but far more telling arguments came from black Mississippians who explained what happened when they tried to vote. Hamer stole the show and won the country's heart with her gripping tale of being beaten in jail "'til my hands was as navy blue as anything you ever seen." She concluded that "all of this is on account we want to register, to become first-class citizens, and if the Freedom Democratic Party is not seated now, I question America. Is this America," she asked, "the land of the free and the home of the brave?"[79]

The millions watching did not see the end of Hamer's live testimony because President Johnson abruptly cut it off with an impromptu press conference. The president, who had ordered the FBI to wiretap SNCC and MFDP phones in Atlantic City (as well as King's), was adamant against seating the challengers—especially Hamer—lest he lose white Southerners in November. But the ex-sharecropper had such an electrifying effect and the public response was so overwhelmingly sympathetic that he had to offer a slight compromise: two at-large votes for the delegation heads and guest passes for the rest, along with a nondiscrimination pledge for the future. The MFDP would have accepted "any honorable compromise" and endorsed the proposal by Congresswoman Edith Green to seat both delegations.[80] But Johnson's offer felt like a slap in the face—two token seats, not even representing their state, hand-picked by the white party bosses. And the nondiscrimination pledge meant little without guaranteeing black voting rights.

Resisting eloquent cajolery by King, Bayard Rustin, and other big guns who feared funding cutoffs by liberal and labor backers—Rustin pleading for the primacy of practical politics over moral protest—the MFDP delegates followed Hamer's lead and voted almost unanimously to reject the offer. "We didn't come all this way for no two seats!" she exhorted her colleagues.[81] Feeling "cheated," the normally gentle Moses stormed out of a meeting with Hubert Humphrey, slamming the door behind him. Hamer told the vice presidential hopeful she would pray for his soul. The battle was lost when their supporters on the credentials committee caved in to intense arm-twisting by the White House and Humphrey forces. "I have never seen such just really blatant use of power" to block her proposal from floor debate, Edith Green recalled.[82] The MFDP's last hurrah was a dramatic, televised sit-in in the empty seats of the regular delegation, whose members had already walked out in protest of the ill-fated compromise.

The boardwalk vigil grew very large on the last night of the convention, as a thousand voices chanted "Freedom now!" and led by Hamer, sang the movement's anthem, joining hands more tightly than ever. The grass-roots army that had valiantly tried to inject moral passion and commitment into cautious electoral politics returned to the Southern battlefield dejected, disillusioned, angry, but far from giving up. Many had learned that, whether or not they could ever hope to build alliances with white liberals, they had to first have power of their own.

A harsh critic of the Atlantic City setback was thirty-nine-year-old Malcolm X, who was rapidly emerging as the leading spokesperson for the emotions and aspirations of the black poor in the nation's large cities. He called 1964 "the Year of Illusion and Delusion," the year of the "great doublecross" of blacks.[83] Tall, slim, and pensive, Malcolm Little was the son of a Baptist preacher who in the 1920s had organized for Marcus Garvey's black nationalist Universal Negro Improvement Association. A high school dropout, Malcolm was educated in the ghettos of Roxbury and Harlem, making his way as a hustler, drug dealer, and pimp. In the middle of a six-year prison term for robbery, he converted to the separatist Nation of Islam, or Black Muslims, founded by Elijah Muhammad. He gained increasing recognition as a phenomenal stump speaker and organizer for the Muslims, but conflicts with Muhammad led to his departure in March 1964. In a hurricane of activity he set up his own Muslim group, founded the Organization of Afro-American Unity, and took two long journeys to the Mideast and Africa, during which he converted to orthodox Islam and talked deeply with African revolutionary leaders.

Back at home he lectured to countless audiences—shifting expertly from focused fury to incisive reasoning and pungent wit—about what he had learned in his explorations and his evolving vision of black liberation. In late December 1964 he spoke to black teenage activists from Mc-Comb, whom SNCC had brought to New York for the Christmas holidays:

Never at any time in the history of our people in this country have we made advances or progress in any way based upon the internal good will of this country. . . . The only time the black man in this country is given any kind of recognition, or even listened to, is when America is afraid of outside pressure, or when she's afraid of her image abroad. So we saw that it was necessary to expand the problem and the struggle of the black man in this country until it went above and beyond the jurisdiction of the United States. . . . The greatest accomplishment that was made in the struggle of the black man in America in 1964 toward some kind of real progress was the successful linking together of our problems with the African problem, or making our problem a world problem. . . . I wanted to point this out to you because it is important for you to know when you're in Mississippi, you're not alone.[84]

This was Malcolm's grand strategy: to internationalize the struggle of African-Americans, to ground it firmly in the global context in which people of color were the majority, and to get moral, diplomatic, and material help from Third World countries; to "expand the civil-rights struggle to the level of human rights," and as a first step to put American racism on trial before the United Nations.[85] No longer was Malcolm an absolute separatist, except as a temporary necessity, and his commitment to black nationalism was tempered by his newfound internationalism. Nor was he a Marxist, though he identified with African-style socialism. Despite his criticism of civil rights leaders like King for their caution and subservience to white money, he wanted to cooperate with the freedom movement. He argued that it had to play by different rules, however, and that the chief priority was for blacks to unify themselves before they could think about making alliances with whites, rich or poor. He felt that freedom would ultimately come either "by ballots or by bullets."[86] He had little tolerance for the "masochism" of nonviolence and adamantly justified not only armed self-defense but "tit for tat" revenge against the Klan and other white terrorists. That issue divided him most sharply from the movement mainstream, from its leaders anyway, though not so much from SNCC, which by that time tacitly supported the right of armed self-defense.

On 21 February 1965 Malcolm X was assassinated (apparently by Black Muslim loyalists) as he was about to unveil a new political program at Harlem's Audobon Ballroom. He had just started to forge closer ties with the Southern movement. Two weeks before SNCC had brought him to Selma, Alabama, where he was warmly cheered by young protesters getting ready to march; though he had toned down his remarks, SCLC officials worked hard to calm the marchers' excitement. Malcolm's promise was cut short, but his vision and legacy were to loom large over the rest of the decade and beyond.

In January SCLC had decided to conduct a major voting rights campaign in Selma, where a small band of SNCC activists had been organizing ward meetings and registration marches for two years, braving fierce attacks by Sheriff Jim Clark and his volunteer posse. They were ambivalent about King's people coming in, but gave the effort full support, knowing it would boost the registration drive even if it might weaken indigenous leadership. Out of 15,000 eligible black voters in the county, only 300 were registered, most of them professionals; the percentage was lower in neighboring rural counties. Registration was permitted only two days per month, and black applicants were processed so slowly that even if everyone passed the fraudulent exam, it would take years to enfranchise all of Selma's black citizenry.

Fresh from the pinnacle of world acclaim for winning the 1964 Nobel Peace Prize, King led a march toward the courthouse where, after kneeling in prayer, he, Abernathy, and hundreds of others were jailed. Protests grew during the week until over 3,000 had been arrested. Two weeks later black people in the nearby town of Marion were savagely set upon by a squad of state troopers when they marched peacefully at night, and twenty-six-year-old Jimmie Lee Jackson was shot in cold blood trying to protect his mother and grandfather, both of whom were badly beaten. When he died a few days later, local blacks decided to march on the state capital. SCLC's James Bevel had the same idea.

On Sunday, 7 March, Hosea Williams of SCLC and SNCC's John Lewis led 600 people out of Brown AME Chapel, defying Governor George Wallace's ban on marching. King was back in Atlanta. As they crossed the Edmund Pettus Bridge—named for Selma's own Confederate general—on the highway to Montgomery, forty-five miles away, they were halted by a solid phalanx of helmeted and gas-masked state troopers, who with little warning lunged at them, smashing heads and lobbing tear-gas grenades. The troopers and Sheriff Clark's posse, on horses, chased and trampled the marchers all the way back to the church, madly flailing whips, clubs, and cattle prods, and hurling one youth through a stained-glass window that depicted Jesus. Despite a fractured skull, Lewis found strength to direct his fallen comrades out of danger. Protests against "Bloody Sunday," demanding federal action, erupted in cities all over the country, including a SNCC sit-in at the attorney general's office and an expanded vigil and picket line at the White House.

SCLC flashed telegrams to hundreds of Northern clergy urging them to join King two days later to pick up the march. When federal judge Frank Johnson issued an injunction against it, King wavered but then decided to proceed. When the singing and chanting marchers, their ranks swelled by many religious notables, recrossed the Pettus Bridge, troopers stopped them again. As King led the gathering in prayer, the troopers strangely moved out of the way; but instead of pushing on, he ordered his followers to turn back. They retreated to the church singing "Ain't Gonna Let Nobody Turn Me 'Round," the Selma theme song—an irony not lost on everyone. King's maneuver, the result of a last-minute agreement with federal officials, angered the more militant protesters and furthered SNCC's distrust of King and SCLC.

Yet the rapid-fire series of events, including the murder of a white Unitarian minister from Boston—which, predictably, prompted the national concern that Jackson's death had not—already had worked magic on Washington politicians, not least the supreme politician in the Oval Office whose own residence was briefly disrupted by a sit-in. As demonstrations continued around the country, Lyndon Johnson finally resolved to make a voting rights bill—with key provisions for federal registrars and a ban on literacy tests—his highest domestic priority. Virtually overnight he and Attorney General Nicholas Katzenbach crafted a congressional coalition to enact it.

On Monday evening, 15 March, Selma protesters huddled around television sets to watch the president plead for the bill, with uncharacteristic passion, before a joint session of Congress. "At times history and fate meet in a single time in a single place," he began, his big frame hunched over the podium, "to shape a turning point in man's unending search for

Kneeling Selma to Montgomery marchers look at John Birch Society billboard of
Martin Luther King, Jr., at Highlander workshop, March 1965.
© 1978 Matt Herron

freedom. So it was at Lexington and Concord. So it was a century ago at Appomattox. So it was last week in Selma, Alabama." After promising the nation that "we shall overcome," he closed by reminiscing about his own encounter with discrimination against Chicanos as a young Texas teacher and declared: "I do not want to be the President who built empires, or sought grandeur, or extended domain. I want to be the President who helped to feed the hungry."[87] It was his finest hour, though the bill did not reach his desk until late summer.

Despite this high-level attention, the march to Montgomery would not be held back. With a go-ahead from the federal court and careful logistical preparation, hundreds of marchers set off for the Alabama capital, closely guarded by nearly ten times as many National Guard and Army troops deployed by the president. For five days the "mudcaked pilgrims" trekked through the heat and drenching rain, through the dense swamps of Lowndes County, past half-collapsed shacks, rickety Baptist churches, and a dilapidated black school in Trickem without a roof.[88] Their numbers multiplied on the final night, and they were regaled by famous entertainers in their campground.

The next day, as Governor Wallace peered out sheepishly at the surging mass of humanity below his office window—impressed in spite of himself—Martin Luther King, Jr., stood near the bronze star marking the site of the inauguration of Confederate president Jefferson Davis. Down beyond the protesters he could see the church he had pastored, where the bus boycott had been launched a decade before. The decentralized movement had traversed the South and grown into, perhaps, the nation's preeminent political force; now thousands of participants had returned to its birthplace. "How long?" King asked the marchers. "Not long," he answered, repeating the litany again and again as more and more voices joined the surging rhythm. "How long?" he concluded. "Not long, because mine eyes have seen the glory of the coming of the Lord; tramping out the vintage where the grapes of wrath are stored. . . . His truth is marching on!"[89]

One of his rapt listeners was Viola Liuzzo, a white volunteer from Detroit who had labored with boundless energy to make the march a success. That morning she had felt a strong premonition that someone would be killed. As she drove her conspicuous green Oldsmobile back to Montgomery with a black teenager to ferry another carload home, she was shot to death by four Klansmen, one of them an FBI informer, on a desolate highway in the swamps of Lowndes County.

Marchers from Selma enter Montgomery in the rain, March 1965.
© *1978 Matt Herron*

A Dream Deferred

What happens to a dream deferred?

Does it dry up
like a raisin in the sun?
Or fester like a sore—
And then run?
Does it stink like rotten meat?
Or crust and sugar over—
like a syrupy sweet?

Maybe it just sags
like a heavy load.

Or does it explode?

—Langston Hughes, "Harlem"

The day after Viola Liuzzo's murder, and partly in response to it, seasoned SNCC organizer Stokely Carmichael arrived in Lowndes County,
Alabama, with a sleeping bag and the name of someone to stay with.
SNCC had decided that if they could get impoverished blacks to vote in
this "totalitarian" county—where they were four-fifths of the population
and not a single one had been able to vote—it could be a model for the
entire black belt.[90] Born in Trinidad, Carmichael grew up in New York
ghettos and graduated from the select Bronx High School of Science,
where he hobnobbed with children of the Old Left, black and white. Then
he attended Howard University in Washington and threw himself into the
sit-ins and freedom rides—one of those whose baptism by fire was Mississippi's Parchman Penitentiary. He had recently gained recognition as
a district director of the Mississippi Summer Project.

Having learned from the MFDP that blacks could not rely on white
allies and must create their own base of power independent from the
Democratic party, Carmichael and his cadre carefully mobilized local citizens, notably ministers and older women, to form the Lowndes County
Freedom Organization (LCFO), aided by an obscure law making it not
hard to qualify an alternative county party. Its symbol was a black
panther, an animal "that when it is pressured it moves back until it is
cornered," explained LCFO chair John Hulett, a longtime local activist
and father of seven, "then it comes out fighting for life or death. We felt
we had been pushed back long enough."[91] The plan was simple, wrote
SNCC program secretary Cleveland Sellers: "We intended to register as
many blacks as we could, all of them if possible, and take over the
county. . . . After achieving success in Lowndes, we intended to widen
our base by branching out and doing the same thing in surrounding counties. We were convinced that we had found The Lever we had been
searching for."[92]

Black enfranchisement took hold, boosted by new federal registrars,
bringing with it a rise in white retaliation. An LCFO convention nominated candidates for all county offices and conducted a remarkable grass-
roots campaign during summer and fall 1966. At a large, spirited church
rally on election eve, the candidate for tax assessor, Alice Moore, gave
a very short speech: "My platform is tax the rich and feed the poor," she
announced to roaring applause.[93] Hulett promised that they would govern
the county "as a model for democracy."[94] Though they lost every seat,
the party of the black panther had made a good start toward building a
network of indigenous black political organizations.

During this period SNCC was beset by growing pains and battle fatigue, new political questions, and a need to look for new directions. An influx of white organizers after Mississippi Freedom Summer intensified black-white friction, and conflict arose between the more individualistic "freedom high" faction trying (as they saw it) to carry on the original SNCC spirit and lifestyle, and the "hardliners," led by Forman and Sellers, who wanted a more disciplined, centralized, and politically effective organization and were challenging the leadership style championed by Bob Moses and Ella Baker.

A heated issue that could not be ignored was the sudden escalation of the Vietnam War by President Johnson. Moses and others had taken part in the earliest antiwar rallies. In January 1966 SNCC came out against the war with a strong statement condemning the government for its hypocrisy in ostensibly defending freedom and democracy in the Third World when it refused to do so in the American South. In fact, SNCC felt growing affinity with national liberation movements in Vietnam and elsewhere. Since SNCC men were vulnerable to conscription and were harassed by their local draft boards, the statement also supported those who resisted the draft in order to build democratic forms at home: "Where is the draft for the freedom fight in the United States?"[95] Despite blistering attacks by the media, politicians of all stripes, and black moderates, SNCC did not retreat, which cut it further adrift from the civil rights mainstream. SNCC organizer Julian Bond, just elected to the Georgia legislature, was barred by fellow legislators from taking office for backing the Vietnam stand. SNCC did antidraft organizing in its communities, and several staff members refused induction—Sellers was sentenced to five years. The organization led disruptive protests at the Atlanta induction center, where they invented a famous slogan, "Hell no, we won't go!" Later they would help create the National Black Anti-War Anti-Draft Union.

In early June 1966 James Meredith, who had integrated "Ole Miss" with the aid of federal troops, set off on a solitary march through Mississippi to make the point that black people could live like human beings. His ambush by shotgun, seriously injuring him, precipitated a dramatic conflict among the movement's leaders that had vast repercussions. The chief civil rights leaders converged at Meredith's hospital bedside in Memphis and resolved to jointly continue his "march against fear," to reunify the movement and to push registration in places where the government was delinquent in enforcing the new voting law. King had just started an SCLC campaign in Chicago, ultimately unsuccessful, to force Mayor Richard Daley to end racism in hiring and housing and to prove that nonviolent action could work in explosive Northern ghettos. To symbolize his commitment he had moved with his family into a dingy, urine-stenched tenement in one of the Windy City's worst slums. Stokely Carmichael had been elected chair of SNCC in May, along with dynamic ex–freedom rider Ruby Doris Smith Robinson replacing Forman as executive secretary, at a pivotal meeting in which it was decided that white SNCC members should organize only in white communities. Roy Wilkins and Whitney Young angrily packed their bags, however, when Carmichael, backed by CORE's Floyd McKissick, got King's reluctant assent for the march to minimize white participation, to have protection from the armed Deacons for Defense, and to aim at promoting independent black organizations.

As the marchers trod through familiar SNCC territory in the Delta, they roused the local folk and expanded voting rolls but were met by ferocious police assaults. After his jailing for setting up sleeping tents, Carmichael was warmly welcomed by a huge night rally in Greenwood. "This is the twenty-seventh time I have been arrested—and I ain't going to jail no more!" The crowd cheered him on. "The only way we gonna stop them white men from whuppin' us is to take over. We been saying freedom for six years and we ain't got nothin'. What we gonna start saying now is Black Power!"[96] SNCC organizer Willie Ricks led the assembly in passionate cries of "Black power!" repeated over and over. The expression, which starkly encapsulated SNCC's political vision, had been used before by Richard Wright, Paul Robeson, and Adam Clayton Powell, but now caught on and electrified black youth all over the country as it ignited a storm of criticism from older leaders and white liberal allies. On the march the nightly rallies turned into contests over which chant, "Black power" or "Freedom now," could drown out the other.

In Yazoo City, where to his chagrin he had been booed by some marchers, King held a long summit meeting with Carmichael, McKissick, and other leaders to try to resolve the antagonism. He said he understood the new slogan's magnetic appeal to young blacks, whose expectations had been lifted by himself and others but who felt bitter and betrayed because their elders were unable to deliver on promises. Yet he argued that the slogan would be self-defeating for the movement. Leaders must be concerned with how their rhetoric is interpreted, he counseled. While the *concept* of Black Power was sound, the slogan had the "wrong connotations." He worried about the violent images it conjured up and the media's alarmism. Carmichael replied that every other ethnic group had created its own power base to advance itself, why not black people?

Leaders meet during the spring 1966 Mississippi march in Greenwood just after
Stokely Carmichael's "Black Power" speech. Bernard Lee (*left foreground*),
Carmichael (*on floor*), Andrew Young and Martin Luther King, Jr. (*left and right on
couch*), and Lawrence Guyot (*upper right*). *Bob Fitch*

"That is just the point," King answered.

No one has ever heard the Jews publicly chant a slogan of Jewish power, but they
have power. . . . The same thing is true of the Irish and Italians. Neither group
has used a slogan of Irish or Italian power, but they have worked hard to achieve
it. This is exactly what we must do. We must use every constructive means to
amass economic and political power. This is the kind of legitimate power we
need. We must work to build racial pride and refute the notion that black is evil
and ugly. But this must come through a program, not merely through a slogan.

"Martin," Carmichael confessed, "I deliberately decided to raise this
issue on the march in order to give it a national forum, and force you to
take a stand for Black Power." King laughed. "I have been used before.
One more time won't hurt."[97] Neither side swayed the other, but out of
respect for De Lawd the SNCC and CORE chiefs agreed to stop using
either slogan until the expedition was over. Later King disavowed the
Black Power slogan, but he never repudiated Carmichael or SNCC. He
still hoped for a united black movement.

Despite the acrimony, some SNCC activists were very impressed with King when they made friends with him hiking along the hot highway, "discussing strategy, tactics and our dreams." He had an engaging sense of humor and an open mind, Sellers discovered, and was "much less conservative than we initially believed. . . . I will never forget his magnificent speeches at the nightly rallies. Nor the humble smile that spread across his face when throngs of admirers rushed forward to touch him." He was "a staunch ally and a true brother."[98]

There is no question that King was moving leftward as the decade of the 1960s raced along at its relentless pace. And in direct proportion, he became an increasing threat to the higher circles, especially the president and J. Edgar Hoover. The latter had called him "the most notorious liar in the country" for criticizing the FBI's collusion with Southern police.[99] Obsessed with hatred, the FBI czar had conducted unremitting espionage against King—to which the Kennedys and Johnson acquiesced—aimed at smearing him with alleged Communist ties and sexual improprieties. What began as a personal vendetta turned into a major, covert federal program to harass and discredit the potential "black Messiah" after he spoke out against the war in Vietnam.

King had agonized about his moral responsibility in regard to Vietnam at least since the bombing began in early 1965. Overriding objections from his aides, who were worried about losing financial donors, he started criticizing Johnson's policy that August, but his public comments were restrained. By spring of 1967, prodded by the burgeoning antiwar movement and one of its advocates, Coretta Scott King, his soul-searching led him to believe that he must be more forthright. Speaking before 3,000 at New York's Riverside Church in early April, he declared that he had been moved to "break the betrayal of my own silences" and condemn "the greatest purveyor of violence in the world today—my own government. . . . Somehow this madness must cease." He opposed the war not only because it was morally wrong, he said, but because it robbed the country of resources needed to fight racism and poverty, and because young black men were dying for a freedom in Vietnam they could not have at home. He could no longer segregate his moral concerns: Vietnam and civil rights were intertwined. Thus, "we must combine the fervor of the civil rights movement with the peace movement."[100] The most prominent American to join the antiwar forces, the Nobel Peace Prize winner was denounced by the *New York Times* and other liberal media for linking the issues and for incompetence in foreign affairs, and by black leaders like Wilkins and Young for alienating LBJ and jeopardizing the delicate civil rights coalition.

During the same period that King emerged as probably the most influential critic of the war, he was also critical of past civil rights strategies, particularly his reliance on dramatic short-run confrontations to shake the nation's conscience, and he moved closer to SNCC's belief in long-term community organizing. He eventually came to see that what was most needed was not the elite coalitions so jealously guarded by Wilkins, Young, and their ilk, but grass-roots, class-based, interracial alliances of the poor. His ultimate goal was now "a reconstruction of the entire society, a revolution of values," and the building of a "socially conscious democracy which reconciles the truths of individualism and collectivism."[101] His first concrete step toward this vision was to try to mobilize an army of poor people to shut down the nation's capital until they were given butter instead of guns—to win the war against poverty once and for all. He saw it as a supreme test of nonviolent action.

But on 4 April 1968—just when King might have begun to forge the grand alliance against poverty and militarism that was his final dream— he was shot dead on a motel balcony in Memphis, where he was supporting a strike by sanitation workers. The thirty-nine-year-old leader, who had suffered more and more from the government's incessant hounding and from attacks within his own movement and had readied himself for his death, was laid to rest at his father's church in Atlanta. While many Americans grieved quietly, black youth in a hundred cities expressed their rage in the most widespread urban violence the country had ever seen. Overtaken by the tornado of events, the poor people's army in Washington fizzled in the hard spring rain.

The conflagration that greeted King's killing followed half a decade of escalating rebellions in black ghettos, where racist police practices, lack of jobs, inhumane housing, and associated ills had produced an "explosive mixture which had been accumulating in our cities since the end of World War II," concluded the national commission on civil disorders the same month that King fell.[102] Moreover, the unfulfilled promises of the freedom movement, and its minimal attention to cities outside the South where segregation was not the issue, persuaded many young ghetto dwellers that they would have to act on their own, without plan, organization, or allies. Most of the urban uprisings were ignited by instances of police misconduct. The white cops who patrolled the ghettos both symbolized and actualized the power, racism, and repressiveness of "the Man." They gave the "mean streets" the feel of a Third World colony.

In August 1965, four days after President Johnson signed the Voting Rights Act, the first large-scale "riot" broke out during a sweltering heat

Newly registered voter, Batesville, Mississippi, summer 1966. *Bob Fitch*

wave in the vast Watts section of Los Angeles. For five days black men and women looted stores and firebombed buildings, their principal intent "to destroy property owned by whites, in order to drive white 'exploiters' out of the ghetto."[103] The California National Guard belatedly restored order using excessive firepower. Thirty-four people died, mostly black; hundreds were injured, nearly 4,000 jailed. Despite the loss of black lives, the young insurgents of Watts believed they had won—they had drawn the nation's attention to their plight.

Two summers later, in July 1967, the ghettos' spontaneous combustion verged on outright civil war in two cities; half a dozen others had lesser disturbances. Pent-up political powerlessness in Newark, New Jersey, resulting from an unresponsive, white-dominated city hall, fueled a rampage of looting and property wreckage triggered by the police beating of a black cab driver. Poorly coordinated police and National Guard troops stifled the revolt with much indiscriminate gunfire, some of it against imaginary snipers. Nearly half of the twenty-one blacks they killed were uninvolved, including a seventy-three-year-old man, six women, and two young children.

The most catastrophic urban rebellion in U.S. history erupted a week later in Detroit, which had seen a major race riot in 1943, mainly whites attacking black newcomers. By the mid-1960s, after further migration from the South, the once-integrated area centering on 12th Street was among the nation's most densely populated urban districts, with overcrowded, dilapidated apartment buildings and rampant unemployment among its predominantly black inhabitants. "Open warfare" with police had been growing since the earlier conflict.[104] A late-night raid of a black club drew a furious crowd that started a chain reaction of looting and burning, young blacks seeming to be "dancing amidst the flames."[105] Most of the several hundred gutted buildings were destroyed by spreading, wind-swept fires. Fire fighters reportedly withdrew 300 times when the police failed to protect them. Governor George Romney flew over the battleground at dusk on the second day. "It looked like the city had been bombed on the west side," he testified later, "and there was an area two-and-a-half miles by three-and-a-half miles with major fires, with entire blocks in flames."[106] Five thousand National Guardsmen were reinforced by 2,700 Army paratroopers dispatched by the commander-in-chief. As in Newark and Watts, the devastation was compounded by chaos within the armies of the law, who often did not know who, where, or why they were shooting. Most of the forty-three deaths of men, women, and children—thirty-three of them blacks—were "accidental."

Conditions improved little in the aftermath, and in the long run got worse. More federal effort went into making riot control forces more efficient than into eradicating the underlying problems of poverty and racism. The government, already scaling down its inadequate antipoverty programs, refused to heed its own investigative commission's warning that "our nation is moving toward two societies, one black, one white—separate and unequal. . . . White society is deeply implicated in the ghetto. White institutions created it, white institutions maintain it, and white society condones it." Perhaps the "unprecedented levels of funding and performance" the Kerner Commission called for would have been more available had it not been for the other war 10,000 miles away.[107]

When in the mid-1960s the Southern-based freedom movement turned into a broader nationwide struggle for black liberation, it pursued several paths that intersected but also diverged, ranging from revolt in the ghetto to black capitalism. Black Power emerged as the unifying theme for all those who rejected the goal of integration, but it had various meanings to suit various agendas. Unable to fashion a clear political strategy to implement it, black radicals exploited its ambiguities to widen their appeal. In the most basic sense, inspired by Malcolm X, it stood for racial pride and racial identity—black consciousness—conveyed by the slogan "Black is beautiful." More concretely, it expressed democratic aspirations for collective self-determination and political control of black communities. On the economic front, it was interpreted as a mandate to develop and support black-owned businesses.

More and more, Black Power came to be entwined with a new version of black nationalism—the conception of African-Americans as a colonized people with a rightful claim to nationhood (a perspective antedating the Civil War). Black nationalism implied separatism from whites, but disagreements arose about how far to go, and whether coalitions with whites were acceptable on black terms. Some followed Malcolm X in seeing separatism more as a strategy than as an ultimate aim. Two conflicting strands of nationalism vied for Malcolm's mantle: political nationalists, such as the Black Panthers, who emphasized class oppression as much as race and sought alliance with white radicals; and cultural nationalists, the most well-known of whom were Ron Karenga and playwright Imiri Baraka (Leroi Jones), who celebrated African roots and espoused cultural revolution. Both strands were profoundly influenced by Frantz Fanon's study of the Algerian war against France. Fanon argued that for a colonized people to gain liberation, violence was not only a strategic necessity but a psychological need. Yet the violence of some Black Power groups was mainly on a rhetorical and stylistic level. Despite a fetish with guns, overt violence rarely went beyond armed self-defense, ostensibly a constitutional right.

By the time of the Newark and Detroit disorders, SNCC had shifted its center of gravity to the Northern war zones, setting up shop in a number of cities. Providing a political framework for the growing fury of urban blacks, Stokely Carmichael emerged as the leading popularizer of Black Power and an international celebrity—which rankled many SNCC members who felt his cult of personality violated their ethic of group-centered, accountable leadership. Acting increasingly on his own, Carmichael moved toward cultural nationalism and complete separatism, while under James Forman's tutelage SNCC tried to synthesize class and racial politics. CORE also adopted Black Power, like SNCC removed its white members, and engaged in militant organizing in Northern cities; before long it promoted black capitalism as a solution. Black Power assumed different shapes and textures in different urban locales, some organizers continuing efforts to desegregate jobs, housing, and education, some mobilizing for the expansion of welfare payments and "welfare rights," others creating separate, black-controlled institutions to meet black needs. In several places activists put together all-black, citywide coalitions, or "united fronts"; a model was the Black Congress in Los Angeles, formed after the Watts uprising, in which Karenga's "US" organization played a key role.

One black liberation group seized such extraordinary media attention that it overshadowed all others. Taking its name from the symbol of the Lowndes County Freedom Organization in Alabama and identifying closely with Third World liberation struggles, the Black Panther Party for Self-Defense (BPP) was founded in late 1966 by Huey Newton and Bobby Seale in Oakland, California. The BPP's chief mission was to *enforce* civil rights laws and constitutional guarantees, a task the Southern movement had neglected. In particular, they engaged in "patrolling the police" and informing black people of their rights when facing arrest. This activity led to a sensational shoot-out in the Oakland ghetto during which Newton allegedly killed a white cop. Convicted of manslaughter, the Panthers launched an all-out campaign to "free Huey" that eventually won his release.

Militaristic and highly centralized, the BPP promulgated a ten-point platform centering on community control, freedom for all black prisoners, and "our major political objective, a United Nations–supervised plebiscite to be held throughout the Black colony . . . for the purpose of determining the will of Black people as to their national destiny."[108] Forming chapters in several dozen cities, the BPP organized "survival programs" to help needy blacks, including free breakfasts for ghetto children. In 1968 it formed an electoral coalition with the white-led Peace and Freedom party, whose presidential candidate was the Panther's chief communicator, Eldridge Cleaver. The same year it contrived a short-lived alliance with SNCC to take advantage of the latter's organizing skill and resources, and Carmichael's notoriety. What Cleaver called a "merger" of the two groups was barely more than a tenuous link with Carmichael, appointed BPP "prime minister."[109] Personal and ideological clashes produced deepening distrust and hostility, and the alliance shattered in open recrimination. Unable to surmount its own internal divisions, which were intensified by external repression, SNCC faded into obscurity a year later.

Hampered by their authoritarian leadership and violent image, the Black Panthers never built a solid base in the black community, outside of Oakland; their most reliable support came from the white left. The harder they clung to Marxism-Leninism, the less they were able to reconcile black nationalism and socialism. Though Black Panther violence was far more of word than deed, local and national police agencies teamed up in a concerted effort to extinguish the organization. The campaign included illegal arrests, spurious prosecutions, premeditated murder by police (Fred Hampton and Mark Clark in Chicago), and FBI "Cointelpro" operations that fomented divisiveness and paranoia within the party and toward other militant groups such as SNCC and Karenga's US. (FBI machinations precipitated a Los Angeles gunfight in which US members killed two Panthers.) As with SNCC's demise, it is hard to determine whether warfare from within or without took the heaviest toll—harder still to disentangle the two. With most of its leadership killed, imprisoned, or self-exiled, the Black Panther party survived the decade a shadow of its luminous past.

As it migrated northward, the black freedom movement vividly reproduced the historic duality of separatist versus integrationist perspectives that had always characterized the African-American struggle. If the Southern movement's great achievement was the abolition of legalized segregation, the legacy of Black Power was by and large the fruit of its distinct movement culture, which owed more to African origins and urban folkways than to the black church. Among its enduring contributions are the hard-won black studies programs that have taken hold in many colleges and universities (even high schools), and a flowering of African-American art, literature, music, drama, and film. New generations of black people still face multilayered disadvantages, but thanks to the culture of black liberation they now have an advantage not enjoyed by most whites: a rich heritage to take pride in and a collective identity to celebrate. The resulting self-respect and self-confidence are crucial tools of empowerment in the continuing struggle for black equality.

Political and cultural expressions of Black Power lived on through the 1970s and beyond, but the black liberation movement lost its cutting edge with the collapse of SNCC and the Panthers. Two closely linked episodes in 1971 marked the movement's eclipse. Prison organizer and Panther field marshal George Jackson, locked up eleven years for a $70 robbery—seven of those years in solitary confinement—and author of *Soledad Brother,* a compelling indictment of prison racism, was shot through the head by a guard at California's San Quentin in an alleged escape. "George's death has meant the loss of a comrade and revolutionary leader," black activist/intellectual Angela Davis, a close friend, wrote from her jail cell several miles away.[110] She had been accused of involvement in an attempt to free prisoners from a courtroom during which Jackson's teenage brother had been slain.

The next day, across the country at Attica prison in upstate New York, inmates fasted and protested silently. Jackson's book had uplifted them; he was a hero. Two weeks later over half of Attica's population, mainly blacks and Puerto Ricans, seized control of the prison, took dozens of hostages, and issued demands for long-overdue improvements. They called in an unusual team of "observers," including Panther chair Bobby Seale and *New York Times* columnist Tom Wicker, to negotiate for them. When talks broke down and Governor Nelson Rockefeller refused to step in, helicopters suddenly flooded the interior with tear gas as a battalion of state troopers sneaked in with high-powered rifles and in a few minutes wiped out thirty prisoners and ten hostages. The Attica massacre was the bloodiest crushing of a prison revolt in American history. A survivor, inmate John Lee Norris, wrote a poem about it:

> . . . And another page of history is written in black blood
> And old black mamas pay taxes to buy guns that killed their sons
> And the consequence of being free . . . is death
> And your sympathy and tears always come too late
> And the only thing they do right is wrong
> And it's just another page.[111]

Many others had reason for hope. Dewey Greene of Greenwood, Mississippi, father of two SNCC activists, summed up the meaning of the change wrought by the freedom movement he had participated in: "That Negro won't take no beating," he said. "So, I guess it's coming little by little, but I know it's come that far."[112]

Chapter Two

Everything Is Possible

Phoenix Rising

June 1958. The *Phoenix* left Honolulu harbor under full sail heading southwest into the Pacific. Sailing the fifty-foot ketch were skipper Dr. Earle Reynolds, Barbara Reynolds, their teenage children Ted and Jessica, and Nick Mikami, citizen of Hiroshima, their ultimate destination. Close relatives of Mikami's had been victims of the nuclear holocaust in 1945. Dr. Reynolds was an anthropologist who had done a study for the Atomic Energy Commission (AEC) on the effect of radioactivity on the bones of Hiroshima children born shortly after the bombing. The stunting of bone growth was so appalling that the AEC refused to let him publish it. Infuriated, he quit his job, built the *Phoenix* in Hiroshima, and embarked with his family and Mikami on a four-year journey around the world, a lifelong dream. Stopping in Hawaii to prepare for the last leg, they found that the AEC had cordoned off a vast area of the Pacific for H-bomb tests that summer, blocking their route back to Japan. While on shore they met the crew of the *Golden Rule*, including CORE activist Jim Peck and skipper Albert Bigelow, a former Navy commander and Massachusetts housing commissioner (both future freedom riders)—who had tried twice to sail into the Eniwetok test zone only to be caught by the Coast Guard a few miles out to sea, arrested, and jailed.

Though Earle Reynolds had first thought the pacifist sailors a little crackpot and was interested in the legal and scientific more than the moral issues, his wife persuaded him that they should continue the voyage of the *Golden Rule,* come what may. Mikami and the teenagers were enthusiastic. Reynolds wrote later that he was "just not the lawbreaking type," and that what he feared was not so much the physical danger as "the idea of *doing* such an outlandish thing"—along with the expectation that his career would be finished.[1] Hours after they entered the test zone, the Coast Guard illegally boarded the *Phoenix,* arrested Reynolds, and escorted them to the Navy base on Kwajalein atoll. In the middle of the night Barbara and Ted Reynolds witnessed a dirty orange light, like a "gigantic flash bulb," illuminating the dark clouds.[2]

As it turned out, the expeditions of the *Phoenix* and its precursor garnered worldwide publicity and sparked protests against AEC nuclear testing throughout the United States and in Europe. The *Golden Rule* was a project of the Committee for Nonviolent Action (CNVA), set up the year before by pacifist groups to provide a militant cutting edge for the nascent peace movement. For several years radical pacifists, many of them Quakers, had agitated against nuclear weapons. A favorite target was civil defense drills. But their ranks had been badly depleted by the scourge of McCarthyism. The congressional witch hunts had scared many Americans into believing that all radicals—even committed liberals—were Communists in disguise. In this climate of mass hysteria, *any* dissent was dangerous. Meanwhile, some principled scientists, including a few who had helped develop the Bomb, became alarmed about the dangers of radioactive fallout and educated their colleagues. "Most hoped to bridge the gap between East and West and to rebuild the international scientific community as a force for peace and understanding."[3] Made credible by the technical expertise of some of its members, a movement to stop nuclear tests was galvanized by the issue of atmospheric testing—just when the orbiting of Sputnik, the first artificial satellite, heightened Cold War fears about Soviet potential.

To complement the direct action focus of CNVA, a collection of peace liberals and "nuclear pacifists," among them Nobel Prize–winning chemist Linus Pauling and journalist Norman Cousins, formed the National Committee for a Sane Nuclear Policy (SANE) to educate the public and lobby the higher political circles with rational arguments. SANE quickly grew into a major national organization and, like CNVA, broadened its goal: complete nuclear disarmament. But in 1960, just as it was emerging as a significant political force, a purge of alleged Communist members weakened it, and many radical pacifists resigned in protest.

Though few in number, CNVA members proved to be a remarkable cadre of direct actionists, skilled at attracting the media with daring exploits. Seeing the new development of intercontinental ballistic missiles as a fateful escalation of the arms race, CNVA protested the construction of a missile base near Cheyenne, Wyoming, in late summer 1958; two women and three men were imprisoned for blocking trucks. The next year CNVA launched "Omaha Action," a campaign of community education and civil disobedience to halt the building of missile silos near that city. One of those arrested climbing over a fence was A. J. Muste, the seventy-four-year-old ringleader and chair of CNVA. The most respected and influential radical pacifist in the country, Muste had been fighting for justice and peace for half a century—as a Dutch Reformed minister, a labor leader and strike organizer during the 1920s and 1930s, the head of the pacifist Fellowship of Reconciliation, and an incorrigible civil disobedient. During the early thirties Muste was a leader of the Trotskyist movement, but he soon abandoned doctrinaire Marxism and in many essays and speeches articulated "a vision of nonviolent revolution which included a democratic political order, a socialist economic system, world government, and a nonviolent method of national civil defense."[4]

While in federal prison for the Omaha protest, activist Brad Lyttle thought up the "Polaris Action" as a further step in stimulating public opposition to nuclear arms. CNVA settled in New London, Connecticut, where missile-firing Polaris submarines were built. In the summer and fall of 1960 peace guerrillas invaded the docks, paddled small boats to board the subs or block their launching, and even swam out to throw their bodies on them. The activists had tough encounters with the workers and sailors they tried to talk with, but eventually gained some local support. A few workers offered to quit if CNVA could find them new jobs.

For years pacifists had been told to "tell it to the Russians," but early attempts to do so had little success. The San Francisco-to-Moscow March, commencing in December 1960, made this its mission. After a trek of several thousand miles, enduring weeks with little food, a group of Americans and West Europeans walked through the Iron Curtain into East Germany and Poland—at the height of the second Berlin crisis—and arrived in Moscow in October 1961. They held a vigil in Red Square and passed out leaflets urging disarmament. "I went to jail because I refused to serve in the U.S. Army," Lyttle explained to an audience in Minsk. "I have protested against American rockets aimed at your cities and families. There are Soviet rockets aimed at my city and my family. Are you demonstrating against that?"[5]

Following two more years of peace talks, nonviolent invasions of test sites on land and sea, campus rallies, marches—notably, a simultaneous protest by 50,000 women in several dozen cities organized by Women Strike for Peace—and vigorous lobbying by SANE, the Kennedy administration reached agreement with the Soviets in August 1963 on a limited test-ban treaty prohibiting atmospheric and undersea testing. A good first step, it was nevertheless a half-measure at best. Allowed to continue explosions underground, in which the United States had technological superiority, the AEC conducted over twice as many tests in the next seven years as in the previous eighteen, many more than the Soviet Union conducted. Moreover, the accelerated testing readied a new generation of lower-yield but more accurate weapons, particularly the destabilizing MIRVs (multiple independently targetable reentry vehicles), which were multiple-warhead missiles. Yet for the time being, the end of superpower atmospheric testing, the most immediately harmful symptom of nuclear madness, persuaded many activists that the government was serious about negotiating a halt to the arms race and that a thaw in the Cold War might be at hand. The peace movement was defused. In hardly more than a year it would reemerge and quickly grow larger than ever, focused on another issue more down to earth and peopled by a vast new constituency that would join forces with veteran pacifists—many of whom, however, would ultimately leave pacifism behind.

A year earlier, in June 1962, sixty members of a little-known group called Students for a Democratic Society (SDS) gathered for a conference at the AFL-CIO's wooded FDR Camp at Port Huron on the southern shore of Lake Huron, fifty miles north of Detroit. It had been hard to find a meeting place. A Texas activist had just written to Al Haber, the group's president, "I look forward to hearing from you further about . . . such details as WHERE THE HELL IS IT GOING TO BE?"[6] Under a different name, SDS had been for years the student wing of the League for Industrial Democracy, a tired social democratic outfit, but since 1960 it had been declaring its independence, symbolized by changing its name. SNCC's sit-in movement had spurred its growth; SDS became a major supporter of the Southern black students and in some ways a white counterpart of SNCC, with which it had deep affinities. SDS field secretary Tom Hayden, a journalism student at the University of Michigan and editor of the campus paper, worked with SNCC on voter registration in Georgia and Mississippi, was beaten and jailed, and sent back vivid reports to SDS members. Haber and Hayden foresaw the emergence of a white student movement parallel to the pioneering black student movement, with which it might coalesce. They sensed that what was needed more than theories and programs was a comprehensive moral vision of the possibility of fundamental change in a nation paralyzed by Cold War, both domestic and foreign.

The Michigan conference had been called not only to reshape SDS but to write a manifesto for the white student movement waiting to be born. Delegates divided up into small study groups to revise a rough draft written by Hayden, who had prepared by digesting the ideas of a multitude of political thinkers, including John Stuart Mill, John Dewey, Albert Camus, and especially, C. Wright Mills. The proposed revisions were argued on the principle of "bones-widgets-and-gizmos": "bones (essential matters) could be given an hour's debate, gizmos (effluvia) only ten minutes, and widgets (of medium importance) something in between."[7] Finally, the pieces were sewn together like a patchwork quilt.

The Port Huron Statement was a moral critique of American society—especially of racism, militarism, and citizen apathy—a compelling vision of a regenerated society, and a sketch of a strategy for moving forward. It exalted the aspiration for individual empowerment, for community, and for personal wholeness and authenticity; urged the translation of private troubles into legitimate political concerns; and exposed the invisible connections in the entangling web of issues that plagued the nation and the world. The heart of its message was the call for a new kind of democracy:

> We would replace power rooted in possession, privilege, or circumstance by power and uniqueness rooted in love, reflectiveness, reason and creativity. As a *social system* we seek the establishment of a democracy of individual participation, governed by two central aims: that the individual share in those social decisions determining the quality and direction of his life; that society be organized to encourage independence in men and provide the media for their common participation. . . . [Politics should] have the function of bringing people out of isolation and into community, thus being a necessary, though not sufficient, means of finding meaning in personal life.[8]

All major institutions had to be fully democratized, including economic, cultural, and educational ones.

As it evolved, this new concept of participatory democracy stressed the process of social change but did not lose sight of the need to exercise real power to confront prevailing institutions. In the judgment of historian Wini Breines, it "sought to create both a community within the movement and structural transformation in the larger society," and it "contained the notion of transforming people's relations to institutions and each other in the process of large-scale change." Striving for community and for power were seen as indivisible efforts. But the two poles of this dialectic would soon come unhinged, and a basic conflict would arise in the New Left between what Breines defined as "prefigurative" versus "strategic" politics.[9]

The manifesto made it clear that for good reasons the university, "located in a permanent position of social influence," would be the primary nexus of change, and students the key agents. The "social uses of the universities' resources"—as engineers of the arms race, for instance—made them "functionally tied to society in new ways, revealing new potentialities, new levers for change."[10] Anchored in the "multiversity," which was both target and tool, students and faculty would make forays into the larger world to create alliances with black activists, the peace movement, progressive labor unions, and liberal Democrats. One goal was to realign the Democratic party (pushing conservatives into the GOP) to make it a vehicle of change.

The Port Huron Statement had a big influence on the emerging politics of the New Left, and on the student movement generally. It provided a script that would be acted out by thousands, then hundreds of thousands, with more or less coherence, until SDS would ultimately toss it into a dustbin. The delegates who left the camp at Port Huron after five days of nonstop deliberation did not know that—along with SNCC—they had set the stage for the great surge of grass-roots democracy in the 1960s. But they knew they had charted a new beginning. "It was a little like starting a journey," recalled one participant.[11]

What was this "New Left," and where did it come from? It was new in a double sense: first, as a breaking away from and transcendence of "the memories, the certitudes, and the promises" of the "Old Left" (especially the Communist party), which it dismissed as cranky and hierarchical.[12] In an era heralded by centrists as signifying the "end of ideology," it rebelled against ideology from within the left and embodied a flexible vision at once moral and political, utopian and practical, personal and structural. More important, it was new because it expressed not just a political analysis but a cultural and psychological need—a "union of political reflection and cultural sensibility."[13]

Strictly defined, the New Left was not the student movement as a whole. As sociologist (and Port Huron veteran) Richard Flacks explains, it comprised young activists who were committed radicals but were "disaffected from all 'established radicalisms,' and who self-consciously sought to provide political direction, theoretical coherence and organizational continuity to the student movement."[14] Most were well-educated daughters and sons of well-educated, upper middle–class parents, especially professionals, who politically were liberal or even further left. Relatively few were nonwhite, or from working-class or low-income families. Many of their followers—the larger number of student protesters (from similar backgrounds) who identified with the New Left but were not active members of its organizations—tended to be less intellectually or theoretically inclined, even anti-intellectual (a source of later tension and division).

In an immediate sense SDS and the New Left were catalyzed by the Southern freedom movement—in particular by SNCC, whose organizing style and values SDS imitated and refined, both organizations talking "to people not only about specific issues," Tom Hayden remembers, "but about their lives and feelings"—and to lesser extents by the ban-the-bomb movement and the efforts to restore civil liberties in the wake of McCarthyism.[15] On a deeper level, the New Left was a direct response to the cold, conformist culture of the 1950s, with its ethic of acquisitiveness and its model, the unquestioning "organization man." Stuck in the yawning chasms—on the one hand between American ideals of democracy and self-fulfillment and the felt experience of bureaucratic manipulation and personal emptiness, and on the other hand between the possibilities for freedom and creativity generated by technology and abundance and the harsh realities of material and spiritual poverty—middle-class youth were "growing up absurd," the title of Paul Goodman's path-breaking book. "Our abundant society is at present simply deficient in many of the most elementary objective opportunities and worth-while goals that could make growing up possible," Goodman noted. "It has no Honor. It has no Community."[16] Unable to make sense of their world, angered by universal hypocrisy—many females were awakening to very personal stings of injustice—young people were acting out their semiconscious critique of the "organized system" through "deviant behavior" of one kind or another: as rebels without causes, as followers of the Beat subculture of nonconformity, and more and more through political activism. In fact, Beat figures like Allen Ginsberg and Jack Kerouac were role models for many of the political rebels, and the existentialism of Camus their philosophy of choice.

If the passionate and sardonic Goodman was the chief interpreter and promoter of youthful cultural alienation, the equally passionate, Texas-bred sociologist C. Wright Mills was most responsible for translating it

into political language and commitment. An academic dissident who ana-
lyzed what he considered to be an interlocking "power elite" of corporate,
military, and political leaders, and who engaged in other nonconforming
social science, Mills worried that in both superpowers, "we now witness
the rise of the cheerful robot, the technological idiot, the crackpot realist.
All these types embody a common ethos: rationality without reason."[17]
His solution was to turn reason into the key to fundamental social change:
to convince intellectuals, especially the young intelligentsia, of their
moral responsibility to make their work relevant to the problems of the
era and to lead the academy, then all of society, out of conformity and
apathy and into informed engagement with these great problems. His
words and spirit shone through every page of the Port Huron Statement,
adopted three months after his death from a heart attack at forty-five.

After Port Huron, SDS chapters sprouted at dozens of campuses, and
members worked hard on civil rights and peace. But, ironically, the main
focus for a while was off campus, on building an "interracial movement of
the poor." Through SDS's Economic Research and Action Project
(ERAP), student cadres were recruited for SNCC-style community organizing in white and black ghettos of Chicago, Cleveland, Newark, Baltimore, and other Northern cities. Their objective was to empower
low-income residents to gain greater control over jobs, housing, and services and to create "community unions" through which this power could
grow and endure. Though the ERAP projects won some demands and
offered a testing ground for participatory democracy—downplaying leadership, using consensus decision-making, and so forth—most ended in
failure. Yet ERAP was a radicalizing experience for the organizers. The
intransigence of local bureaucracies taught them the need to confront,
rather than try to reform from within, the controlling institutions of
American life.

By fall 1964 a full-fledged student movement was still not in sight. SDS
and other groups had made some small ripples but had not yet made a
splash.

At noon on 1 October 1964, two deans and the campus police chief
walked up to a young man sitting at a table on Sproul Plaza at the University of California's 27,000-student Berkeley campus. The table dis-
played literature on the Congress of Racial Equality and a collection jar,
violating a campus ban on advocacy and fund-raising for off-campus political causes. When CORE organizer Jack Weinberg refused to take down
the table and was arrested, a large crowd gathered around him and cried,

"Take all of us!" A police car arrived on the plaza, Weinberg was put inside, and a sea of students spontaneously surrounded it and sat down, their numbers multiplying fast. Mario Savio, a philosophy major active in the campus Friends of SNCC who had just returned from Mississippi Freedom Summer, jumped on top of the police car, a perfect soapbox, and after politely removing his shoes demanded Weinberg's release and an end to the free speech ban. Later he led a sit-in at the administration building, following fruitless negotiations with officials. But the police car, with Weinberg still inside, would be held hostage nonviolently for thirty-two hours.

Through the afternoon and evening countless students waited in line to taste the forbidden fruit of free speech atop the car's sagging roof. One of those who gave her first public speech on this occasion was twenty-year-old Bettina Aptheker, daughter of prominent Old Left parents, who as a teenager had marched to ban the bomb and Jim Crow and had picketed her local Woolworth's in Brooklyn in support of the Southern sit-ins. On campus she had been active in the Communist party–oriented W. E. B. Du Bois Club and had been arrested in civil rights protests across the bay in San Francisco. Aptheker recalled that she "got inspired" and felt that she had "something to say." Fending off nervousness, she climbed up to face the TV cameras that pierced the darkness. "There was this tremendous glare of light . . . and every time I said something there was this tremendous roar from the crowd. It came out of nowhere because I couldn't see. I was thrilled." Her talk aimed at keeping everyone there, and she shared the counsel of nineteenth-century black leader Frederick Douglass that "power concedes nothing without a demand."[18] Literally overnight she found herself a leader of the newborn movement. The next evening Savio announced an agreement with administrators, who had realized the students' seriousness. The protesters freed the police car, later paying to repair its badly dented roof, but the peace treaty turned out to be just a temporary truce.

Like the action of Rosa Parks in Montgomery, the peaceful sit-down that gave birth to the Free Speech Movement (FSM) at Berkeley was not planned in advance but was well prepared. The movement had been incubating at least since May 1960 when Berkeley students tried to attend hearings of the House Un-American Activities Committee (HUAC) in San Francisco. Repeatedly denied admission, they borrowed the new tactic of Southern black students and staged a sit-in, only to be washed down the steps of City Hall by high-powered fire hoses; dozens were arrested. A widely shown film HUAC made about the event, "Operation

Abolition," induced such hostility toward the committee, especially among college youth, that it hastened the demise of McCarthyism, and indeed, of HUAC. The triumphant resurgence of the Southern freedom movement in 1963 spurred an effective campaign against racist hiring practices in San Francisco in which Berkeley activists played a central role. Hundreds of students were arrested for sitting in at the Sheraton Palace Hotel and other businesses. Some activists like Savio went to the South for Mississippi Freedom Summer.

Thus when the university—pressured by *Oakland Tribune* publisher William Knowland and other right-wingers—abruptly extended its ban on political activity to a small strip of pavement on the campus border that had been a haven for political educating and recruiting, it unwittingly provoked a public outcry. Activists perceived it as a direct attack on civil rights organizing and felt that they were being treated like Southern blacks. Their *own* civil rights were being violated. "Last summer I went to Mississippi to join the struggle there for civil rights," said Savio. "This fall I am engaged in another phase of the same struggle, this time in Berkeley. The two battlefields may seem quite different to some observers, but this is not the case. The same rights are at stake in both places— the right to participate as citizens in democratic society."[19] It was quite logical, as Jack Weinberg pointed out, that when the administration moved to completely bar organizing for black freedom and other causes, the activist community would respond with tactics they had learned in the freedom movement.[20] But the Berkeley bureaucrats were thrown off guard by the readiness, skill, and confidence of their young adversaries.

In the heady days after the initial victory on Sproul Plaza, an unusually broad coalition of student groups—ranging from Goldwaterites and Young Republicans to socialists and Maoists—formed the Free Speech Movement to carry out the 2 October pact with the administration. Because of the residue of McCarthyism and relentless red-baiting, "we had to convince people that we were small 'd' democrats in addition to whatever else we were," Savio commented later. "We were hung up about democracy."[21] The structure and process of the FSM in fact provided a near-perfect forum for small-scale participatory democracy. Each student group chose representatives to a large executive committee acting as a parliament, which in turn elected delegates to a steering committee that implemented the larger body's policies and made day-to-day tactical decisions. The steering committee arrived at its decisions by the Quaker method of consensus after thorough debate that sometimes took hours, always trying to incorporate dissenting views. The only time they formally voted was to narrowly approve, and then abruptly call off, what became known as the "abortive sit-in." The FSM was also democratic in its openness. Privileged information and secret deals were unimaginable. Aptheker, Savio, and others often stayed up all night churning out leaflets, with detailed accounts of the day's happenings, that were printed by dawn and handed out, 20,000 daily, starting at 8:00 A.M.—an impressive effort at sustained political education. The flaw in FSM democracy was that more women did not hold leadership positions. Even the half-dozen who did play key roles, including Aptheker and two other women on the steering committee, sometimes had trouble getting their ideas taken seriously.

The movement's growth was aided by a string of blunders by their "best organizer," the administration, including crass manipulation of the tripartite committee set up to develop a new policy, and other acts of bad faith. When the FSM seemed to be losing steam after weeks of rallies and hectic organizing, the chancellor rejuvenated it by bringing new charges against Savio and another leader. Incensed, 1,000 students took over Sproul Hall, administration headquarters, as Joan Baez led them in singing "We Shall Overcome." Words just spoken by Savio at a huge rally were ringing in their ears: "There's a time when the operation of the machine becomes so odious, makes you so sick at heart, that you can't take part, you can't even tacitly take part. And you've got to put your bodies upon the gears and upon the wheels, upon the levers, upon all the apparatus, and you've got to make it stop. And you've got to indicate to the people who run it, to the people who own it, that unless you're free, the machine will be prevented from working at all."[22]

After the students spent an exhilarating night nourished by peanut butter sandwiches, Charlie Chaplin films, and "Free University" classes, Governor Edmund G. Brown sent in hundreds of police who dragged them out, one floor at a time, and arrested 800—the biggest campus civil disobedience in the country's history. In response, graduate students organized an unprecedented strike that shut down the university, and many professors were persuaded to back the movement. On 8 December the Academic Senate voted overwhelmingly in favor of the FSM demands—one of the "really courageous moments" in the faculty's history. After the vote, Aptheker recalled, "we students parted rank, forming an aisle through which the faculty seemed to formally march in a new kind of academic procession. Many of us were crying, and so were many of them. There were many among them and among us who finally came to believe that the repression of the 1950s was truly at an end."[23] The Regents announced that university rules would no longer interfere with the First and Fourteenth amendments, the chancellor implemented the faculty recommendations, and the free speech ban was rescinded. Goliath had been vanquished.

The scrupulously nonviolent Berkeley rebellion, the nation's first white student movement since the 1930s and the first ever to use mass direct action on campus, was about more than freedom of speech. Reportedly, most participants, and the silent majority who supported them, felt alienated in the academic assembly line of this huge, impersonal institution that seemed increasingly harnessed to the needs of large corporations and the Pentagon. No one had championed the vision of higher education as a "knowledge industry" with an externally defined social mission more effectively than UC's president Clark Kerr. Berkeley political theorists Sheldon Wolin and John Schaar noted that the students were "ill-housed, and ill-clad, and ill-nourished not in the material sense, but in the intellectual and spiritual senses. As the multiversity has climbed to higher and higher peaks of research productivity, material riches, and bureaucratic complexity, the students have fallen into deeper and deeper abysses of hostility and estrangement."[24] They refused to be treated like cogs in a machine, to be "bent, folded, spindled, and mutilated" by faceless bureaucracies. They were fighting to better, and to gain more control over, their own lives. Beyond the personal realm, many had come to see their university as an indispensable contributor to basic social ills, from automation to the nuclear arms race, and they believed that by changing this institution and forcing it to live up to its original scholarly ideals, they would make a big stride toward reshaping the entire society.

The FSM's remedy for both alienation and powerlessness was to create an authentic intellectual and political community in which students could find the meaning and sense of belonging they longed for, and to multiply and link up such communities across the land. The vital legacy of the Free Speech Movement was the astonishing solidarity it generated, no matter how temporary, between diverse individuals and groups. Aptheker remembers it as "the intense moment of connection between us which infused a spirit of overwhelming and enduring love. . . . This connection frames the essential meaning [of the movement]."[25] In this and in other ways the Berkeley revolt served as an inspiring model for student movements later in the decade. As the Port Huron Statement had predicted two years earlier, the multiversity had now become a legitimate political battleground. Before long, campus insurgency would be the front line of the war at home.

From Protest to Resistance

Early August 1964. Two weeks before he squashed the Mississippi Freedom Democratic party challenge at Atlantic City, President Johnson ordered an attack by sixty-four jet fighters on an oil depot and naval port
in North Vietnam. He announced on television that the bombing, the first
by the U.S. military since the Korean War, was a justified retaliation for
a torpedo assault on the USS *Maddox* in the Gulf of Tonkin the day before. That incident never took place. Three days earlier, several miles
offshore, the destroyer had battled and badly damaged three North Vietnamese patrol boats—sinking one—that were responding to a raid on
two nearby islands by South Vietnamese ships, part of an intensifying
program of covert warfare against the North run by U.S. military advisers and the CIA. The *Maddox* had very likely provided intelligence for
the South Vietnamese action. For a few months Johnson and his inner
circle had been looking for a dramatic provocation to secure explicit congressional backing for deeper military involvement in Southeast Asia.
After meetings between the president and leaders of Congress, especially J. William Fulbright, head of the Senate Foreign Relations Committee, the Gulf of Tonkin Resolution sailed through the House unanimously,
and through the Senate with just two dissents. It gave Johnson authority
"to take all the necessary measures to repel any armed attack against
the forces of the United States to prevent further aggression."[26] Even
Fulbright did not know that the administration considered it a blank
check, the equivalent of a declaration of war. In the short run, by pro-
jecting an image of restrained forcefulness, Johnson's first "crisis" helped
him win a landslide victory over his hawkish GOP opponent, Arizona
senator Barry Goldwater.

The U.S. government had committed itself to the survival of a non-
Communist Vietnam ever since 1949, when the Truman administration
started funding the French war to reconquer its erstwhile colony. This
was the year at the height of the Cold War during which Truman had
"lost" China to its Communist revolution and the Soviets had blockaded
Berlin. Truman's 1947 containment doctrine required that the United
States hold the line at all cost against further Communist expansion. After resisting wartime Japanese occupation, and borrowing the most famous phrases of the American Declaration of Independence, Vietnamese
nationalists under the popular Communist leader Ho Chi Minh had declared independence from French rule in September 1945. Ho's repeated
requests for U.S. assistance were ignored. When his guerrilla forces

finally defeated the French in 1954 after the pivotal siege of Dien Bien Phu, the United States helped engineer a peace settlement, accepted by Moscow and Beijing, that divided the country *temporarily* into a Communist North and a non-Communist South. The Eisenhower administration fully supported the new Saigon regime of Ngo Dinh Diem (which it virtually created), fortifying it with military aid and advisers. Refusing to carry out the reunification election called for by the peace agreement, Diem's dictatorship became increasingly repressive, brutally stifling dissent by Buddhists and a growing underground opposition. The indigenous, Communist-led National Liberation Front (NLF) formed in 1960 and launched a guerrilla war aimed at an independent, neutral South Vietnam. It received little material support from Hanoi until after President Kennedy substantially enlarged the number of U.S. combat advisers in the South. In the aftermath of the disastrous CIA-directed invasion of Cuba (April 1961), Vietnam seemed a more favorable theater in which to apply the young president's new strategy of "flexible response" and counterinsurgency warfare. Hanoi's troops did not enter the South until after Johnson bombed the North and pushed through his de facto declaration of war.

From the outset American policymakers had perceived Vietnam as a "test case." If they could frustrate a successful war of national liberation—significantly, in the only country in the world that had won independence from colonial rule under Communist leadership—it would set an example that might deter misguided national (and regional) self-determination in other parts of the globe more vital to U.S. economic and strategic interests, such as the Mideast. In March 1965 Assistant Secretary of Defense John McNaughton, responsible for Vietnam policy, memoed Defense chief Robert NcNamara that the predominant objective in Vietnam was "to avoid a humiliating U.S. defeat," thereby preserving the U.S. reputation as a guarantor in the rest of the world.[27] And, he might have added, to prevent electoral defeat at home. Every president since Harry Truman had feared the domestic political consequences of "losing" South Vietnam to Communism—a legacy of McCarthyism. Kennedy was apparently convinced that he might not win reelection. Johnson worried that if he lost Vietnam he would lose Congress—as Truman had after the "fall" of China—and that his beloved "Great Society" federal aid programs would go down the drain. Journalists and historians popularized the metaphor of Vietnam as a "quagmire," into which the nation inadvertently slipped deeper, step by step, its leaders mistakenly believing that each short-term measure of incremental escalation would do the trick.

Actually, policymakers understood at each juncture that, as Kennedy and Johnson well knew and national security adviser McGeorge Bundy privately warned, "the struggle in Vietnam will be long"—and costly.[28]

In February 1965, after an attack by NLF guerrillas on the U.S. base at Pleiku in which several GIs were killed, the White House fired up its long-planned strategy of sustained bombing against North Vietnam. The relentless "Rolling Thunder" campaign would last almost four years and despite high civilian casualties would prove spectacularly ineffective, except in strengthening the will of the North Vietnamese population. On 8 March the first two battalions of combat Marines landed on the beach at Da Nang, ostensibly to protect the sprawling air base there. Ground troops "were now necessary to back up an air offensive designed to avoid the use of troops."[29] Unlike the legion of advisers already in-country, these forces—and the additional battalions, then divisions, that quickly followed—had secret orders from President Johnson to engage in offense, in "search and destroy" missions. By the end of the year nearly 200,000 Marines and Army troops had arrived. They had not been requested and were only reluctantly approved by the shaky Saigon regime. (Diem had been assassinated during a U.S.-backed coup in November 1963.) And so, with little light at the end of the twisting tunnel, the United States launched a major ground and air war in spring 1965, carrying out the program championed by Goldwater a few months before that LBJ had publicly spurned. Because of a "policy of minimum candor" demanded by the commander-in-chief, the American people did not know the real meaning of these moves.[30] This was no longer a mere "intervention" like others in the recent past. For the fourth time in the twentieth century, the United States was at war. Besides the death and destruction inflicted on inhabitants and on themselves, the three million GIs who were to serve in South Vietnam would disfigure the traditional culture of a country occupied one last time by foreign troops.

Saturday, 17 April 1965, was a warm cloudless day in Washington, one of those dreamlike spring days that make the cherry blossom city look like a fairy-tale picture book of democracy. Its outward beauty camouflaged the fact that many in its inner corridors were busily engaged even on the weekend in detailed planning for what would in fact turn into the nation's longest and most divisive war. Believing their government would listen to reason, about 25,000 Americans marched on Washington that day to protest Johnson's Vietnam policy. Organized by SDS, it was the first national demonstration against the war and the largest antiwar gathering the country had ever seen. People came on buses and trains from all parts of the country. Many were students, but many were older. A significant number of blacks were there, partly owing to a major effort by SDS to link the war with civil rights.

After picketing the White House the petitioners moved on to the Washington Monument, where they heard peace songs by Joan Baez, Judy Collins, and Phil Ochs and speeches by Bob Moses, Staughton Lynd, radical muckraker I. F. Stone, and Alaska senator Ernest Gruening, the only lawmaker besides Wayne Morse to vote against the Gulf of Tonkin Resolution. SDS president Paul Potter closed the rally with a passionate and prophetic address urging his listeners to try to understand and change the "system" that produced the Vietnam War and to build a broad social movement that "will, if necessary, respond to the administration war effort with massive civil disobedience all over the country, that will wrench the country into a confrontation with the issues of the war."[31] The huge assembly then headed toward Capitol Hill, looking so determined it seemed to Lynd that "the great mass of people would simply flow on through and over the marble buildings."[32] But they stopped at the Capitol steps, dropped off their end-the-war petition, and went home. All of a sudden antiwar protest, SDS in particular, was "big news."[33]

Small protests against Vietnam intervention, organized mainly by radical pacifists, had occurred sporadically ever since an August 1963 demonstration against Diem's harsh persecution of Buddhists, some of whom had immolated themselves. Also worthy of note was a multi-city protest in late December 1964 sponsored by the War Resisters League and other groups. The success of the SDS march had as much to do with luck in timing as careful organizing. Participants at an SDS National Council meeting decided on it after hearing I. F. Stone tell them about the war's hidden history; his small-circulation newsweekly had been an indispensable source of information on U.S. policy. SDS invited all groups to take part, even Communists—a bold move that angered some liberals and social democrats and brought public criticism from prominent peace leaders, including Norman Thomas, Bayard Rustin, even A. J. Muste. But news of Rolling Thunder and the threat of full-scale war made the dispute seem trivial; eventually, nonexclusion came to be an accepted principle of the new movement.

In the wake of the April march SDS membership swelled, and the major media did stories on it; the young activists, however, did not know how to cope with sudden fame. At the June convention in Kewadin, Michigan, delegates decided, by default, not to shape SDS into what it could have become—the premier national antiwar organization. The reasons are complex, but two stand out: the deeply held commitment to decentralism and chapter autonomy, reinforced by the influx of new members attracted to the group's antiwar efforts but wary of top-down authority; and the "old guard" leaders' resistance to "single-issueism." Kirkpatrick Sale comments that the "Kewadin spirit" led SDS "away from the assertion of national leadership and into a continued reliance upon local initiative. It was, in truth, perhaps the easiest and surest direction for the organization, then still young and small, and because of it SDS would be able to grow and prosper at the chapter level as no other campus organization had ever done. But for this, in the long run, it had to pay a price."[34]

The budding movement did not wait for SDS to lead it. In March, University of Michigan students and faculty organized an all-night "teach-in" that drew thousands, an idea quickly copied at a hundred other institutions. Typically, antiwar profs would debate State Department "truth teams" before large audiences. Berkeley's May teach-in was mammoth. In late July troops of the Committee for Nonviolent Action marched on the New York induction center, where a few young men burned their draft cards in a flaming pot. A *Life* photograph of Catholic Worker activist Chris Kearns clenching his burning card so incensed conservative members of Congress that it quickly passed a law making draft card destruction a crime punishable by five years in prison.

During the twentieth anniversary of the Hiroshima and Nagasaki bombings in August, the "Assembly of Unrepresented People" gathered in Washington for four days of workshops and direct action. It was designed to connect Vietnam with black voting rights and other issues, to create a peace *and* freedom movement. On the final day a few hundred were arrested, the most yet in Washington, as they tried to nonviolently invade the Capitol with a "Declaration of Peace." March leaders Bob Moses, Staughton Lynd, and David Dellinger were splattered with stinging red paint by American Nazis. On the West Coast, protesters in Oakland sat down in front of Army trains carrying soldiers bound for Vietnam. The Assembly of Unrepresented People gave birth to the first national antiwar coalition, the National Coordinating Committee to End the War in Vietnam (NCC), which was composed of thirty-three organizations. The NCC and its later incarnations would organize the great peace marches of the next half-decade.

In mid-October the "First International Days of Protest," the NCC's baptism, saw thousands take to the streets in nearly a hundred cities,

Dave Dellinger, Staughton Lynd, and Bob Moses lead the Assembly of
Unrepresented People to the U.S. Capitol to protest the Vietnam War,
9 August, 1965. A heckler threw red paint at them. *Neil Haworth/WRL*

some as far-flung as Tokyo. In New York a big march was organized by
the Fifth Avenue Peace Parade Committee, a wide-ranging coalition that
had just been founded by schoolteacher Norma Becker, a powerhouse of
drive and energy. The day before, pacifist David Miller lit a flame to his
draft card in front of TV cameras at the city's induction center, the first
to publicly defy the new law. Several more burned their cards in the
following weeks. On Thanksgiving weekend SANE sponsored a Washington march at which SDS's new president Carl Oglesby gave an enlight-
ening speech that blamed the war on liberals—not "humanist liberals"
like many in his audience, but the system and ideology of "corporate
liberalism" responsible for an overall foreign policy driven by corporate
needs.[35] As Paul Potter did in April, Oglesby made it clear that Vietnam
was not an aberration. By this point SDS was no longer trying to *reform*
liberalism, but to challenge its legitimacy across the board.

As the war expanded, opponents felt an increasing urgency to end it, testified to by the hundreds who engaged in civil disobedience. A handful chose to sacrifice everything. In early November Norman Morrison, a thirty-two-year-old Quaker from Baltimore, sat down outside Defense Secretary McNamara's office window at the Pentagon, quietly poured kerosene over his body, and died in a small inferno. A week later Roger LaPorte, a young Catholic Worker who had recently witnessed a draft card burning—hecklers had yelled, "Burn yourselves, not your cards!"—immolated himself in front of the United Nations. Earlier, an eighty-two-year-old refugee from Nazi Germany named Alice Herz had set herself aflame on a Detroit street, leaving a note that said: "I choose the illuminating death of a Buddhist to protest against a great country trying to wipe out a small country for no reason."[36]

Surprisingly, the movement that grew so quickly in 1965 appeared to drag its feet the next year. But this surface inertia was deceptive, the calm before the storm. Little noticed by the media, much was stirring and percolating at the grass roots—especially on campuses—and in the higher peace circles. Activists were patiently building for the long haul ahead. Key events took place that enlarged the opposition, including Senator Fulbright's televised Vietnam hearings (he was already questioning the war), a couple of dozen peace campaigns for congressional seats—only one came close—and of course, more marches. In June the movement strongly backed the decision by three Army privates at Fort Hood, Texas—one was black, another Puerto Rican—to refuse to fight in "this unjust, immoral, and illegal war," an omen of things to come.[37] The "Fort Hood Three" were court-martialed and imprisoned.

A potent generator of antiwar sentiment, especially among young people, was the repertoire of "message songs" by popular singers like Pete Seeger, Joan Baez, Phil Ochs, and above all, Bob Dylan, stars of the folk music resurgence that had just reached its peak. Some songs were explicitly antiwar (and antiracist), such as Seeger's "Where Have All the Flowers Gone?" and "If I Had a Hammer," Dylan's "Blowin' in the Wind"—all hit tunes performed by Peter, Paul, and Mary—Buffy Sainte-Marie's "Universal Soldier," and P. J. Sloan's remarkable "Eve of Destruction" (sung by Barry McGuire), one of 1965's biggest hits. Others mocked passive conformity—Simon and Garfunkel's "The Sounds of Silence"—or celebrated youthful rebellion, like Dylan's "The Times They Are A-Changin'." Though several of these political ballads climbed to the top of the charts and touched millions, neither folk nor rock music ever played the central role in movement-building that freedom songs played in the black movement. The antiwar movement never became a "singing movement," in part because, except for Pete Seeger and others less known, these musicians were not song leaders—they were pop stars who sang at peace rallies yet remained distant from the grass roots.

Though belied by his official rhetoric, the commander-in-chief seemed to be getting the message. With the failure of air attacks on oil storage depots in North Vietnam, the Joint Chiefs of Staff pushed Johnson to order unrestrained bombing of Hanoi and Haiphong in late 1966. At his request they brought a team of Pentagon computer whizzes to the Oval Office to prove their case. "I have one more problem for your computer," said Johnson. "Will you feed into it how long it will take five hundred thousand angry Americans to climb that White House wall out there and lynch their President if he does something like that?"[38] Though some populated targets remained off-limits, the bombing steadily expanded. U.S. troops kept pouring into South Vietnam, to reach half a million by the end of 1967. The war seemed as relentless and intractable as it was indeterminate—truly a "stalemate machine."[39]

The national antiwar coalition had trouble staying intact during 1966 owing to the insistence of some on nonexclusion and the factional conflicts of Communists, Trotskyists, and pacifists. A fragile unity was maintained by the war's urgency and the skillful piloting of A. J. Muste, by then eighty-one, whose openness, honesty, and universal respect enabled him again and again to cut through sectarian squabbles and find common ground. In November 1966 the Spring Mobilization Committee was born, replacing the NCC, to mount mass marches in New York and San Francisco aimed at bringing out impressive numbers of "ordinary" Americans to give a true picture of public opposition. In December Bettina Aptheker called a conference in Chicago that formed the Student Mobilization Committee to build campus support for the April marches. Muste did not live to see the climax of his life's work for peace and justice. He died in February 1967, and the movement would never again have a leader acknowledged by every faction. Shortly after his death, 2,500 well-dressed, middle-class women from Women Strike for Peace marched into the Pentagon, demanding to see "the generals who send our sons to Vietnam."[40]

Despite rain, light then heavy, at least a quarter of a million people gathered at the sprawling Sheep's Meadow in New York's Central Park on Saturday, 15 April 1967—a diverse assemblage of all ages and races, but predominantly young, white, and middle-class. Quite a few hippies showed up with painted faces and flowered hair. A front line of notables, including Martin Luther King, Jr., Dr. Benjamin Spock, Stokely Carmi-

Bettina Aptheker (with bullhorn) leads women's antiwar march from the University of California's Berkeley campus to the Oakland induction center, ca. 1966.
© *1969 Ted Streshinsky*

chael, head organizer James Bevel (from SCLC), and a towering photograph of Muste led the overflowing peace army along 59th Street and down Madison Avenue to the United Nations. The crowd was so vast that thousands never got out of the park. The organizers were dizzied by the size and success of the New York march (and by the San Francisco one that drew about 50,000). King turned to Dellinger on the speakers' platform at the UN and told him that more people had turned out than for the 1963 March on Washington. Dellinger believed that at last they had a real movement: "I somehow felt like 'we're in.'"[41]

Earlier at Sheep's Meadow, in an action not sanctioned by the march officialdom, seventy young men, mostly Cornell students, stood on a rocky cliff in front of TV cameras and burned their draft cards in a coffee can filled with paraffin. A few were lit by supportive wives and women friends. As they finished their task, the contagious spirit of collective action moved a hundred more to come up from the edges and put their cards to flame.

In February 1966 crusty General Lewis Hershey, czar of the Selective Service System since its inception, declared that draft boards could begin inducting male college students with lower standing, to be determined by class rank and national examinations. With draft calls approaching 40,000 per month, middle-class students were suddenly no longer insulated from the military. The Vietnam War became very real to them for the first time. The SDS National Office wrote up a "counter-exam"—on the war—half a million of which were handed out at the official tests in May. Anxiety turned to anger when college administrators routinely agreed to send class rank to local boards, showing how little they seemed to care for students' welfare. SDSers and other activists galvanized this discontent into widespread protest, especially sit-ins, from San Francisco State to Brooklyn City College, including a five-day takeover of the University of Chicago administration building. Continued agitation pressured enough institutions to refuse cooperation that Selective Service abandoned the ranking procedures and the plan to systematically draft students. Only a small proportion of undergraduate males were inducted while in college; many of these were black, brown, or working-class. Yet the draft, seen as inseparable from the war that it fueled, had emerged as the most critical issue facing students. It became the driving force of mass antiwar opposition among the younger generation.

The energy produced by the class rank fight helped to catalyze far-reaching changes in the leadership and direction of SDS. Chapters and

Draft card burning in Sheeps Meadow, Central Park, New York City,
15 April 1967. *Dave McReynolds/WRL*

membership were multiplying geometrically. The bulk of the newcomers
were younger, came from west of the Mississippi, often from big state
universities, and their style was more militant yet more libertarian, re-
flecting the influence of the blossoming "counterculture" that both shaped
and was shaped by the New Left. The new breed of activists, dubbed
"prairie power," took the reins from the old guard. In August 1966 the
national convention in Iowa elected a new set of leaders, two of whom
would play key roles as New Left strategists in the coming year. These
were Carl Davidson, vice president, an SDS regional "traveler" and philosophy instructor at the University of Nebraska; and twenty-nine-year-
old Greg Calvert, national secretary, from a poor working-class family in
southern Washington—his father worked in a lumber mill, his grandpar-
ents were Finnish-born Wobblies—who had been teaching Western Civilization at Iowa State.

The delegates decided on a full-scale "organizing thrust" on issues of
student power and university complicity with the war machine, but also
committed SDS to further decentralization, "operating not with a national

program but by energizing local people in local chapters around local grievances."[42] An implicit consensus had been reached that it was time to up the ante to match the gruesome escalation of the war, to move "from protest to resistance," a popular slogan Calvert coined.[43] If the war could not be stopped, as many believed, SDS might succeed in raising its cost at the same time that the group radicalized a new generation of students and created the foundation of a broad American left.

That fall and winter "complicity" and "resistance" were the guiding themes as SDS groups led militant confrontations against war research, ROTC, and most of all, campus recruiting by the military, the CIA, and Dow Chemical, maker of napalm bombs. Harvard SDS won the prize for sensational media coverage when its members trapped Defense chief McNamara's car, after he refused to debate the war on campus, and then heatedly interrogated him. As if mirroring their guerrilla tactics, he escaped through underground tunnels.

SDS had a knack for creative direct action, but its real prowess lay in painstaking research and analysis of all facets of the American "empire" at home and abroad. Peter Henig and Cathy Wilkerson unearthed an jofficial memo by the Selective Service System that they published in the SDS paper *New Left Notes* in January 1967. Entitled "Channeling," the document explained that the agency's function was only partly to induct men into the military. Its main purpose was "pressurized guidance," using deferments and the "club of induction" to force young men into occupations in the national interest—especially in the defense industry— that they might not choose otherwise. This strategy provided the benefits of totalitarian control without the moral or financial costs: "The psychology of granting wide choice under pressure to take action," the memo asserted, "is the American or indirect way of achieving what is done by direction in foreign countries where choice is not allowed. Here, choice is limited but not denied."[44] Draft resistance leader David Harris called this state of affairs "participatory totalitarianism."[45] The memo was a smoking gun that seemed to confirm SDS's accusations about the bureaucratic state and its nefarious objectives. The New Left's most widely distributed pamphlet, "Channeling" was a powerful eye-opener for legions of draft-age youth. It inspired a favorite SDS button that said: "Not With My Life You Don't."

As both hard data and grand metaphor, "channeling" offered ammunition for a New Left strategic vision (formulated by Calvert, Davidson, Wilkerson, and David Gilbert) that took off from Port Huron but was more radical and theoretically sophisticated. Philosopher Herbert Marcuse and French neo-Marxists shaped the new thinking as much as Mills and Camus influenced the original vision. Calvert spelled it out eloquently at a Princeton SDS conference in February 1967. When Guatemalan guerrillas enter a village, the national secretary began, they don't hand out tracts by Marx or Mao; instead,

[they] talk to the villagers about their own lives: about how they see themselves and how they came to be who they are, about their deepest longings and the things they've striven for and hoped for, about the way in which their deepest longings were frustrated by the society in which they lived. Then the guerrillas encourage the villagers to talk about their lives. And then a marvelous thing begins to happen. People who thought that their deepest problems and frustrations were their individual problems discover that their problems and longings are all the same . . . and, finally, that out of the discovery of their common humanity comes the decision that men must unite together in the struggle to destroy the conditions of their common oppression. That, it seems to me, is what we are about.

Calvert suggested that an authentic revolutionary movement was a struggle by those engaged in it for their own freedom. Radicals, as distinguished from liberals, perceive themselves as "unfree" and must unite with others to overcome shared oppression. Though they might not recognize their unfreedom, white middle-class students were in fact manipulated to be the "trainees" of the "new working class," the highly skilled technicians and professionals required by advanced capitalism, and "the factory-like multiversities are the institutions which prepare them for their slots." Thus, white students were a legitimate agency of change in their own right. They had to fight, without guilt, for their own freedom— not serve as missionaries to another group's oppression, whether blacks, industrial workers, or Vietnamese. Campaigns for democratic control in the university (the student population more than doubled during the 1960s) would mature into a groundswell of democratic struggles in the workplace that could lead to decentralized revolutionary change.[46] Around this time "revolution" started to become a household word in New Left circles.

The increasingly conscious need, desire, and responsibility for self-liberation animated the rising public defiance of the draft. As an organized movement, draft resistance grew up both in and outside of SDS. Several strands of antidraft activism since 1965 converged: pacifist draft card burning, conferences on noncooperation in New Haven, Des Moines, and

Chicago, the signing of "We Won't Go" statements by college students, and class rank and other SDS antidraft work. The influence of SNCC was pervasive and included its early support of draft resistance, the exemplary induction refusal of several black activists, and the controversial decision that whites should leave SNCC and organize their own people. With the draft as the overarching issue, the December 1966 SDS National Council meeting adopted a bold, multifaceted antidraft program that entailed protests at induction centers and the creation of unions of draft resisters. Two weeks earlier eighteen-year-old Cornell SDS president Bruce Dancis tore up his draft card at a demonstration outside a faculty meeting on class rank policy. His dramatic act motivated the Cornell "We Won't Go" group he had cofounded to organize the collective draft card burning at Sheep's Meadow in April.

Draft resistance organizers on both coasts formed an independent organization to launch what they hoped would be a mass movement of noncooperation with the draft. This was partly because SDS never made draft resistance its central activity, partly because of political and stylistic differences with SDS, and partly to make a fresh start. In March 1967 David Harris, Dennis Sweeney, and other members of the Peace and Liberation Commune in Palo Alto, California, joined with Berkeley activists to create "the Resistance." The next month at the Spring Mobilization rally in San Francisco, Harris announced the group's call for a nationwide draft card "turn-in" in October. An ex–high school football star from the farming capital of Fresno, where he was "Boy of the Year," Harris had recently resigned as Stanford student body president to pour his energy into antidraft organizing. He and other commune members had already sent back their cards to the government and were prepared to go to prison.

Harris and Sweeney had worked with SNCC in Mississippi and envisioned the Resistance as a "white SNCC."[47] It came to life as a blending of the risk-taking, openness, and direct democracy of SNCC, the principles of Gandhian nonviolence, and the flourishing California counterculture's libertarian values, which centered on an "exploration of selfhood."[48] Much in the spirit of Calvert's Princeton speech, resisting the draft was seen as an existential act of self-liberation—from the dehumanization of channeling, from the "white skin privilege" of deferments, and above all, from immoral complicity in the war machine. It was a "personal, deep communication type of politics," as SDS activist Tom Bell put it, a fusion of the personal and the political that would build, so they dreamed, toward a nonviolent revolution.[49] As an immediate strategy, it could provide crucial leverage to end the war. Organizer Paul Rupert commented later that the Resistance "had a very material grasp of the fact that we were potential cannon fodder and could have a real part in making it impossible for the war to be waged."[50] But success hinged on getting enough people to take the first big step of renouncing their deferments and facing induction.

The summer and fall of 1967 Harris, Sweeney, and cohorts roamed the West Coast from San Diego to Seattle, searching out prospective noncooperators, telling their story to small groups or one-to-one, and explaining why they had chosen the role of "criminal." Sometimes they played music and smoked marijuana together. "Part of the process was creating a sense of intimacy between us which . . . we felt was the basis of our organization," Harris recalled.[51] The organizers planted a seedbed of local Resistance groups that by the end of the year had sprouted in all parts of the country and had coalesced into a loosely structured national federation linked by common action and political style. Rejecting formal leadership, stressing consensus decision-making, Resistance groups did not have officers (unlike SDS), partly because draft resisters faced a common risk of prison and thus, at least rhetorically, all were leaders or none. This concealed a benign "tyranny of structurelessness," however, in which more articulate spokespersons like Harris exercised dominant leadership that was informal and sometimes unaccountable.[52] But that organizational style had its advantages, too. During this period draft resistance took hold as the moral cutting edge of the antiwar movement.

Despite the competition, SDS was growing faster than ever; the chapters forming in every state except Alaska eventually numbered over 300. The main target was still university complicity, particularly war-related recruiting, and confrontations proliferated during the fall of 1967. Many were aimed at Dow Chemical, whose flesh-ripping jellied gasoline, napalm, served as the most glaring symbol of the Vietnam carnage. The most explosive campus action erupted at the University of Wisconsin in Madison, where a determined but nonviolent obstruction of Dow recruiting by a few hundred students brought about a ferocious assault by riot-clad police who bloodied students in the manner of Selma and Birmingham. A stunned crowd of people outside the building did what they could to aid the injured and stymie the cops, including letting air out of a paddy wagon's tires and immobilizing it with their bodies. The police responded with more beatings, tear gas, and Mace, a paralyzing nerve gas, and the furious crowd finally counterattacked with rocks and bricks until the battle died down. Never before had an American campus witnessed such flagrant police brutality. It sparked a short-lived strike by students and sympathetic teachers.

That same week in mid-October about 1,500 young men turned in their draft cards at churches and federal buildings in the first National Day of Noncooperation, surpassing Resistance organizers' expectations. Thousands more would follow suit in later turn-ins. Dr. Benjamin Spock, Yale chaplain William Sloane Coffin, and other representatives of Resist, a support group of older adults, delivered the relinquished cards in a briefcase to the Justice Department. Spock, Coffin, and two others were later convicted in a celebrated trial of conspiring to "aid and abet" draft refusal.

In the San Francisco Bay Area the Resistance had joined in coalition with SDS and pacifist groups to mount Stop the Draft Week, aimed at shutting down the Oakland induction center. It was a way to involve women and others not subject to the draft, and those not willing to openly defy it. But the tense coalition broke apart over tactics: traditional and symbolic civil disobedience versus something more militant that might actually close the facility. Some of the latter camp, wanting to march in step with Black Power, sought to demonstrate the seriousness of white radicals. The two factions compromised by dividing up the week. The Resistance and the War Resisters League conducted a peaceful sit-in the same day that cards were collected. The next day troops led by Berkeley SDS aggressively blockaded the induction center and nearby streets in a taste of guerrilla warfare (though with little actual violence); they were soon routed by the police.

In a return engagement on Friday they outwitted the cops and kept them at bay, and for a while kept them surrounded, using cars, benches, and potted trees as barricades. Resistance activist Stuart McRae recalled that the blockaders acted spontaneously and "did not rely on the direction of their leaders: using some of the ideas generated on Tuesday, they developed a form of resistance which no one had planned. The action consisted of rapidly clearing the area around the induction center as the police advanced, and then joining together to cut off the induction center by blocking intersections ouside the police lines. This prevented the buses, filled with inductees, from arriving for about three hours."[53] In the heat of battle they had invented a controversial new weapon, "mobile tactics," that lay in a gray area between militant nonviolence and armed struggle.

The Oakland skirmishes served as prelude to the frontal assault that weekend on the headquarters of the American military-industrial juggernaut. Organized by the National Mobilization Committee, successor to the Spring Mobilization and the widest left coalition yet—ranging from liberal clergy to SNCC—the spectacle drew a potpourri of participants by offering a legal march and rally for beginners, a "be-in" for hippies, and militant civil disobedience for those choosing to put their bodies on the line. The last action was planned as a "creative synthesis of Gandhi and guerrilla," as chief organizer David Dellinger described it, nonviolent but forceful.[54] SDS, which had reluctantly endorsed the April mobilization—like SNCC's criticism of King, they felt that big media-centered marches stifled long-term grass-roots organizing—decided to fully back this one when it appeared a real confrontation was brewing. The feds delayed granting permits and deployed thousands of combat-ready troops to defend the Pentagon. Up to 100,000 people marched from the Washington Monument to a subdued rally at the Lincoln Memorial. About half of them crossed the Potomac River and congregated in a vast Pentagon parking lot, where they witnessed an odd spectacle. A collection of "witches, warlocks, holymen, seers, prophets, mystics, saints, sorcerers, shamans, troubadours, minstrels, bards, roadmen, and madmen" led by a counterculture cadre called the Diggers and a rock band named the Fugs invoked every bit of magic they could muster to levitate the Pentagon and exorcise its evil spirits.[55] Chants of "Out, demon, out!" filled the crisp autumn air.[56]

An SDS vanguard and a "Revolutionary Contingent" broke through a cordon of MPs and National Guard and seized high ground on a plaza at the Pentagon's north entrance. A few made it inside but were beaten and busted by troops lying in wait. By late afternoon several thousand had maneuvered to the plaza and the steps above, and their front lines pressed up against solid rows of rigid young soldiers carrying bayoneted M-14s. Following a scenario that the steering committee had dreamed up late the night before, the protesters conducted a teach-in, both through bullhorns and face-to-face, to win the hearts and minds of the troops, their peers in age if not race or class. Over and over they urged the young soldiers to "join us!" They talked gently—"You are our brothers"—and sang to them, even stuck flowers in their gun barrels.[57] Two or three put down their rifles and seemed about to switch sides when MPs swiftly stole them away.

As night fell and cold set in, protesters in the rear built campfires out of posters and debris. Marijuana joints were freely shared. Someone yelled, "Burn a draft card! Keep warm!" and shortly thereafter hundreds of little flames flickered in the darkness—the grandest "burn-in" of all. In an intense moment of solidarity and "religious awe," people sang "Silent Night."[58] But the military's high command would not let all be calm. The MPs and U.S. marshals had beaten and arrested people sporadically all evening, but late at night, with the TV cameras gone, the troops formed a flying wedge and fiercely attacked their unarmed foes, thrashing them with clubs and rifle butts. Women were singled out for the cruelest treatment. Peace had returned by Sunday dawn, and many of the weary protesters departed. But a hard core of several hundred stayed put until midnight, when they were ordered to disperse. Singing "This Land Is Your Land" and—again and again—"We Shall Overcome," they calmly offered themselves for jail and were taken away.

The nonviolent siege of the Pentagon, along with Stop the Draft Week, marked a turning point for the antiwar movement, which would now become both broader and more assertive. It was a turning point too for the Johnson administration, which, despite LBJ's smug pronouncements, was startled by the size and militance of the Pentagon invasion. The military chiefs were berated for inadequate intelligence, and Johnson ordered the FBI, the CIA, and other agencies to drastically step up surveillance and infiltration of antiwar groups. Soon the FBI would have over 1,000 agents assigned to the New Left, plus several thousand informants, buttressed by countless spies carrying out the CIA's "Operation Chaos." But it was too late for the Johnson administration to stem the tide.

In fact, the Pentagon was at war with itself. Inside its mighty walls a cluster of high civilian officials had already grown disenchanted with the apparent stalemate in Vietnam, and the rising public protests deepened their doubts. The clincher was the spectacular Tet offensive starting on the Vietnamese New Year, 31 January 1968. In a sudden blitz NLF guerrillas backed by North Vietnam invaded every major city and town in South Vietnam and even occupied part of the U.S. Embassy in Saigon. "What the hell is going on?" newscaster Walter Cronkite exclaimed off camera in his CBS studio. "I thought we were winning this war."[59] An authoritative source reported that the brilliantly coordinated offensive caught the military and the White House by surprise, and "its strength, length, and intensity prolonged this shock."[60] Though it ended in military defeat for the NLF—"We lost our best people," an NLF leader ruefully admitted later—it was, with the help of American television, a stunning political and psychological victory, the kind that mattered most in a guerrilla war.[61] Tet finally shattered the illusion that the United States could win in Vietnam, at least on the ground and without nuclear weapons.

In early March Clark Clifford, an influential corporation lawyer and former adviser to Kennedy and Truman, replaced McNamara as secretary of defense. The latter's mounting misgivings about the war had estranged him from LBJ and his inner circle, and Johnson had sent him off to run the World Bank. But his lieutenants stayed put. These civilian dissenters led by Assistant Secretary Paul Warnke and his deputy Morton Halperin saw Clifford's arrival as a crucial chance to reappraise Vietnam policy. For the first time even the military gave the president a pessimistic report, but still asked for 200,000 more troops on top of the half-million already there. (General William Westmoreland, the U.S. commander, later disclosed that he intended to use them for an invasion of North Vietnam.)

Johnson set up a task force under Clifford to advise him on the post-Tet crisis. The Pentagon "doves" felt that the troop request marked a watershed between all-out escalation and scaling down the war. They lobbied hard for a more defensive strategy and negotiations. Assistant Secretary Phil Goulding argued that if the troop request were granted, requiring bloated draft calls and full mobilization of reserves, "the shock wave would run through the entire American body politic. . . . The antiwar demonstrations and resistance to the draft would rise to new crescendos, reinforced by civil rights groups who would feel the President had once again revealed his inner conviction that the war in Vietnam was more important than the war on poverty."[62] Air Force Undersecretary Townsend Hoopes sent a memo to Clifford stating that "the war is eroding the moral fibre of the nation, demoralizing its politics, and paralyzing its foreign policy." More troops "would intensify the domestic disaffection, which would be reflected in increased defiance of the draft and widespread unrest in the cities."[63]

Though the task force recommended giving the military most of what it wanted, Clifford was persuaded that the policy must change. He convened a meeting of the "Wise Men"—pillars of the national security establishment like Dean Acheson, John McCloy, McGeorge Bundy, and Cyrus Vance—who had counseled Johnson on Vietnam and had always backed him fully. Now they informed the president diplomatically that his policy was bankrupt. The cost, political and financial, was too high. Vance said later that a key factor in their turnabout was the group's awareness that the "divisiveness in the country was growing with such acuteness that it was threatening to tear the United States apart."[64]

On 12 March, two weeks before LBJ's fateful meeting with the Wise Men, Senator Eugene McCarthy came close to beating him in the New Hampshire primary (and in fact won most delegates). The pious, poetry-writing Minnesota senator and his battalions of hard-working student volunteers had campaigned for an end to "Johnson's war." Since the previous summer Congressman Allard Lowenstein and other progressive Democrats alienated by LBJ's intransigent Vietnam stance had been searching for someone to challenge his renomination in the primaries on a forthright antiwar platform. When dream candidate Robert Kennedy demurred, the "Dump Johnson" activists turned to McCarthy. Four days after the latter's unexpected triumph in New Hampshire (and after failing to get LBJ to appoint a national commission on the war), Senator Kennedy threw his hat into the ring. The president made a dramatic television speech on 31 March, on the eve of the Wisconsin primary, announcing that he had cut back the bombing of North Vietnam in hopes it would lead to peace talks. Then he astounded the nation by declaring that he would not run for reelection. He seemed finally to be convinced that his fellow Americans were turning against the war.

"I felt that I was being chased on all sides by a giant stampede coming at me from all directions," he confided later to biographer Doris Kearns.

On one side, the American people were stampeding me to do something about Vietnam. On another side, the inflationary economy was booming out of control. Up ahead were dozens of danger signs pointing to another summer of riots in the cities. I was being forced over the edge by rioting blacks, demonstrating students, marching welfare mothers, squawking professors, and hysterical reporters. And then the final straw. The thing I feared from the first day of my Presidency was actually coming true. Robert Kennedy had openly announced his intention to reclaim the throne in the memory of his brother. And the American people, swayed by the magic of the name, were dancing in the streets. The whole situation was unbearable for me. After thirty-seven years of public service, I deserved something more than being left alone in the middle of the plain, chased by stampedes on every side.[65]

To the surprise of U.S. officials, Johnson's speech did prompt negotiations with Hanoi. He rejected Westmoreland's troop request, replaced him as supreme commander, and put a ceiling on U.S. forces. The bombing of the North was reduced in scope (but not in tonnage) and later halted, but the air war in South Vietnam and Laos substantially expanded. The peace talks deadlocked from the start, and the ground fighting actually intensified. The policy changed, but not enough to end the war. Yet it proved to be an irreversible step in that direction.

During this period SDS weathered another sea change. Since late 1967 many members had begun to see it as an explicitly revolutionary organization, indeed a revolutionary vanguard. Many were rushing to adopt Marxist-Leninist mind-sets of one variety or another, partly to cope with an invasion of disciplined cadres from the Maoist Progressive Labor party (PL). The majority lost interest in the "new working class" strategy that put students at the center. Chapters decided to work with constituencies other than white students. In late March the National Council in Kentucky resolved that the priority was racism and support of "the black struggle for liberation."[66] President Johnson's speech, which implied that the war might not be interminable, and King's murder four days later followed by unprecedented black revolt, seemed to vindicate the new SDS line.

Though from then on SDS downplayed the war to some extent, opposition to it jumped sharply during the first half of 1968 among liberals and the middle class. Liberal students, intellectuals, and politicians started to play a bigger role in the broadening movement, notably in marshalling antiwar forces within the Democratic party. Already in 1967 liberal activists and New Leftists had joined forces to organize "Vietnam Summer" (loosely modeled on Mississippi Freedom Summer), involving 20,000 volunteers nationwide, largely students, an impressive effort of doorbell-ringing and public education to reach mainstream Americans. Unlike other presidential election years, however, radical protest was not overshadowed or assimilated by presidential politics, at least not until the fall. Two historic events would demonstrate that the New Left still set the agenda, that the radical tide had not yet crested.

Columbia. The April upheaval began inauspiciously with a noon rally at the "Sundial" in the middle of the Upper Manhattan Ivy League campus. The students were protesting the punishment of SDS activists who had demonstrated inside Low Library, the administration building, against the school's ties with the Institute for Defense Analyses (IDA), a Pentagon think tank that did war research. For two years Columbia SDS had done patient educational work on complicity issues and led nonviolent protests against class rank and CIA and Marine recruiting. Now that the "action faction" had taken over chapter leadership from the "praxis axis," which was oriented to the new working class strategy, many members were eager for more militant tactics. The rally participants tried to enter Low once again, but after making it past conservative counterdemonstrators, found that the doors were locked. A few hundred then broke ranks, marched across Amsterdam Avenue, and descended into the hilly Harlem park—a buffer zone between the elite university and the teeming ghetto below—where Columbia was building a controversial gymnasium whose bottom level would offer a separate-but-unequal facility for its Harlem neighbors. The students tore down the fence at the gym site and scuffled with police before heading back to campus to regroup at the Sundial.

Newly elected SDS head Mark Rudd, a brash young demagogue from suburban New Jersey, proposed that they seize the main undergraduate building, named after alumnus Alexander Hamilton. The building was soon jammed with students, who imprisoned the acting dean, crew-cutted Henry Coleman, in his office. They held him hostage until the next afternoon. A contingent of black students from the Student Afro-American Society, heretofore little involved with the gym issue, had joined the takeover. Just before dawn they asked their white allies to leave, impatient with their slow decision-making process and not trusting them to "go all the way."[67] The black activists barricaded the doors with a mountain of desks, chairs, and file cabinets and renamed their building "Malcolm X Hall." Undaunted, many of the evicted SDSers surged toward Low Library, heaved a board through a window, and made themselves at home in the plush suite of Grayson Kirk, Columbia's aloof chief executive, who perfectly personified the hated "Establishment." They sat behind his big mahogany desk, sipped his sherry, smoked his "President" cigars, and pored over incriminating files.

After settling into Hamilton Hall the day before, a steering committee drafted six demands that the black students, adhering to a more hierarchical leadership model, did not want debated by the whole body. The crux of the demands, which would gain a sanctified status, was to stop "Gym Crow," sever all ties with the IDA, and grant amnesty to the occupiers. By welding together the issues of racism, Vietnam, and the university's "archaic power structure," the radicals were "able to mobilize a wide range of support, and could capitalize on three separate sources of frustration."[68] During the next two days, as formal and ad hoc faculty committees hastily gathered to deal with the crisis, students mostly not connected with SDS captured three more buildings. Occupiers elected a "Strike Central" coordinating committee that in mildly bureaucratic fashion handled thorny logistical problems and galvanized campuswide support. In contrast to the austere atmosphere in Malcolm X Hall, the whites experimented with novel forms of participatory democracy—tutored by Tom Hayden in one building—and with communal living and a "liberated" life-style. It turned out to be more liberated for men than for women since the latter did most of the housekeeping chores, in one "commune" cooking for 300 "in a kitchen the size of a telephone booth."[69]

While supportive Harlem residents rallied outside the university gates and well-organized jocks blockaded food deliveries, threatening their own rebellion to restore the status quo, negotiations mediated by the faculty reached a dead end. Kirk and his heir apparent, once-popular vice president and ex-dean David Truman, remained even more unyielding than their adversaries. They had received hundreds of calls from university presidents urging them to hold the line. The stickler was amnesty, since for each side it symbolized their power and legitimacy; if granted, it would likely ensure further growth of the movement.

Kirk and Truman blundered badly. Instead of trying to co-opt the students with procedural reforms, or calling the police right away, they delayed taking action for nearly a week while the revolt built momentum. Late at night on 30 April, 1,000 of "New York's finest" smashed through the barricades and, except in Hamilton where the blacks were arrested peacefully, removed the occupants with "grim, methodical cruelty."[70] Over 700 were arrested, and 150 injured. The scale and ferocity of the big bust outraged most students and many faculty and brought about a widely supported strike that ended classes for the year. An improvised "liberation school" sprung up, allowing anyone to teach. Those taking part in the protracted protest were heartened by the simultaneous student rebellion in Paris that led to a nationwide general strike in May. Activists at Columbia never won amnesty, but both the gym and IDA were abandoned. Kirk and Truman left the university.

The media went wild over the Columbia uprising and made it the enduring symbol of 1960s campus revolt. It succeeded to the extent that it did not only because of antiwar fever and the college administration's rigid incompetence, but also because of general discontent with the lack of community at Columbia, exacerbated by demeaning institutional regulations, about which students had no say. Though scores of smaller campus protests swept the country in April and May, Columbia was unique in at least one respect. It was the first actual coalition of black and white students (though tense and distrustful), which enhanced the latter's confidence and sense of legitimacy; in Carl Oglesby's words, it was "the most concrete unification yet of the antiracism and antiwar fights."[71] The white and black radicals' biggest failure was their inability, or refusal, to stake out a middle ground between co-optation and "revolution" that might have enabled them to direct a broad campus movement for fundamental university reform. Instead, the cutting edge was blunted, and SDS shunted to the sidelines, by the ensuing clamor, led by liberal students and faculty, for superficial "restructuring" of decision-making.

During the spring the two Democratic challengers were battling in the hustings. Kennedy won primaries in Indiana and Nebraska, McCarthy in

Wisconsin and Oregon. Vice President Humphrey finally announced his candidacy and gained a delegate lead running in the back rooms. After winning the key California contest on 4 June, Kennedy appeared to be moving toward a convention victory. That night, after celebrating with his campaign workers in Los Angeles, he was shot dead in a hotel kitchen on his way to a press conference. "I just found myself sobbing hysterically," one man who knew him recalled, speaking for millions who did not. "I just hadn't realized fully how many hopes I'd pinned on him, feeling that he was just indispensable to the country, and feeling that I had loved him . . . that he couldn't really be replaced."[72] The two leaders who represented the greatest hope for peace and social justice had been assassinated two months apart. Like King, the young New York senator had been maturing politically in the last years of his life and moving leftward. He seemed genuinely committed to a progressive agenda. For many the message of Kennedy's killing was that the door had been shut to the possibility of change through electoral politics. Those who did not give up altogether began to pursue other options more seriously.

Chicago. The National Mobilization Committee ("the Mobe") had intended it as another Pentagon action, only bigger. Its purpose was to confront the Democratic convention on Vietnam; "demonstrate that the politicians do not speak for us; [and] encourage and help discontented Democrats to seek new and independent forms of protest and resistance."[73] Rennie Davis, ex-ERAP organizer and now codirector with Tom Hayden of the Mobe's convention project, recalled that "our idea of Chicago was a rank-and-file walkout of ordinary Democrats, spearheaded by the campus, but much, much broader than that."[74] Hayden hoped to build a large antiwar coalition, balancing "militance and breadth," that would link New Leftists with Kennedy and McCarthy supporters and put pressure on reformers within the Democratic Party.[75]

They would have to share the Windy City turf with a less nonviolent outfit, the Youth International Party, or "Yippies," which aimed at shaping the youth culture into a revolutionary force, utilizing sensational "media events" in lieu of real organizing. An outgrowth of the Pentagon protest, it had been founded by Jerry Rubin, a creative antiwar organizer from Berkeley and a key architect of the October siege; Abbie Hoffman, colorful New York hippie leader who had incited the exorcism of the Pentagon's evil spirits; and Paul Krassner, editor of the *Realist*, a counterculture journal. The Mobe and the Yippies, very different in style and purpose, joined in an uneasy alliance to orchestrate a week of convention protests—the former to focus on a decentralized "counterconvention" with rallies and marches, the Yippies to concoct a "Festival of Life" abounding in rock music and nominating for president a live pig named "Pigasus."

But not very many people came to Chicago at the end of August— several thousand in all—owing to lackluster organizing by the Mobe and all-out preparation for war by Mayor Daley. If the mayor's overkill (and hints of violence from the movement) scared many away, the Daley machine "partially saved us," Mobe leader Dellinger believed, when it refused permits and unleashed the roughneck Chicago cops.[76] The main gathering place for protesters was Lincoln Park, miles from the convention amphitheater. Every night with escalating fury the police attacked the crowd to enforce the midnight curfew. "A truly stupefying sight," novelist William Styron wrote of night four, "100 or more of the police in a phalanx abreast, clubs at the ready, in helmets and gas masks, just behind them a huge perambulating machine with nozzles, like the type used for spraying insecticide, disgorging clouds of yellowish gas, the whole advancing panoply illuminated by batteries of mobile floodlights," verily a "night-scene out of Armageddon."[77] The next afternoon antiwar delegates staged a raucous protest inside the convention hall, singing "We Shall Overcome" and chanting "Stop the war!" after the peace plank's defeat by a relatively close margin. That night a few hundred of them marched downtown where they vigiled by candlelight.

Earlier the Mobe had held a big rally at Grant Park. When an overzealous protester shimmied up a flagpole and put the Stars and Stripes at half mast, and others (including an undercover cop) pulled it down and put a red T-shirt in its place, the cops charged in and cracked heads, scattering thousands in all directions. Some of the more aggressive "park people" bombarded the cops with rocks, chunks of concrete, and other makeshift ammunition. As the ralliers regrouped, Dellinger announced a march on the convention hall, where presidential nominee was to be named later on. After gleefully merging with a civil rights procession from the Poor People's Campaign led by a three-wagon mule train, which was allowed to get through, the marchers were trapped by police and machine gun–toting National Guard outside the Conrad Hilton Hotel, the Democrats' headquarters. Painted by the eerie glare of TV lights, the police— some reportedly screaming, "Kill, kill, kill, kill!"—lunged at protesters and bystanders alike, flailing clubs wildly and spraying Mace everywhere.[78] A small portion of the 7,000 demonstrators taunted the police

with obscenities and fought back fiercely. Beaten to the ground and trampled, shoved through plate-glass windows, lying bloody in the street, the
injured and others around them shouted over and over, "The whole world
is watching!"

Mobe leader and college professor Sidney Peck was targeted by the
deputy police superintendent he had negotiated with earlier. "The main
thing I was concerned about was protecting my head, because that's how
I earn a living," Peck remembered, "so I put my arms over my head and
they gave me a real beating with nightsticks. I had to have twenty-two
stitches in my head, surgery on my finger, they pounded all over my
kidneys, one of them jammed a nightstick between my legs."[79] According
to a reporter, the police went "quite literally, berserk."[80] In the convention hall, just before Hubert Humphrey clinched his long-sought reward,
Connecticut senator Abraham Ribicoff told the delegates that "with
George McGovern we wouldn't have Gestapo tactics on the streets of
Chicago," turning Mayor Daley purple with rage.[81]

In its official report *Rights in Conflict,* the Walker Commission, which
investigated the convention protests, concluded that although during the
week police had been provoked by obscene epithets and flying objects,
their violence was "unrestrained and indiscriminate," especially at night.
Moreover, police violence was "made all the more shocking by the fact
that it was often inflicted upon persons who had broken no law, disobeyed
no order, made no threat. . . . Newsmen and photographers were singled out for assault and their equipment deliberately damaged."[82] Some
protesters, trying out spontaneous mobile tactics, had engaged in violence of their own, even if it was mainly retaliatory. Much of it was per-
petrated by paid informers and provocateurs—how much may never be
known. Army Intelligence admitted years later that "about one demonstrator in six was an undercover agent."[83]

For many radicals the lesson of Chicago was that from now on violent
tactics would be a legitimate recourse to meet the "fascism" of the enemy
and to make the war more costly. Few held out hope for the broad antiwar coalition that had initially fired up Davis and Hayden, or agreed with
Arthur Waskow that what was needed now was "guerrilla politics, not
guerrilla war."[84] Dellinger spoke for some in drawing another conclusion.
Regretting that Chicago had not been more like the Pentagon action, he
criticized fellow leaders who "found it hard to move from protest to resistance without adopting some of the cynicism and *realpolitik* of the society we were resisting."[85]

Festivals of Life

"New tribes will gather in Chicago," blared the much-ballyhooed Yippie manifesto in January 1968.

We will be completely open, everything will be free. Bring blankets, tents, draft cards, body paint, Mrs. Leary's cow, food to share, music, eager skin and happiness. The threats of LBJ, Mayor Daley and J Edgar Freako will not stop us. We are coming! We are coming from all over the world!

The life of the American spirit is being torn asunder by the forces of violence, decay and the napalm, cancer fiend. We demand the politics of ecstasy. We are the delicate spoors of the new fierceness that will change America. We will create our own reality, we are Free America. And we will not accept the false theatre of the Death Convention.[86]

The Yippies' Festival of Life turned out to be poorly organized and almost a mockery of its prodigious media buildup. Only a few thousand youth gathered in Chicago's Lincoln Park on Sunday afternoon to "get high" on marijuana and psychedelics and shake their bones to the "acid rock" of Detroit's MC-5. This was the only band that dared to risk police attack, and the least known of the pantheon of rock stars, from Bob Dylan to Jefferson Airplane, originally invited. When Abbie Hoffman brought in a flatbed truck to use as a stage (the MC-5 could be heard but not seen), defying police orders, cops moved in to make arrests. Some of the park people yelled, "Pigs eat shit!" and a handful threw bottles and stones; police screamed back, "Get the fuck out of town!" and, "Go back where you came from, fags!" The convention week's first bloody skirmish quickly escalated. Unlike the night before, Allen Ginsberg failed to calm things with his beatific *Om*'s, though he solemnly chanted for seven hours while the violence swirled around him.[87]

Both as grandiose myth and more prosaic reality, the Festival of Life dramatized the interconnection of the militant New Left and the effervescent counterculture, which, like the New Left, reached its pinnacle of influence in 1968. The previous autumn's hippie pageantry at the Pentagon, exorcising its evil spirits, followed that cold night by the intermingled lighting up of joints and draft cards in the face of the Army's assaults; the communal (if male-dominated) life-styles explored in Columbia's "liberated territory"; the Yippies' celebration of armed love in the Windy City—countless breathtaking moments like these made the political and cultural strands of the multidimensional youth rebellion look and feel like a seamless fabric. But it was never free from frays and tears. Participants and historians looking back had difficulty detecting the borders between radical politics and full-scale cultural revolt, which converged and overlapped but still had fundamental and growing cleavages between them. Was it, as one reflected who lived both fully, "a hydra with two heads," appearing to be two things from the front, one from the back?[88]

Ten years before, writer Norman Mailer had prophetically explored a unifying psycho-social dimension of the next decade's politico-cultural upheaval: a shared existential style and outlook deriving from black artists and hipsters. "If the fate of twentieth century man is to live with death from adolescence to premature senescence," he conjectured in the 1957 essay,

why then the only life-giving answer is to accept the terms of death, to live with death as immediate danger, to divorce oneself from society, to exist without roots, to set out on that uncharted journey into the rebellious imperatives of the self. . . . One is Hip or one is Square (the alternative which each new generation coming into American life is beginning to feel), one is a rebel or one conforms, one is a frontiersman in the Wild West of American night life, or else a Square cell, trapped in the totalitarian tissues of American society, doomed willy-nilly to conform if one is to succeed.

. . . So it is no accident that the source of Hip is the Negro for he has been living on the margin between totalitarianism and democracy for two centuries.

The common ethos of hip blacks and whites was their "burning consciousness of the present"; more, "to be engaged in one primal battle: to open the limits of the possible for oneself. . . . Yet in widening the arena of the possible, one widens it reciprocally for others as well," so that each individual's fulfillment contains "its antithesis of human cooperation."

Writing soon after the triumph of the Montgomery bus boycott, Mailer foresaw that if black people continued to break free from their oppression, it would catalyze the unleashing of the hipster's "psychically armed rebellion" upon the broad expanses of American life; to "bring into the air such animosities, antipathies, and new conflicts of interest that the mean empty hypocrisies of mass conformity will no longer work. A time of violence, new hysteria, confusion and rebellion will then be likely to replace the time of conformity."[89] The armies of the night were already stirring.

Perhaps as profound as the multifaceted influence of the Southern black movement on the New Left, and later, on feminism, was the sub- tler pull of urban black culture on both of these, on the rise of the coun- terculture, and on SNCC and Black Power. This cultural heritage reached these groups directly or through the Beat writers and artists who tried to fashion a white version of it. Younger black and white activ- ists, and eventually the larger host of counterculture "freaks," dressed themselves in the "cool" existential style of the rebel, the "psychic out- law"—starting in the era of Kennedy and Camelot, when style really mattered.

Many of the attributes that characterized the later counterculture (emerging as a mass phenomenon between 1966 and 1967) were staples of the subcultures of early SNCC and SDS, which played a key role in transmitting them to a broader audience of young people, initially in col- leges and universities. These included love of jazz, folk, and rock, rec- reational marijuana smoking, freer sexual connections, more intimate relationships generally, and the "alternative life-style," that is, seeking to integrate work and play. Some more overtly political elements, which SNCC and SDS eventually turned away from, infused their organizing style and practice and constituted a shared creed, later adopted by many in the counterculture: the beliefs that one's whole life has political mean- ing ("Politics is how you lead your life"), and that inner and outer domains of politics need to be connected; in the words of Michael Rossman, a leader of Berkeley's Free Speech Movement, the dream that "recon- structing the society, reconstructing the self . . . can happen simultane- ously, interpenetrating as they must."[90] Changing consciousness was seen as a pivotal tool in both realms. If anything seemed new in all this it was the notion (never accepted by all activists and increasingly chal- lenged as time went on) that transforming one's individual life and con- sciousness was not only a high value in itself but would lead to changing the world—would be a step in that direction, at least.

Flowing out of these precepts was the overriding impulse to create and live the future society in the present, a feeling as prevalent in SNCC's sit-ins and freedom rides as in the early New Left. Rossman happily recalled the first student takeover of a campus building, by the FSM in 1964: "We dance, we sing, we show movies. What we were doing in that short space of time was a prophetic action. We were acting out the dimensions of a new society . . . on an improvised basis, in a very small space. We were acting as if we could make our own future."[91] Acting as if.

Prefigurative efforts, animated by what might be called a prefigurative ethic of immediacy, claimed center stage in the myriad dramas of both activists and hippies. Counterinstitutions, higher on the agenda in some milieus than others, mushroomed all over. A kindred spirit brought to life SNCC freedom schools and rural cooperatives in Mississippi; underground newspapers and "free universities" in big cities and campus towns; the panoply of alternative structures (stores, community services, and so forth) in hippie enclaves like Haight-Ashbury; feminist publishing collectives, health clinics, rape crisis centers; and the thousands of intentional communes, urban and rural, that ranged from disciplined revolutionary (or religious) cells to apolitical living groups.

Whether through new social forms or be-ins, "happenings" and other modes of living life as public theater, hippies played with participatory democracy and—children of Walt Whitman and the Transcendentalists— took it to deeper regions of soul and psyche. The counterculture offered a world of spontaneous pleasure to shape cooperatively with others. "It is, at last, reality itself that must be participated in," wrote Theodore Roszak, "must be seen, touched, breathed with the conviction that *here* is the ultimate ground of our existence, available to all, capable of ennobling by its majesty the life of every man who opens himself. It is participation of this order—experiential and not merely political—that alone can guarantee the dignity and autonomy of the individual citizen." As Roszak saw it, counterculture pioneers aspired "to ground democracy safely beyond the culture of expertise."[92]

While the New Left arose partly as a response to psychological and cultural alienation and this remained basic to its collective identity, the counterculture that grew out of it (but never left it behind) made alienation, and the older generation deemed responsible for it, its prime adversary. Regardless of the fact that many adherents had little political awareness (on an articulated level), the counterculture's motley mobilization had the effect if not the intention of assaulting the mores of the technocratic "death culture," down to the scientific worldview of instrumental reason and, especially, the Protestant work ethic. They were subverting technique, efficiency, and joyless labor with the power of the imagination, challenging not just authority but its scientific and moral foundations. A new culture was gestating, Roszak speculated, in which "the non-intellective capacities of the personality—those capacities that take fire from visionary splendor and the experience of human communion—become the arbiters of the good, the true, and the beautiful." Many of the disaffected young gave only lip service to tangible goals, like ending the war and racism, and spurned direct action tactics. Others were quite involved, or had been. But whether cognizant or not, all were engaged in a broader project with the potential of "altering the total cultural context within which our daily politics takes place."[93]

Three interrelated pursuits staked out the common ground of white radical activism and hippiedom: community, drugs, and rock music. Many New Left groups considered community-building (among themselves) part of their work, though a lower priority. Groups typically drew a line between working and living together; it was unusual for the same collective to combine both spheres. One that did was the Peace and Liberation Commune in the small black ghetto of East Palo Alto, California (comprised of a dozen young men, including several Stanford dropouts and two blacks), which birthed the Resistance.

"For us," David Harris recalled, "resistance began when that community began." Creating community was integral to the initial organizing process of persuading others to return their draft cards. "I remember hours at Ken Swanson's playing guitars, and autoharps, and talking, and making merry with each other, and trying to create a relationship before you left . . . instinctively feeling that that closeness had to be there for the thing to function." Rather than being oriented toward "objective conditions" like most of SDS, the West Coast Resistance saw noncooperation with conscription partly "as a means of expression of the lives we were trying to do. We were into the idea that your life was your art."[94] Of the whole New Left, the Resistance was probably most suffused with countercultural values and life-style and felt the strongest need for a supportive community to help sustain those who faced prison. But within the Palo Alto Resistance, as elsewhere, divisions grew between those more caught up in the counterculture and "personal liberation" (faithful to the original Resistance worldview) and others drifting toward hard-line Marxism-Leninism.

The Peace and Liberation Commune had an unexpected offspring. In March 1968 Harris married folksinger Joan Baez, who had founded the Institute for the Study of Nonviolence with Ira Sandperl and Roy Kepler. Just before he went to prison, Harris helped the institute get free access to a rustic 750-acre ranch in the golden, rolling Palo Alto foothills to use as a rural center for workshops and conferences. The owner was a sympathetic industrialist who had invented color videotape. As the word spread, several dozen Resistance folk and friends, many from the Los Angeles area, moved onto "the Land" without permission and raised cabins, domes, yurts, tepees, and other creative dwellings in the woods.

A few self-reliant women arrived singly and built their own homes. The institute staff was unable to remove the interlopers. Before long the back-land homesteaders (and kids), whose population peaked at nearly 200, overshadowed the handful of nonviolent activists who lived communally in the old ranch buildings by the road. The two communities became one, gardening, volleyballing, and "boogying" together, until finally evicted by a new owner in the late 1970s; bulldozers obliterated their homes.

Across San Francisco Bay, fifty miles northeast, occurred the most fateful attempt to hatch a prefigurative community mixing radical politics and oppositional culture—for a few enchanting weeks in spring 1969, "a perfect representation of the Movement's utopian impulse."[95] The university in Berkeley had torn down houses it owned to make way for dorms or a soccer field but had left the three-acre lot empty. Backed by local businesses, hundreds of radicals, "street people," students (some from fraternities and sororities), younger professors, and neighbors joyfully packed sod, planted vegetables and flowers, made music, danced and frolicked in their patch of Eden. With no bosses, and making decisions cooperatively, "what we were creating was our own desires," Stew Albert exulted in the alternative *Berkeley Barb,* "so we worked like madmen and loved it." Black Panthers came over and got into the spirit. "Are you going to call it PEOPLES Park," asked Bobby Seale. "Listen we got to have some Panthers down here working, this is really socialistic."[96] The little park "touched some deep hunger for a common life," recalled another participant, Todd Gitlin. "It consolidated the community, made it palpable."[97]

Neither the university administrators nor Governor Ronald Reagan liked what they saw sprouting, and they squelched the minicooperative commonwealth with tactics normally reserved for violent ghetto uprisings. Deputy sheriffs fired shotguns freely at the crowds, killing one bystander, blinding another, and injuring more than one hundred people. Reagan called in the National Guard, 3,000 of whom bivouacked in the park and occupied downtown Berkeley, making it feel strangely like Saigon. At one point a Guard helicopter sprayed the entire square-mile campus with debilitating tear gas. Outside of the South, it was the era's bloodiest premeditated repression of essentially unviolent activity—Vietnam come home to roost, some thought. Many were so shocked, then demoralized, that the utopian experiment intended "to fuse movement and counterculture ended up driving a wedge between them."[98] Two months later the most spectacular (and short-lived) hippie commune of

National Guard troops detain demonstrators and bystanders at People's Park,
Berkeley, California, May 1969. © *1969 Ted Streshinsky*

the age, the huge Woodstock rock festival in rural upstate New York,
appeared to have little interest in any cause beyond itself.

No one will ever be able to measure the impact of drug use on the
New Left's journey, and to exaggerate would mislead; yet it clearly made
a difference. Marijuana and, much less common, psychedelics (LSD,
mescaline, and psilocybin) facilitated uninhibited explorations of the self
at the same time that they fortified feelings of community and solidarity,
the connectedness embellished by the shared rituals of partaking. Drugs
amplified, if not stimulated, the sense that "everything is possible" and
enabled one to visualize the texture of such possibilities. It made it easier
to dream, to savor ideals, to envision alternatives, and to live these out
in the moment, thus intensifying the prefigurative ethic of immediacy. As
a case in point, grass-smoking and "tripping" were conspicuous sacra-
ments at the inception of the West Coast Resistance and helped to nourish the participants; though quite a few resisters rarely if ever used
drugs. On the downside, drugs abetted the ethereal thinking ("sunshine
language") and air of unreality in pockets of the New Left that fed into a
growing flight from reality by many. And an untold number abused these
chemicals with harmful personal consequences.

In the larger arena of the counterculture, illicit drug consumption—along with related symbols of defiance such as long hair on men, wild clothes, and hippie lingo—encouraged legions of politically uninvolved youth to experience their lives outside the law as vaguely political. The authorities came to treat them like criminals no less than those who put their bodies on the line. Indeed, many got an inkling of what it felt like to be black or brown. "When you smoked dope," explained Rossman, "you inhaled an entire complex of attitudes and culture. . . . You couldn't smoke dope without being an outlaw and being against the state, because the state was out to get your ass." It was inherently a political act "not because the politics was in the chemistry but in the social situation. One chose to enter into conspiracy, breathing together as an outlaw together."[99] How often this outlaw stance turned into overt activism is a different matter.

What activists and counterculturalists (many were hybrids of both) had most in common was immersion in the culture of rock music—born out of black rhythm and blues—that pushed, pulled, and pervaded all dimensions of the youth revolt. It was not just the booming background behind it all; the music helped "to define and codify the mores and standards" of the youth subculture.[100] Rare was the rock tune that did not convey a political message, if implicit. Unlike folk music and "folk rock," not many were overtly antiwar; songs like "I Feel Like I'm Fixin' to Die Rag" sung by Country Joe and the Fish ("One, two, three, what are we fighting for?") were the exception. Fewer still were antiracist. Antisexist songs were yet unheard of, sexist lyrics being the norm. Yet most in some manner mocked or condemned the perceived hypocrisy, authoritarianism, artificiality, or sheer deadness of the dominant culture and its older guardians; the pounding beat and rhythm as much as the lyrics belted out good-bye to all that. On the positive side rock music clamored for unlimited personal freedom, living life fully, spontaneously, without inhibition, in the now—the ethic of immediacy unleashed with abandon. No song reveled in the youthful yearning for an unbridled self (freed with help from friendly drugs) more tantalizingly than Bob Dylan's "Mr. Tambourine Man," a 1966 hit by the Byrds. And numerous rock hits celebrated togetherness and community—for example, "Let's Get Together," popularized by the Youngbloods:

> C'mon people now, smile on your brother
> Everybody get together, try to love one another, right now![101]

More than any other rock band, the Beatles' later repertoire blended pleas for peace (John Lennon's "Give Peace a Chance") and peaceful revolution with mystical explorations of inner domains ("Strawberry Fields Forever," "Lucy in the Sky With Diamonds"); of course, the latter was their favored path to the former.

To a degree, through its overpowering medium, rock momentarily reconciled some of the tensions between the values of the New Left and the counterculture, and within each of these—particularly the antinomies of individualism and community. Discordant notes seemed to merge in the surging rhythms and harmonies. And if they didn't, it all seemed to matter less anyway. But one disharmony that could not easily be drowned out was the contradiction that many young people began to sense between rock's clarion call for a new consciousness and "energy force" and the commercialized rock music industry manipulating youth as an unprecedented mass market. This multibillion-dollar industry proved to be as impersonal and exploitative as any other and played a decisive role in commodifying the once-oppositional culture, which slipped into a morass of passive consumerism.

As antiwar protests, campus uprisings, black militancy, and the hippie revolt swept to epic proportions in the late 1960s, all magnified in the media's glare, and as currents of each spilled into the others, many were the hip radicals and radical hippies who believed that a momentous convergence might be in the making, that the new cultural sensibilities could be the common denominator of an all-embracing politico-cultural revolution. Journalist Andrew Kopkind wrote that "political radicals have to see the cultural revolution as a sea in which they can swim."[102] Disaffected middle-class youth began to be perceived as a bona fide agency of change, even if apolitical in conventional terms. Like any other constituency, "flower power" would have to be organized. The longer haired, more libertarian activists who gained ascendance in SDS in the mid-1960s intuitively grasped that their effectiveness in reaching students and other youth would partly depend on how well the organizers resonated with countercultural styles and symbols.

The first counterculture group to pursue this mission was San Francisco's Diggers, their name deriving from the antiproperty, communist revolutionaries of the seventeenth-century English civil war. Renowned for their "free stores," free money, and free-food programs in Haight-Ashbury and elsewhere, their chief organizing tool was guerrilla theater (a political art form they pioneered) and various creative put-ons—such as the practice of "public nuisance," which they called "new sense." Diggers specialized in public drama that would "create the condition it describes," whether burning dollar bills, handing out free marijuana, or slaughtering a horse to protest capital punishment.[103] They attracted an ardent following in hippie enclaves West and East. Through one of its disciples, ex–SNCC organizer Abbie Hoffman, the Diggers inspired the birth of the Yippies, one of whose key purposes, in Hoffman's words, was the "blending of pot and politics into a potlitical grass leaves movement—a cross-fertilization of the hippie and New Left philosophies."[104] But with their deliberate emphasis on distortion, myth-making, and manipulation of media, the projection of mass guerrilla theater onto a televised national stage, and disdain for grass-roots organizing, the Yippies lost in authenticity what they gained in celebrity. Some of those most determined to weld political and cultural transformation violated the counterculture's own values and spirit.

The foregoing sketch shows that the New Left cannot be understood without taking into account the larger cultural maelstrom in which it was moored, if not submerged. If one looks hard one can see the permeable boundaries distinguishing the two phenomena—which on a superficial level was the divide between those who saw themselves as political activists and those who did not. But many New Leftists had dual identities restlessly coexisting—head in one world, perhaps, heart and hormones in the other. And conflicts arose within SNCC, SDS, and the Resistance about the proper role of counterculture values in radical organizing work. From start to finish New Left groups danced around the creative tensions between "expressive" and "strategic" inclinations, which, unresolved, contributed to the New Left's demise.

New Left and counterculture, both influenced by the cultural renaissance of "black consciousness," constituted interwoven strands of a broad-gauged youth revolt. Yet each had a distinct core of values, motives, and aspirations that set it apart. The New Left was a bona fide social movement. The counterculture incurred no less of an upheaval, but (similar in this respect to the ghetto uprisings) was far more spontaneous, amorphous, and by and large, unorganized. Nor can it be said that the counterculture functioned as the New Left's own "movement culture," though it offered elements of such. Unlike the shared church culture of the Southern crusade, much of the counterculture had little in common with the New Left and even felt alienated from the radicals, seeing their self-righteous seriousness as reproducing the social neuroses it rejected. And the "do your own thing" ethic of self-reliant independence that overshadowed the counterculture's communitarian urges was a far cry from the black church, which provided the protective, nurturing sanctuary of a real-life "beloved community" in the heat of struggle. When the going got tough, the New Left had no such shelter from the storm—only the survival tools of rugged individualism.

A House Divided

The day before Richard Nixon swore to uphold the Constitution as the nation's thirty-seventh president, the Mobe organized a nonviolent counterinauguration to protest the continuing war. Led by four active-duty GIs, 10,000 "militant but genial" demonstrators marched toward the Capitol. [105] The next day, in the cold and drizzly air, Nixon solemnly promised to bring unity to his country and peace to the world. "The greatest honor history can bestow," he proclaimed, "is the title of peacemaker."[106] Armed only with banners and chants, Mobe troops peacefully invaded the inaugural ceremony and the parade to the White House. But as the presidential motorcade crawled down Pennsylvania Avenue, a shower of projectiles—sticks, stones, bottles, cans, smoke bombs, and a ball of tinfoil—landed on the limousines of the new regime. The Mobe publicly condemned this action by an SDS faction. Nonviolent, then briefly violent, it was the first time an august inauguration had been disrupted.

Nixon inherited the deadlocked war when he narrowly won the presidency in November 1968. (His margin of victory over Humphrey was less than one percent of the popular vote; independent candidate George Wallace, the Alabama governor, garnered ten million votes, or 14 percent.) One of Nixon's first decisions was to appoint Henry Kissinger—Harvard expert on NATO and nuclear weapons, White House consultant, adviser to his defeated rival, Nelson Rockefeller—to be his assistant for national security. They formed a close, exclusive partnership in the making of foreign policy. The two men had learned a vital lesson from the breaking of President Johnson: that dissent either within the administration or from outside could not be tolerated.

They decided early on to try to win the war quickly by threatening the destruction of North Vietnam. But first they had to make this threat credible to Hanoi, and to Moscow. Nixon apparently believed that he could get a favorable settlement the way Eisenhower had in Korea—by threatening massive escalation, including the use of nuclear weapons. Ike's nuclear warning to the Chinese in 1953, when Nixon was vice president, hastened the Korean War's end and convinced him that such a credible threat could work against another obdurate Asian enemy. "I call it the Madman Theory, Bob," chief of staff H. R. Haldeman reported Nixon telling him during the 1968 campaign. "I want the North Vietnamese to believe I've reached the point where I might do *anything* to stop the war. We'll just slip the word to them that, 'for God's sake, you know Nixon is obsessed about Communism. We can't restrain him when he's angry—and he has his hand on the nuclear button'—and Ho Chi Minh himself will be in Paris in two days begging for peace."[107]

To build his credible threat, Nixon expanded the bombing of Laos, sending in B-52 "stratoforts" for the first time, and started a secret air war in Cambodia in March 1969. For over a year the Cambodia bombing orders were burned after each sortie because the White House demanded "maximum security."[108] By extending the war to all of Indochina, Nixon and Kissinger were showing Hanoi and Moscow that they would break restraints imposed by Johnson, that there were no limits to what they might do—and that they would not be affected by protests, no matter how big.

During the first hundred days of the Nixon administration, white and "Third World" student activism escalated in size and militance. About one-third of all students took part in protests on 300 campuses, a quarter of which included strikes or building takeovers. In many cases these actions involved property destruction or violence. Fighting institutional racism, black and Chicano students at San Francisco State, backed by white radicals, sustained the longest student strike ever, punctuated by police battles almost daily. At Cornell black students occupied a building to make a stand on the same issue. Fearing attack, they armed themselves in self-defense but left the building peacefully after reaching a fair agreement with administrators. A nine-day nonviolent takeover of a war-related electronics laboratory at Stanford led to a ban on classified research and severance of the Stanford Research Institute, which was deeply involved in counterinsurgency studies for the military.

By 1969 draft resistance (openly refusing to cooperate) and draft evasion (avoiding induction any way possible) had become a mass phenomenon. During the Vietnam era over 200,000 men refused induction. Though most were never prosecuted, 8,750 were convicted—generally those more vocal about it—and 3,000 were sent to prison, serving an average of eighteen months. As many as half a million failed to register for the draft, only a few of whom were jailed. Tens of thousands fled to Canada and other countries. The Resistance spearheaded the swelling movement of draft refusal. But most Resistance groups limited their effectiveness by being overattached to renouncing deferments and returning draft cards—a choice more appropriate for some than for others less privileged; they did not gear their strategy to the class and racial inequities of the draft system. Many resisters were not prepared for the harshness of prison, and some were embittered by it.

Winter and spring 1969 marked the point when a significant number of men and women in the military first openly protested the war, in Vietnam as well as at home. "GI coffeehouses" and underground papers helped galvanize the discontent at many bases. Twenty-seven soldiers in the brig at San Francisco's Presidio were charged with mutiny when, singing "We Shall Overcome," they staged a sit-down strike. Thousands of soldiers and sailors went AWOL to avoid going to Vietnam. A few were given temporary sanctuary in churches and movement dwellings. In April many GIs in uniform joined peace marches all over the country.

Five women calling themselves "Women Against Daddy Warbucks" darted into thirteen Manhattan draft boards and, to block inductions, stole thousands of draft files, plus the "1" and "A" typewriter keys ("1-A" signifying "draft eligible"). Two days later they surfaced at Rockefeller Center and tossed the confettied draft records into the noontime air; they had sent a message explaining their action to all the multinational corporations headquartered there. This was the latest in more than a dozen nonviolent raids on draft boards (and Dow Chemical) that had started in October 1967 when Jesuit priest Phillip Berrigan and three others poured their own blood on draft files in Baltimore as a further experiment in combining Gandhi and guerrilla action, pushing nonviolent direct action to its outer limit—or, as activist Jim Forest put it, to "open up a new phase of resistance."[109] The most celebrated raid was done by the "Catonsville Nine"—Berrigan, his brother Daniel, also a Jesuit priest, and seven other radical Catholics—who made a bonfire of draft files with homemade napalm and declared that "we believe some property has no right to exist."[110] Participants in these actions carefully avoided harm to any person, either waited around until arrested or turned themselves in, and accepted the consequences, although after their trial the Berrigans and others of the Catonsville crew did go underground until caught by the FBI. In part this "ultra resistance" was an effort to halt the relentless spiral toward outright armed struggle by offering an alternative. But some New Left activists had lost patience with even the most militant expressions of nonviolent action.

Although SDS now put less stock in the revolutionary role of students, it played a central role in many campus protests that spring. Except at a few places, like Stanford, where they won partial victories, SDSers by and large felt frustrated with their lack of success in building a more radical movement. Nationally and locally, the previous year had been taken up as much with bitter quarrels and shouting matches over the correct line—"vanguarditis," Carl Oglesby called it—as with actual organizing.[111] To fend off Progressive Labor's growing clout, the National Office had turned itself into a disciplined cadre and won adoption of a proposal to forge a Revolutionary Youth Movement (RYM) of the working class.

The sectarian madness culminated at the June convention in Chicago. National officers handed delegates a long-winded treatise entitled "You don't need a weatherman to know which way the wind blows"—a line from Bob Dylan—which set forth the rationale for their new strategy while refuting all the main tenets of PL's politics. According to Kirkpatrick Sale, it was "a peculiar mix of New Left attitudes clothed in Old Left arguments, the instincts of the sixties ground through a mill of the thirties, the liberating heritage of SDS dressed up in leaden boots from the past."[112] The assembly soon degenerated into mindless name-calling and slogan-shouting and a few fistfights in the back. RYM leader Bernardine Dohrn, a brilliant young attorney who had worked with the National Lawyers Guild, led a walkout by the majority united in their opposition to PL. Later she returned to the rump session with her forces and declared that PL members were expelled from SDS; the RYM faction, several hundred strong, marched out into the Chicago night. Over the summer RYM in turn split into two parts, one of which became "Weatherman," which was committed to urban guerrilla warfare in support of Third World revolution. As a national organization SDS was dead. Richard Flacks concludes that the "organized New Left disintegrated into warring factions over precisely the question of how to transcend the limits of student radicalism. . . . The era of *campus* confrontation and *student* revolutionism has ended not because it failed, but because it reached the limit of its possibilities."[113]

Compelled to do something to quell the political earthquake, President Nixon lowered draft calls, pledged to end the draft, set up a lottery to make conscription less inequitable, and brought home some troops. He also announced a peace proposal calling for mutual withdrawal from South Vietnam, which was rejected out of hand by Hanoi. In early summer 1969 Nixon decided to "go for broke" to end the war, according to his memoirs, "either by negotiated agreement or by an increased use of force. . . . Once the summer was over and Congress and the colleges returned from vacation in September, a massive new antiwar tide would sweep the country during the fall and winter. . . . After half a year of sending peaceful signals to the Communists, I was ready to use whatever military pressure was necessary.

"I decided," Nixon's account continues, "to set November 1, 1969— the first anniversary of Johnson's bombing halt—as the deadline for what would in effect be an ultimatum to North Vietnam." In August Kissinger met secretly with North Vietnamese diplomats in Paris and personally delivered the threat "to take measures of the greatest consequences." He warned them not to allow the war to become Nixon's war, since, he said, "if it is Mr. Nixon's war, then he cannot afford not to win it." A month later Ho Chi Minh, Vietnam's George Washington, died at seventy-nine. Nixon had just received a response to a letter he had sent him. Ho's message hinted at flexibility, but not capitulation. "After receiving this unpromising reply," he recalled, "I knew that I had to prepare myself for the tremendous criticism and pressure that would come with stepping up the war."[114]

The commander-in-chief ordered Kissinger to draw up a plan to force Hanoi to its knees. His national security czar assembled a team of trusted aides and instructed them to "examine the option of a savage, decisive blow against North Vietnam." "I refuse to believe that a little fourth-rate power like North Vietnam doesn't have a breaking point," Kissinger declared. "The Johnson administration could never come to grips with this problem. We intend to come to grips."[115] The resulting "Duck Hook" plan included B-52 carpet bombing of Hanoi and other cities; mining Haiphong Harbor and inland waterways; bombing dikes on the Red River delta to cause catastrophic flooding; a ground invasion; and the use of tactical nuclear weapons to cut off supply routes from China and Russia. Kissinger aide Roger Morris reported seeing photographs of proposed nuclear targets, one of which lay a mile south of the Chinese border. The "savage blow" would take four days, to be repeated until Hanoi cried uncle.[116]

Four blocks from the White House another team of planners was hard at work organizing the October Moratorium, a day of nationwide protest against the war. A few months before, millionaire industrialist Jerome Grossman, a major McCarthy backer in 1968, dreamed up an idea for a national strike that would grow one day longer each month until the war ended. It caught the imagination of Sam Brown, a twenty-six-year-old Harvard Divinity School student who had won acclaim as McCarthy's youth coordinator. Brown named it a "moratorium" on business as usual, rather than the radical-sounding "strike," and planned decentralized grass-roots actions expressing moderation, not militance. Brown and other young liberals from the McCarthy and Kennedy campaigns formed the Vietnam Moratorium Committee in June, their first task being to activate hundreds of student body presidents.

By late September the Moratorium plan seemed to be taking the country by storm, aided by an unprecedented media buildup. About thirty members of Congress supported it, and both *Time* and *Newsweek* put it on their covers, the latter's blaring in big letters, "Nixon In Trouble." Columnist David Broder prophesized in the *Washington Post* that "the men and the movement that broke Lyndon Johnson's authority in 1968 are out to break Richard M. Nixon in 1969. The likelihood is great that they will succeed again, for breaking a President is, like most feats, easier to accomplish the second time around."[117]

The mighty tidal wave engulfed the nation on Wednesday, 15 October. In thousands of cities and towns, students, workers, homemakers, politicians, executives—people from all walks of life, but mostly middle-class and young—left their routines to join marches, rallies, vigils, teach-ins, doorbell-ringings, and readings of the U.S. war dead in Vietnam. An incalculable number simply wore black arm bands to work or school. Hundreds of colleges and high schools closed for the day, while hundreds more sponsored official gatherings. Few campuses or communities were untouched.

At Whittier College, Nixon's alma mater in California's conservative Orange County, the college president's wife lit a "flame of life" to burn until the war was over. Women in Los Alamos, New Mexico, birthplace of the atomic bomb, blocked a bridge leading to war plants. Students at Bethel College in Kansas borrowed an old church bell and rang it once for each of the 40,000 U.S. soldiers who had died. One hundred workers at a New Jersey factory that made body bags for Vietnam demanded an end to the war, even though it would have meant an end to their jobs. In New York City thousands of people, some of them bankers and stockbrokers, joined a noontime "walk for peace" up Wall Street to old Trinity Church, where a hundred leading Establishment figures took turns reading out loud the names of American war dead. At a similar observance in Houston a student wept when he announced the name of a close friend whose death he had not known about. At the county courthouse in Lexington, Kentucky, a large assembly listened to the reading of Kentucky's war dead. A woman walked up to the microphone and uttered a single name. "This is my son," she said. "He was killed last week."[118] In South Vietnam thousands of GIs wore black arm bands, among them half of a platoon that slayed two guerrillas that day. With several million participants, the prim and proper outpouring broke all records for popular protest in the United States.

As the last peace candles flickered into darkness on that historic autumn day, the White House faced the chilling prospect that the Moratoriums would grow steadily larger. Nixon realized that M-Day had knocked the wind out of his ultimatum to Hanoi. In late October he met with his war cabinet and reluctantly called off the escalation plan. "I'm not sure we're ready for this," he told them.[119] Duck Hook was set aside.

On 3 November 1969 the president made a dramatic television speech that, between the lines, heralded a decisive shift in his Indochina policy: to prolong the war indefinitely (since he could not win it on the cheap), but to try to make it invisible to the American public. Nixon and Kissinger would fortify the Saigon regime with military aid to fight the ground war mainly on its own, while further expanding the air war, which was less accessible to the media. By reducing American troops, draft calls, costs, and above all, the caskets returning from combat, they would make it appear that they were "winding down" the war, which would become more destructive than ever to the Indochinese. For this strategy to work they had to buy time. Nixon made it clear that the war could not end unless he had the firm support of "the great silent majority." "Let us be united for peace," he said that night. "Let us also be united against defeat. Because let us understand: North Vietnam cannot defeat or humiliate the United States. Only Americans can do that"—a direct slap at the peace movement.[120]

Nixon and Kissinger knew they could not achieve their goals unless they disabled the mounting movement. They set out to do just that, combining public measures with various covert activities. The White House marshalled its forces to undercut the two-day November Moratorium, which would be followed by mass marches in Washington and San Francisco. Their task was made easier because the marches were organized by the radical New Mobilization Committee. The Moratorium and the New Mobe—the center and left of the movement—had worked out an uneasy alliance. White House aide Dwight Chapin drew up an elaborate "game plan": warnings to M-Day backers in Congress that the next one, led by "fringe groups," would be violent; talking "cold turkey" (threats to cancel licenses and pursue antitrust suits) to the TV networks; denunciations of the movement and its media sympathizers by Vice President Spiro Agnew and others; and a statement by Nixon that he was obliviously watching football during the Washington march.[121]

Night and day for forty hours, while thousands of other Moratorium events took place elsewhere, a long line of protesters walked silently in dark robes from Arlington National Cemetery to Capitol Hill. Each one wore a placard with the name of an American soldier killed or a Vietnamese village destroyed. When they passed the iron gates of the White House, they shouted the names they wore to the commander-in-chief holed up inside. At the Capitol each cardboard name was placed in one of twelve hardwood coffins that were lying in state. On Saturday morning, 15 November, the twelve coffins were carried at the head of a vast procession from the Capitol back past the White House to the Washington Monument. Three quarters of a million people gathered in the cold, the largest single demonstration (up to that time) in American history. Though the New Mobe's marshals worked hard to keep the peace, a few violent incidents occurred, including a skirmish at the Justice Department that "looked like the Russian Revolution going on" to Attorney General John Mitchell.[122] In San Francisco more than 100,000 rallied peacefully in Golden Gate Park.

But the White House game plan squarely hit its mark. The media played down the November protests and cancelled live coverage of the big Washington march, creating the impression that the storm was dying down. By year's end the Moratoriums had faded into history. The peace movement, deserted by much of the media and by many radicals, did not have any idea how remarkably effective it had been. The White House had won a quiet victory in its war against dissent.

With a somewhat freer hand President Nixon sent U.S. troops to invade Cambodia in late April 1970, partly to destroy North Vietnamese supply depots and partly as a show of force to renew his strategy of threat. Outraged college students immediately launched a coordinated national strike that spread to at least 350 campuses, some of which closed for the year. Over half the student population protested in one form or another. Many did canvassing and educational work in nearby communities. After a weekend of turmoil at Kent State University in Ohio, during which the ROTC building was gutted, weary National Guardsmen—ordered to disperse even peaceful assemblies—opened fire on a large crowd of demonstrating students on Monday, 4 May. Two women and two men were killed; nine others were injured, including one man paralyzed for life. Two of the dead were bystanders. The slaying of unarmed students stunned the nation and heightened the angry mood on campus. Much less noticed was the killing of two black students by police at Jackson State College in Mississippi. The powerful surge of protest spurred Congress to force all troops out of Cambodia within two months (the only restraint imposed by lawmakers until after U.S. withdrawal), though the invasion had already done its job.

The most important antiwar event of the summer was the National Chicano Moratorium at the end of August. Concerned above all with the disproportionate number of young Latinos dying in Vietnam, a coalition of Chicano organizations mounted an impressive march and rally in the East Los Angeles barrio—the biggest antiwar protest yet in Southern California. Before the first speaker finished, however, a minor incident on the outskirts led to a ferocious police assault on the rally. Highly armed sheriff's deputies killed three participants, including *Los Angeles Times* columnist Ruben Salazar, who was hit by a tear-gas grenade while sitting in a cafe.

While many student activists shifted to antiwar electioneering in the summer and fall, a small number expressed their frustration and revolutionary fervor by torching or bombing dozens of ROTC buildings and other tainted facilities, including a Bank of America near Santa Barbara and a military research center at the University of Wisconsin where the bomb (apparently provided by an FBI informer) took a graduate student's life. By February 1970 the SDS remnant called Weatherman, dispersed into a web of small communal cells, had gone underground. In March three members of one cell were blown to bits while making a bomb in a Greenwich Village townhouse owned by the family of activist Cathy Wilkerson, who survived the blast. From this point on the Weather Underground took credit for a spate of bombings, including ones at the Capitol and the State Department, that lasted into the mid-1970s. Though the FBI hunted them all over, putting Bernardine Dohrn on its most-wanted list, few were apprehended. The climate of intentional violence, much of it instigated by government provocateurs, was just the rationale Nixon needed to intensify the surveillance, harassment, and prosecution of black and white activists, culminating in the notorious Huston Plan, which lifted restrictions on wiretapping, mail-opening, surreptitious entry, and other illegal measures and provided for direct White House control over the jumble of federal intelligence units. It was never officially approved because J. Edgar Hoover balked at losing FBI autonomy, but most of it was carried out informally.

The most celebrated prosecution was the "Chicago Eight" conspiracy trial of the convention protest organizers—Dellinger, Hayden, Davis, Hoffman, Rubin, Lee Weiner, and John Froines. Black Panther chair Bobby Seale, who had little involvement, was also prosecuted, but his case was eventually separated from that of the white activists. After months of wild verbal warfare between the defiant defendants (and attorneys) and the harsh federal judge Julius Hoffman, all but two were convicted of inciting to riot (but acquitted of conspiracy charges). Moreover, the judge vindictively gave defendants and lawyers hefty sentences for contempt of court. Convictions and contempt citations were overturned later by federal appeals courts.

Though antiwar pressure diminished after the uprising against the Cambodia invasion and seemed to have little effect on the 1970 election, the movement resurged the next spring, making up in diversity what it lacked in numbers. If draft resisters had once been the cutting edge of protest, Vietnam combat veterans now took on that role. In early February 1971, while Lieutenant William Calley was on trial for the massacre of civilians at My Lai village, a formidable new group called Vietnam Veterans Against the War (VVAW) held its "Winter Soldier Investigation," in which 100 veterans testified about numerous other U.S. atrocities they had witnessed or participated in. In late April, climaxing a week of rallying and lobbying by a large veteran encampment—a reincarnation of the Depression "bonus marchers"—almost 1,000 Vietnam vets hurled their combat medals over a hastily built wire fence guarding the Capitol, accompanied by tart one-liners. "Medals for murder!" they shouted. "This is the first honorable service I've done my country!"[123] (At Christmastime fifteen VVAW members, in "Operation Peace on Earth," would occupy the Statue of Liberty as a war protest, hanging the American flag upside down from Liberty's crown, and then from her torch.) The day after the medal turn-in, half a million people assembled in Washington for the last great peace march of the Vietnam War.

A week later, taking "mass mobilization to the civil disobedience level" in the manner of Martin Luther King, the "May Day Tribe" attempted to shut down the government by nonviolently blocking traffic at strategic points.[124] Police scooped up over 12,000 people during the three days, many of them passersby, and held them—for a time without food, shelter, blankets, or latrines—on the Washington Redskins football field and in the Coliseum. But the prisoners improvised imaginatively to meet their needs and created a makeshift community of sharing, humor, and "living theater" that won the hearts and minds of some of their captors.[125]

In mid-June 1971 Randy Kehler opened the Sunday *New York Times* in his cell at the grim, fortress-like Latuna Federal Prison near El Paso, Texas, where he was doing two years for draft resistance. Splashed across the front page was the first installment of the Pentagon's own secret history of the Vietnam War. It might never have seen the light of day without him. The unprecedented study had been ordered by Defense Secretary McNamara to find out what went wrong. Completed in late 1968, the forty-seven volumes of historical analysis mixed with classified memos, cables, and reports examined U.S. involvement from the end of World War II until the opening of the Paris peace talks. Among other things it documented a long pattern of presidential lying and deception that could be extrapolated to the current administration. If only for a few weeks, publication of the "Pentagon Papers" in the *Times* and the *Washington Post*, the nation's preeminent newspapers, made the war sharply visible once again.

The man who leaked the secret history was forty-year-old ex–cold warrior Daniel Ellsberg, once a true believer in the Vietnam cause. After a stint as a Marine infantry commander, he was for years a dedicated national security bureaucrat, an expert on crisis decision-making. He had been a high-level researcher on nuclear command and control at the RAND Corporation, the prestigious Pentagon think tank; a consultant to JFK on nuclear planning; a special assistant to McNamara's deputy in charge of Vietnam policy in 1964–65; a "pacification" official in South Vietnam; and an author of the Pentagon history. In spring 1967 Ellsberg came home from two years in Vietnam opposed to the war effort—initially not because it was wrong or immoral, but because of its dishonesty, corruption, and futility. For the next two years he crusaded in the corridors of power, lobbying high officials such as McNamara and national security adviser Walt Rostow and counseling presidential candidates in 1968, especially Robert Kennedy. None of it seemed to work.

At a conference on social change Ellsberg met Janaki Tschannerl, a nonviolent activist from India, who as a little girl had played with an old man named Gandhi, a family friend. She caught Ellsberg's attention by asserting that "for me, the concept of enemy doesn't exist."[126] She taught him about Gandhian truth force and about Martin Luther King—slain that week—and the next year invited him to the triennial meeting of War Resisters International (WRI) at a Pennsylvania college. "I wanted to see," he explained later, "whether the stereotypes of pacifists and antiwar activists had any validity—namely, that they were guilt-ridden, fanatic extremists." He joined the participants in a vigil outside the Philadelphia courthouse where one of them, Quaker activist Bob Eaton, was to be imprisoned for refusing nonmilitary alternative service. It was his first picket line, crossing the divide to leave behind the faceless anonymity of a bureaucratic insider. "I found it psychologically very liberating," he remembered, "to conquer the small worries of humiliation, ridicule, and risk to one's job that are involved in declaring yourself publicly."[127]

Tschannerl introduced him to Randy Kehler, the twenty-five-year-old leader of the War Resisters League on the West Coast, with whom Ellsberg was quite taken. Kehler gave a talk about how the antiwar community had become a family to him. He concluded:

Yesterday our friend Bob went to jail. This is getting to be like a wedding we had a month ago, when Jane and I were married on the beach in San Francisco, because I always cry a lot. Last month David Harris went to jail. Our friends Warren and John and Terry and many others are already in jail and I'm really not as sad about that as it may seem. There's something really beautiful about it and I'm very excited that I'll be invited to join them very soon. . . . There's one other reason why I guess I can look forward to jail, without any remorse or fear, and that's because I know that everyone here and lots of people around the world like you will carry on.[128]

Ellsberg was so shaken by these words that he went to the men's room and sobbed. He identified with Kehler, not just as a bright Harvard graduate like himself but as someone willing to take serious risks for his ideals.

I remember thinking, this is our best, our very best, and we're sending them to prison, more important, we're in a world where they feel they just had to go to prison. . . . All of a sudden, it set new standards for me of what one could be expected, or asked, to do, in the way of resistance to the war. I realized that these young men were very much like my friends in the Marine Corps who had gone into combat for their country. I saw that what these draft resisters were doing was entirely in that spirit. That they were very patriotic. And suddenly I realized that I too would have to enter a kind of resistance to the war even if I too had to go to prison.[129]

Kehler provided the spark that he needed.

Ellsberg's son Robert, then thirteen, commented years later that his father "returned from the conference with Gandhian books and ideas, pamphlets on anarchism, civil disobedience, and civilian resistance—all of which he insisted that I read—as he set out to make sense of these new perspectives and to relate them to his preconceptions. They were strange indeed to someone whose specialties had been guerrilla warfare, counterinsurgency, nuclear planning, and crisis decision-making. I remember one night he finished reading Thoreau's 'On the Duty of Civil Disobedience' and said, 'This may be the most important essay I've ever read.'"[130]

In October 1969, one month after the WRI conference, Ellsberg decided that he could be an accomplice no longer. With the help of fired RAND colleague Tony Russo, his son Robert, and his eleven-year-old daughter Mary, he photocopied the top-secret volumes that he had in his Los Angeles RAND office. He hoped the history would ignite a full-fledged congressional investigation of the war—but Senator Fulbright and other lawmakers would not touch it. Agonized more and more by the relentless bombing and the invasions of Cambodia and then Laos, he finally turned it over to the *Times*. In the meantime he experimented with other forms of nonviolent direct action. He was beaten by police in Boston when he came to the aid of a fellow demonstrator, and he dazzled his friends Noam Chomsky and Howard Zinn with his daring at Washington's May Day in 1971. Chomsky, the famed linguist and social critic, recalled that "Howard and I, who've been in the Movement for years, kept asking ourselves, 'What the hell are we doing here disrupting traffic?' But Dan maneuvered our little affinity group like a platoon in Vietnam."[131]

When the Pentagon Papers appeared in print a month later, the Justice Department won injunctions against further publication in the *Times* and the *Post*, a "prior restraint" on press freedom that was soon nullified by the Supreme Court. While a collective of nonviolent conspirators led by Janaki Tschannerl quickly spread the contraband to other major dailies, Ellsberg slipped underground to keep the spotlight on the Papers, not the perpetrator. He turned himself in after the FBI fingered him, and he was indicted for espionage. (Charges were dropped two years later.)

But the White House had bigger plans than to just put Ellsberg away. Nixon saw his latest crisis as an opportunity to create another Alger Hiss, the high State Department official he had accused in the late 1940s of spying for Russia—a precursor of McCarthy's investigations. If the first Hiss case had catapulted Nixon to the vice presidency, the second might ensure his reelection as president. By painting Ellsberg as the symbol of the "radlibs" (radical liberals) and then smearing him, they could tar with the same brush both the New Left and antiwar Democrats, gluing them together in the public mind. But Kissinger, who had known Ellsberg for years and had hired him as a Vietnam adviser in early 1969, felt the massive disclosure of state secrets was a serious threat to national security, and to his own; it was imperative to keep his ex-colleague from revealing more. Accordingly, to slander and silence Ellsberg and to stop further leaks, Nixon and Kissinger set up a miniature CIA in the White House known as the "Plumbers." Its chief sleuths were Howard Hunt, former CIA operative and a mastermind of the failed 1961 Cuban invasion, and ex–FBI agent Gordon Liddy. To get the dirt they needed, Hunt and Liddy sent three Cuban-Americans, veterans of many secret missions against Castro, to steal records from Ellsberg's psychiatrist in Beverly Hills—an action instigated by Nixon, if not formally approved by him. The presidential burglars did not find what they were looking for, however, and the anti-Ellsberg campaign fizzled out. But Nixon's direct role in the Ellsberg break-in would come back to haunt him.

As things turned out, Nixon would have little need for Ellsberg as his whipping boy in 1972. His trip to China, negotiations with the Soviets, and the withdrawal of most ground troops from Vietnam transformed the political landscape and enabled him to wear the mantle of peacemaker. He seemed so confident of reelection that in response to the spring 1972 North Vietnamese offensive, he resumed intensive bombing of that country and mined Haiphong harbor for the first time. The Soviet Union, whose ships were endangered, did not cancel the approaching summit talks in Moscow. The antiwar movement revived to challenge the new escalation—including efforts on the West Coast to stop aircraft carriers from steaming back to the Gulf of Tonkin by organizing sailors to jump ship and launching "people's blockades" with flotillas of canoes, kayaks, and speedboats in San Francisco Bay. Antiwar pressures and the inexorable election timetable spurred Kissinger and his counterparts from Hanoi to reach a tentative settlement in October that permitted North Vietnamese troops, and the Saigon regime, to remain in the South. After Kissinger publicly promised that "peace is at hand," Nixon won reelection over George McGovern—the true peace candidate—by the largest margin ever in a presidential election.[132] The president and his partner then reneged on the agreement. When North Vietnam would not accept tougher terms, Nixon sent 100 B-52s and 500 jet fighters to devastate Hanoi over the Christmas season, the heaviest bombing of the war, perhaps of any war. At least two B-52 pilots refused to fly. A world outcry, and the shooting down of about one-fifth of the giant stratoforts, stayed Nixon's hand after thirteen days of carnage. All told, the United States had dropped over twice the bomb tonnage on Indochina as in World War II and Korea combined. Nixon had ordered over half of it—four million tons.

The porous peace agreement signed in January was virtually the same as the October draft. The bottom line was that all U.S. military personnel would leave South Vietnam in exchange for release of the POWs. Yet American bombing of Cambodia continued until Congress, emboldened by disclosures about the infamous Watergate cover-up, outlawed it in August 1973. The ground war, fueled by massive U.S. aid, still raged at a reduced level. Nixon's final crisis forced him to resign the next summer in the face of certain impeachment. Watergate so weakened the presidency that President Gerald Ford and Secretary of State Kissinger were unable to send in the bombers when the Saigon government lurched toward collapse the following spring.

On the last day of April 1975, North Vietnamese troops seized control of Saigon and renamed it Ho Chi Minh City. As the Stars and Stripes were hurriedly hoisted down and the last Americans scrambled aboard the big choppers on the embassy roof, a final message was flashed back to Washington from a deserted office underneath. "It has been a long and hard fight and we have lost . . . ," typed the CIA station chief. "Those who fail to learn from history are forced to repeat it. Let us hope that we will not have another Vietnam experience and that we have learned our lesson. Saigon signing off."[133]

Chapter Three

Sisterhood Is Powerful

Liberty and Justice for All?

In November 1964, a few months after the heady Mississippi Freedom Summer and the defeat at Atlantic City, SNCC held a retreat in Waveland, Mississippi, on the calm waters of the Gulf of Mexico. In an atmosphere of deep political and intellectual ferment and questioning of many things, the weary activists tried to grapple with pressing internal conflicts (especially between blacks and whites) and chart future goals and strategy. Two respected white organizers, Mary King and Casey Hayden, thought it was an appropriate moment to raise certain questions that had been troubling them, that they felt had to be addressed if SNCC was to remain an exemplary model of true democracy and self-determination. King, coming South to SNCC after graduating from an Ohio college, was head of the communications section. Casey Hayden, a Texan and ex–philosophy graduate student in Austin, had been a key leader of SNCC since its inception, most recently in Jackson. (She was briefly married to SDS organizer Tom Hayden, on whom she had had a decisive political influence.) Fearing scorn and ridicule from their cohorts, King and Hayden wrote a position paper for the meeting, one of a few dozen circulated, on the role of women in SNCC. After detailing glaring instances of sexual discrimination in this organization that fought fiercely for equality, the anonymous paper explicitly drew a comparison with white society's treatment of black people: "Assumptions of male superiority are as widespread and deep-rooted and every much as crippling to the woman as

116

the assumptions of white supremacy are to the Negro. Consider why it is in SNCC that women who are competent, qualified, and experienced, are automatically assigned to the 'female' kinds of jobs such as: typing, desk work, telephone work, filing, library work, cooking, and the assistant kind of administrative work but rarely the 'executive' kind."

They presented this paper because, as with blacks, "many women in the movement are not 'happy and contented' with their status. It needs to be made known that much talent and experience are being wasted by this movement, when women are not given jobs commensurate with their abilities. It needs to be known that just as Negroes were the crucial factor in the economy of the cotton South, so too in SNCC, women are the crucial factor that keeps the movement running on a day-to-day basis. Yet they are not given equal say-so when it comes to day-to-day decision making." What they called "male supremacy" felt especially disturbing to King and Hayden because they were part of a movement community in which they and other dynamic women like Ella Baker, Ruby Doris Robinson, and Fannie Lou Hamer played vital leadership roles, yet did not get the recognition they deserved and were still expected to do most of the menial labor. The two women were taking seriously, and wanted to implement more fully, SNCC's commitment to encouraging leadership in everyone. (King commented later that Baker had a marked influence on their awakening feminist consciousness.)

The paper ended on a prophetic note. "Maybe sometime in the future the whole of the women in this movement will become so alert as to force the rest of the movement to stop the discrimination and start the slow process of changing values and ideas so that all of us gradually come to understand that this is no more a man's world than it is a white world."[1]

The authors did not expect immediate changes; they only hoped to spark discussion. Their courageous words did not get much support, however, and were criticized by black women like Robinson who had other priorities. But they had planted a seed. Just as the nineteenth-century women's rights movement emerged out of the participation of black and white women in the crusade to abolish slavery—and out of their awareness of their second-class status in that movement—so the feminist revolt of recent times gestated in the Southern freedom struggle of the 1960s. Though it may seem ironic that women passionately engaged in social activism would precipitate a mass movement centering on ostensibly personal matters, this was the point: that women's inequality in the public world resulted largely from inequality in personal life, that in a deeper way than the New Left understood, "the personal is political."

Undaunted, Hayden and King drafted a longer paper one year later examining the peace and freedom movements' own "sex-caste system" that mirrored the larger society and violated the values these movements stood for. They sent it to forty female activists in SNCC, SDS, and other organizations. Written partly to heal rifts with black women who often felt mistrusting and resentful toward their privileged white sisters, the "kind of memo" was eagerly read by white women taking part in the New Left's first workshop on women at the SDS "rethinking conference" in December 1965.[2] Men were ousted when they failed to listen to the concerns women articulated about their subordinate status in SDS. From that moment on, SDS women organized separate workshops and caucuses at every national meeting and in local chapters, to discuss their grievances and build solidarity.

What were these grievances? "We were still the movement secretaries and the shit-workers," three SDSers wrote later. "We served the food, prepared the mailings and made the best posters; we were the earth mothers and the sex-objects for the movement men. We were the free movement 'chicks'—free to screw any man who demanded it, or if we chose not to—free to be called hung-up, middle class and uptight. We were free to keep quiet at meetings—or if we chose not to, we were free to speak in men's terms."[3] This predicament was hardest for those who had proven themselves to be accomplished organizers in Northern ghettos and the South, often the best. Though there were important exceptions like Jane Adams and Cathy Wilkerson, at some point most found themselves barred from influence and leadership by the "competitive intellectual style" and arrogance of the male elites.[4] (Not all the men, of course, were part of the elite or fit this pattern of behavior.) Male dominance increased as SDS multiplied rapidly and put a premium on machismo posturing—promoted by the media—that women could not easily emulate (even if they wanted to). And the fact that females were not subject to conscription meant that though they played an indispensable role in organizing draft resistance, they were excluded from being its "heroes," adding to their feelings of invisibility.

As women grew more and more aware and angry about the sharp contradictions all but a few experienced between the New Left's egalitarian and democratic ideals and the reality of subordination and exploitation, they fought back with the movement's own ideology and tools. They furthered the analogy between their condition and that of blacks and Third World peoples, rejuvenated the fading commitment to "personal liberation" and organizing against one's own oppression, used movement arenas and resources to reach other alienated women, and engaged in direct action tactics.

At the June 1967 SDS convention in Ann Arbor, Michigan, the "Women's Liberation Workshop" culminated months of agitation by offering a bold resolution on the floor, not open to debate. It declared that "women are in a colonial relationship to men" and "have to fight for their own independence"; demanded that "our brothers recognize that they must deal with their own problems of male chauvinism in their personal, social, and political relationships"; and urged women to insist upon "full participation in all aspects of movement work," especially leadership.[5] Predictably, many SDS men were appalled by the statement and railed against it. But the determined women prevailed over a "constant hubbub" of invective and catcalls and the resolution passed, the first time the New Left took a public stand against what would soon be called sexism.[6] Yet the gap remained between principle and practice, and as women's groups mushroomed in SDS chapters, many questioned whether they could stay within the fold.

Women were agitating for change in other quarters, too. The year before a more sedate controversy over another resolution far less inflammatory had momentous consequences. In June 1966 professional women from every state gathered in Washington for the third conference of the state commissions on the status of women. Formation of these commissions had been spurred by the national commission on the status of women set up by President Kennedy at the urging of Esther Peterson— assistant secretary of labor and head of its Women's Bureau, a former AFL-CIO lobbyist, and a longtime advocate for working women who was the administration's highest female. Chaired by former first lady Eleanor Roosevelt, a revered role model for many professional women and a feminist in deed if not in word, the national commission was actually run by vice-chair Peterson, especially after Roosevelt's death in 1962. Its fact-finding report, released in 1963, documented vast discrimination against women, particularly in employment. The proposed remedies were mild, however, and it opposed the Equal Rights Amendment (ERA), which had been championed by many feminists for four decades. Despite its shortcomings, the commission publicized and legitimized women's issues and solidified an underground network of feminist activists who had been working quietly in Washington bureaucracies. The proliferation of state commissions made this "seething underground of women" national in scope.[7]

A small cadre of these insiders hoped to get the Washington conference, entitled "Targets for Action," to pass a resolution demanding that
the Equal Employment Opportunity Commission (EEOC) carry out its
ban on sexual discrimination in employment. The EEOC had been established by Title VII of the 1964 Civil Rights Act to address complaints of
job discrimination by race, color, religion, national origin—and sex. Black
leaders from the Southern freedom movement, then at its peak, and
congressional allies pushing the act had not wanted to muddy the bill's
chances by including discrimination by gender, which was not mentioned
once in committee hearings. Representative Martha Griffiths, Democrat
from Michigan, planned to introduce an amendment to add "sex" to Title
VII on employment, but Howard Smith of Virginia, conservative czar of
the House Rules Committee, beat her to it. For him it was a ploy to help
defeat the entire bill. Since he had the votes, she let him offer it, prompt-
ing guffaws and ridicule during what was dubbed "Ladies Day in the
House." But the amendment passed the House and stayed in, despite
White House queasiness, as the omnibus civil rights bill meandered
through the Senate. Not only did many lawmakers consider inclusion of
gender discrimination a joke; the EEOC's first executive director typified
the agency's stance with his public remark that it was a "fluke . . . conceived out of wedlock."[8] This scornful attitude coupled with the EEOC's
lack of enforcement power meant that little or no action was taken on
thousands of complaints filed by women—almost one-third of the total
number of discrimination complaints received by the EEOC.

The resolution on EEOC enforcement did not even get to the floor of
the women's conference in Washington. Proponents were told by officials
that the meeting could not pass resolutions on anything—not even discrimination against women! Stunned that so modest a proposal would be
stymied, the women turned to feminist author Betty Friedan, there to
get material for her next book. Friedan, born in Peoria, Illinois, and a
forty-five-year-old Smith graduate and former writer for mass-circulation
women's magazines, had spent five years laboring at her carrel in the
New York Public Library—taking the bus every day from her suburban
home—to produce *The Feminine Mystique,* published in 1963. The book
unflinchingly dissected the web of myths and self-defeating ideals that
kept middle-class women chained to the one-dimensional role of house-
wife and mother, and the cultural forces that created and bolstered those
myths. She showed how after World War II (when many women employed during the war returned to full-time homemaking), educators, social scientists, the mass media, corporate advertising, and above all,

Freudian theories of female sexuality—regarded as a "scientific religion"—had all coalesced to instill in intelligent and talented women the belief that their only source of fulfillment was home, family, and sex.[9] These not-so-hidden persuaders convinced women that domesticity was their essential commitment, thereby tightening the grip of the age-old sex-role division just when many were beginning to let go of it.

Friedan discovered that the mostly well-educated and financially secure suburban housewives she interviewed lived lives of silent desperation; they felt inadequate, anxious, and often depressed because they were not satisfied with an existence ruled by traditional feminine values, but did not see a way out. Her conclusion was that

> the core of the problem for women today is not sexual but a problem of identity—a stunting or evasion of growth that is perpetuated by the feminine mystique. It is my thesis that as the Victorian culture did not permit women to accept or gratify their basic sexual needs, our culture does not permit women to accept or gratify their basic need to grow and fulfill their potentialities as human beings, a need which is not solely defined by their sexual role. . . . Encouraged by the mystique to evade their identity crisis, permitted to escape identity altogether in the name of sexual fulfillment, women once again are living with their feet bound in the old image of glorified femininity. And it is the same old image, despite its shiny new clothes, that trapped women for centuries and made the feminists rebel.[10]

Friedan's solution to "the problem that has no name" was for women to find their identity by making their own "life plans" and doing meaningful work outside the home.[11] Though she skillfully demonstrated that the problem was social and structural, not personal, her proposed remedy was the reverse—the exercise of individual will and choice. This perspective (which she soon left behind) was based on the tacit assumption that at least for white middle-class women (her subject), institutions did not have to change substantially. *The Feminine Mystique* had an electrifying effect on millions of women and made its author an instant celebrity. While many read their own story in it, others were too threatened by its implications to take it seriously. The best-seller stirred up no small number of future feminists in search of a movement.

Friedan had been approached earlier by feminists in Washington's underground network urging her to start such a movement modeled on that of black people, or at least an organization to push for legal reforms, like the NAACP. In fact, black attorney Pauli Murray had shocked a convention of women's clubs by saying that Title VII would never be enforced "unless women march on Washington like the blacks."[12] At the 1966 Washington conference Friedan, Murray, and Dorothy Haener of the United Auto Workers broached the idea of a feminist organization to the antidiscrimination activists, but at first the latter were not convinced of the need. The next day, however—the silencing of their resolution having been a sobering moment of truth—they were firebrands. During the final plenary session two dozen women from government, state commissions, and unions—including black EEOC commissioner Aileen Hernandez, who quit her post in frustration—hastily gathered to make plans. Friedan later wondered "if Esther Peterson and the other Women's Bureau officials and Cabinet members who talked down to us at lunch knew that those two front tables, so rudely, agitatedly whispering to one another and passing around notes written on paper napkins, were under their very noses organizing NOW, the National Organization for Women, the first and major structure of the modern women's movement."[13]

When officially founded in October 1966, NOW had about 300 charter members, a few of whom were men. The delegates to the organizing meeting in Washington elected Friedan president and Hernandez vice president. The officers, board, and early membership were mainly middle-class professionals in their mid-twenties to mid-forties.

"We, men and women," NOW's statement of purpose began,

who hereby constitute ourselves as the National Organization for Women, believe that the time has come for a new movement toward true equality for all women in America, and toward a fully equal partnership of the sexes, as part of the world-wide revolution of human rights now taking place within and beyond our national borders. . . . We organize to initiate or support action, nationally or in any part of this nation, by individuals or organizations, to break through the silken curtain of prejudice and discrimination against women in government, industry, the professions, the churches, the political parties, the judiciary, the labor unions, in education, science, medicine, law, religion and every other field of importance in American society. . . . We do not accept the traditional assumption that a woman has to choose between marriage and motherhood, on the one hand, and serious participation in industry or the professions on the other.[14]

The document set forth a formidable agenda of reform.

NOW started out as a hierarchically structured organization that made up for its lack of a mass base by expert use of the media. Due to her celebrity status, organizational skill, and boundless energy, Friedan played a key leadership role, serving as president until 1970. Though it operated most visibly in Washington and New York, dozens of local and state chapters grew up as word of NOW was broadcast by the media. From the beginning, Friedan recounted, "there was great reluctance among NOW members to hand over their individual autonomy and decision-making power to any body of leaders. Women had had enough of being manipulated, passively, into performing other people's agendas. . . . The local autonomy and individual participation built into the structure of NOW insured the continued development and emergence of leadership among women at the grass roots, as they took responsibility for actions."[15]

Such a balance of hierarchy and autonomy eluded the higher-ups' good intentions. National leaders encouraged local initiative while they generally ran the show and took the limelight, leading to conflicts between local chapters and the central body that were typically expressed in terms of feminist ideals. Sociologist Maren Carden found some at the grass roots who felt national NOW "works too independently, failing to take account of the majority's interests or to draw upon the ideas and talents of the whole membership. These people believe that national NOW is an elitist clique, whose actions deny the organization's democratic principles." Members urged that "we must break away the elitist values of the male world." Locals desired less top-down control—including calls to action that "sounded like orders to troops"—and more information and resources. The higher circle saw themselves as pressure-group activists, not servants of the locals' needs. For them, grass-roots organizing and the tedious labors of movement-building were a low priority. Yet, according to Carden, the source of these conflicts was not so much political or stylistic differences as the "severe communications gap" between chapters and the national office, and among the chapters.[16] This resulted from "constant administrative chaos" (in Friedan's words)—despite being a fairly hierarchical organization—and a shortage of funds to pay for housekeeping details.[17] An unknown number of budding feminists never got replies to their inquiries, or could not find the nearest chapter.

Dividing up into a myriad of national and local task forces on such issues as discrimination in employment and education, marriage and divorce laws, and women's image in the media, NOW activists proved remarkably effective in changing certain laws relating to women, though the battle for enforcement often took years. Their first victory was getting President Johnson to issue Executive Order 11375 barring sexual discrimination in federal contracts; this order applied not only to academic institutions but to the government itself. As the self-appointed watchdog of the EEOC, NOW successfully filed suit against the agency's upholding of sex-segregated want ads; the group's first direct action was to dump piles of newspapers at EEOC offices, followed by a national day of picketing. And it compelled the airlines to end the involuntary retirement of flight attendants when they married or turned thirty-two. NOW won other campaigns against job discrimination, including a historic settlement with AT&T, which the EEOC had singled out as the "largest oppressor of women workers."[18] It lobbied hard for the 1972 EEOC reform that strengthened that agency's enforcement powers. Moreover, NOW spearheaded congressional passage of the Equal Rights Amendment that year, along with the rest of the "bumper crop" of women's rights legislation in the Ninety-second Congress, "considerably more than the sum total of all relevant legislation previously passed in the history of this country," in political scientist Jo Freeman's judgment.[19]

Yet NOW did not achieve these gains without dissension and division. When the organization had earlier ratified a "Bill of Rights for Women" to be pushed on candidates and parties in 1968, delegates from labor threatened to leave because their unions opposed the ERA (fearing it might nullify hard-earned protective legislation for working women), and a group of more conservative members walked out in protest of NOW's controversial support for reproductive freedom and repeal of abortion laws—the first time that "control of one's body" was officially articulated as a woman's right. This group formed the Women's Equity Action League, which concentrated on ending discrimination in education and employment and later rejoined forces with NOW on these issues and the ERA. Friedan reported that "in facing and airing our 'honest differences' over abortion and the Equal Rights Amendment . . . we forged the crucial generational links between the century-long battle for women's rights that was our past and the young women who were the future."[20]

A vivid linkage across time between the old suffrage crusade and the new movement for emancipation was the Women's Strike for Equality on 26 August 1970, commemorating the fiftieth anniversary of women winning the vote upon ratification of the Nineteenth Amendment. Sensing that something grander than lobbying and litigation was needed, Friedan conceived it as a way to channel the energy of the burgeoning movement toward concrete political objectives. It would show women, the media, and the whole society "how powerful we were."[21] She proposed the idea during her farewell speech as head of NOW in March 1970. Most delegates cheered her suggestion, but the new president, Aileen Hernandez, and other officials worried about squandering scarce resources on a half-baked plan that was likely to fail. Friedan and hundreds of NOW activists pulled out all the stops to bring together a broad coalition of women's groups, including many younger and more militant movement participants, working out differences along the way. As a down payment toward equality, the Strike called for abortion on demand, twenty-four-hour child care services, and equal opportunity in jobs and schooling.

Locking arms with Judge Dorothy Kenyon, an eighty-two-year-old suffrage veteran, and with a young radical in blue jeans, Friedan led a huge march of women, and some men, down New York's Fifth Avenue. Defying police orders to stay on the sidewalk, they overflowed the street, holding banners high and calling out "Come join us, sisters" to women waving from office windows and to bystanders along the route. "This is not a bedroom war," Friedan proclaimed at an evening rally next to the public library where she wrote her path-breaking book. "This is a political movement."[22] Women marched for equality in every other large city that day and in quite a few smaller ones. It was the first nationwide mobilization of women for women since the direct action by suffragists, and the first time that the new crusade was covered seriously by the media. NOW was suddenly famous, and its membership swelled. A majority of the newcomers were homemakers and clerical workers rather than professional women. Freeman and others believed that the Women's Strike marked a turning point for the whole movement, its coming of age.

The Personal Is Political

NOW had initiated the growing wave of feminist activism that led up to the Strike for Equality, but what made it a mass movement were the thousands of younger women, many of them veterans of the black freedom movement and the New Left, who were not satisfied with improvements in the public world of education and employment that seemed like tokenism. The "younger branch" of radical feminists dug down to the root of the problem: the fundamental subjugation of women in relationships with men and in domestic roles. This subjugation put severe limits on opportunities for women outside the home and could be little affected, they thought, by public policy. What they scornfully called "careerism"—Friedan's remedy—was no solution. It did not challenge the domestic division of labor and was an option only for a minority. They demanded not equality of sex roles, which they likened to the Jim Crow doctrine of "separate but equal," but their elimination. This perspective struck chords in a multitude of young, mainly white, middle-class women who became convinced that, like men, they had the right to define themselves as they chose and to shape their own destinies. "For most American women," concludes historian Sara Evans, "only a movement that addressed the oppression at the core of their identity could have generated the massive response that in fact occurred."[23]

As with Rosa Parks and Jo Ann Robinson in Montgomery, the lunch counter integrators, and Berkeley's free speech activists, these radical women were ready to move; all they needed was a triggering incident. The stimulus for the creation of an independent movement for women, outside the confines of the New Left, came in early September 1967 in Chicago at the National Conference for a New Politics (NCNP), which was an abortive attempt to forge a militant black-white alliance. When in a condescending manner NCNP leaders blocked Shulamith Firestone and other women from reading a radical resolution by the women's caucus, on the ground that women's oppression was insignificant compared to racism, the women had had enough. Firestone, Jo Freeman, and others formed the first autonomous women's liberation groups in Chicago.

Later that fall Firestone and Pamela Allen started New York Radical Women. The group helped organize an antiwar march in Washington by the Jeannette Rankin Brigade, a coalition of women led by the eighty-seven-year-old Rankin, the first woman in Congress and the only lawmaker to vote against World War II. Along this march they handed out leaflets announcing that "sisterhood is powerful." The event included a controversial torchlight procession at Arlington National Cemetery symbolizing "the burial of traditional womanhood." New York Radical Women and other feminists talked with many Rankin Brigade participants, many of whom went home to form their own collectives.

Charlotte Bunch started a group in Washington after the protest. Raised in a small town in New Mexico and a graduate of Duke University, she had been a youth leader in the Southern Methodist church, founding president of the short-lived University Christian Movement, a civil rights activist who had marched from Selma to Montgomery, and a community organizer in a Washington ghetto. She had identified both with the New Left and with the "radical wing of Christianity—influenced by the Southern black church—that sought to put the gospel into action for social justice."[24] Later a leading theorist of radical feminism, Bunch remembered that in her first women's group, "we spent months convincing our-

LOOK CINDERELLA...MAYBE YOU SHOULD SKIP THE BALL, AND JOIN A CONSCIOUSNESS RAISING GROUP INSTEAD.

Feminist humor and creativity. *Bülbül Cartoon Service,* © *1973*

selves that it was politically okay to meet separately as women and to focus on women's concerns. We felt somewhat more secure because we saw a parallel to the arguments of blacks who had been establishing their right and need to have their own space."[25]

The desire for a feminist group that was radical on its own terms and not just an extension of New Left ideology prompted Firestone and Ellen Willis in early 1969 to establish Redstockings, which aimed initially at abortion law repeal. About the same time a dissident faction of the New York NOW chapter (by far the largest chapter) tried to change its by-laws to do away with hierarchy. When the chapter majority voted down a proposal by its flamboyant president, Ti-Grace Atkinson, to either abolish offices or spread them around, she resigned in protest, declaring in a press conference that the division was between "those who want women to have the opportunity to be oppressors, too, and those who want to destroy oppression. . . . You cannot destroy oppression by filling the position of the oppressor. . . . Since I have failed to get rid of the power position I hold, I have no choice but to step out of it."[26]

Atkinson and other NOW insurgents joined ex-members of New York Radical Women to form a new group, called The Feminists, whose highest priority was equal participation. To prevent those with more skills and experience from dominating meetings and restoring hierarchy, they set up the Lot and Disc systems. The first of these divided all tasks by lot; the second gave members an equal number of discs, one of which had to be spent for each utterance. Legend has it that at the first meeting members used up their discs in fifteen minutes; at the next meeting they hoarded their discs and said little. To further equality and solidify commitment, the group later decided that no more than one-third of its members could be living with men, and that meeting attendance would be compulsory. They also had rules to prevent "star making," with media spokespersons chosen by lot. Though The Feminists set an example for structuring participatory democracy, its moral absolutism led to its demise. Meanwhile, other collectives arose—such as Boston's Bread and Roses (a rallying cry of the 1912 Lawrence textile strikers, many of whom were women)—that acted autonomously but did not want to extinguish all ties with New Left thinking. They called themselves "socialist feminists" and would deal more with economic issues affecting women.

Despite differences in style and politics, radical feminist groups sprouted at an "astounding rate" as word spread quickly through preexisting networks of New Left women.[27] "I had never known anything as easy as organizing women's groups—as easy and as exciting and as dramatic," recalled Heather Booth, later a prominent organizer of "citizen action" groups in the Midwest.[28] The ranks of the New Left were depleted as legions of radical women declared their independence and applied their abundant organizing skills to fashioning a community and a movement of their own.

What bound all of them together was a shared view of their reality as women. Taking off from French philosopher Simone de Beauvoir's insight that the world treats man as subject, woman as object—as "Other"—they came to see that women constitute an oppressed caste or class, that the male-female division was the "primary class system" underlying all other class distinctions.[29] "We are exploited as sex objects, breeders, domestic servants, and cheap labor," the Redstockings Manifesto proclaimed. "We are considered inferior beings, whose only purpose is to enhance men's lives. Our humanity is denied. . . . Male supremacy is the oldest, most basic form of domination. All other forms of exploitation and oppression (racism, capitalism, imperialism, etc.) are extensions of male supremacy: men dominate women, a few men dominate the rest. All power structures throughout history have been male-dominated and male-oriented. Men have controlled all political, economic and cultural institutions and backed up this control with physical force. They have used their power to keep women in an inferior position."[30]

Women experienced their oppression through sex roles that were socially constructed to a large extent and internalized. While "male" and "female" are biological, Kate Millett suggested, one's gender ("masculine" or "feminine") is cultural and thus learned; anatomy is not destiny. Women, and men, would be truly liberated, she thought, when they could free themselves from "the tyranny of sexual-social category and conformity to sexual stereotype."[31]

If the goal of expunging sex roles was the touchstone of radical feminism, how was it to be accomplished? As one vital step, most advocated removing social barriers to alternative forms of intimacy and child-rearing—"relaxing marriage and divorce laws, changing housing policies that prevent or discourage communal living, challenging social attitudes toward 'illegitimate' children, unmarried couples, group living, and so forth. Only through experimentation can we discover what variety of social units meet different people's needs for love and security, without oppressing women, men, or children."[32] Some went further and advocated abolishing marriage and the traditional family, which were seen as irreparably antiwoman institutions. In her widely read book *The Dialectic of Sex,* Shulamith Firestone called for a full-fledged feminist revolution, made possible by technological advances, in which women would seize control of reproduction and make childbearing and child-raising the responsibility of society, not (solely) of individual women. "For unless revolution uproots the basic social organization, the biological family," she concluded, ". . . the tapeworm of exploitation will never be annihilated. We shall need a sexual revolution much larger than—inclusive of—a socialist one to truly eradicate all class systems."[33]

If the foe of radical feminism was sex roles and the "patriarchy" that fostered them, its burning motivation was the aspiration for self-definition and self-determination, growing out of a woman's sense, wrote Vivian Gornick, that

she is 'invisible' upon the earth; that the life she leads, the defining characteristics that are attributed to her, the destiny that is declared her natural one are not so much the truth of her real being and existence as they are a reflection of culture's willful *need* that she be as she is described. The feminist movement is a rebellious *no* to all that; it is a declaration of independence against false description of the self; it is a protest dedicated to the renunciation of that falsity and the courageous pursuit of honest self-discovery. The whole *point* of the feminist movement is that each and every woman shall recognize that the burden and the glory of her feminism lie with defining herself honestly *in any terms she shall choose.*[34]

Because it was seen as the key to liberation, the courageous pursuit of self-discovery became the central mission of the movement's younger branch through the vehicle of the ubiquitous "consciousness-raising (CR) group." Though informed by the "speaking bitterness" method of the Chinese Revolution, SNCC's testimonials on experiences of racism, and the "Guatemalan guerrilla" organizing approach of SDS and the Resistance, the CR group was a unique creation of radical feminists—at once a recruitment tool, a process for shaping politics and ideology, and a microcosm of an egalitarian community that prefigured a feminist society. To begin with, it brought women together out of isolation. Charlotte Bunch wrote that in these groups,

women begin to discover ourselves as an oppressed people and struggle against the effects of male supremacy on us. It happens when we describe and share our individual problems so that we can understand the universality of our oppression and analyze its social roots. It is learning to take pride and delight in our female-ness, rejecting the need to follow the feminine mystique or to copy men as our models; it is learning to trust and love each other as sisters, not competitors for male approval. It is deciding and redeciding each day, individually and together, that we will take control over our lives, create and support each other in alternative ways of living, and struggle together for the liberation of all women.[35]

Whether set up by a larger feminist entity or spontaneously, a typical CR group had not more than ten or fifteen members. The participants usually met weekly in a safe, nurturing atmosphere and shared their most intimate feelings and perceptions. Realizing that they were not alone, and not powerless, they eventually understood that their personal problems were political in nature and required collective solutions. Many CR groups followed the four-stage process pioneered by the Sudsofloppen group in San Francisco: opening up, sharing, analyzing, and abstracting. These stages involved, respectively, "keeping in touch with our emotions, giving one another information regarding experiences we have had, trying to understand the meaning of those events, and finally fitting that understanding into an overview of our potential as human beings and the reality of our society, i.e., of developing an ideology." In the last two stages, using readings by and about women, they would look for more general causes and solutions, connecting their own experience with that of other women past and present to "gain a sense of the whole."[36] The "free space" of CR groups bestowed self-confidence and a sense of empowerment on an inestimable number of young women and nudged them into the movement. But some who took this journey felt that, though an indispensable first step, the process of enlightenment became too much of an end in itself. They were frustrated that it did not lead more often to immediate action or concrete programs.

Though direct action to change women's lives had less priority than raising consciousness, it still played a big role. In September 1968 about 200 women arrived on the Atlantic City boardwalk to protest the Miss America Pageant. They targeted it, explained Robin Morgan, a key organizer, because it was "patently degrading to women (in propagating the Mindless Sex Object Image); it has always been a lily-white, racist contest (there has never been a black finalist); the winner tours Vietnam, entertaining the troops as a Murder Mascot; the whole gimmick of the million-dollar Pageant Corporation is one commercial shill-game to sell the sponsors' products. Where else could one find such a perfect combination of American values—racism, militarism, capitalism—all packaged in one 'ideal' symbol, a woman."[37]

The women picketed and performed guerrilla theater, auctioned off a dummy Miss America, crowned a live sheep as their winner, and tossed dishcloths, steno pads, women's magazines, girdles, bras, high heels, "and other instruments of torture to women" into a "Freedom Trash Can."[38] An "inside squad" disrupted the nationally televised contest by hanging a banner from the balcony that said "Women's Liberation" and yelling "Freedom for women!" One was arrested for "spraying Toni hair-conditioner (a vile-smelling sponsor of the pageant) near the mayor's box."[39] After a year of quietly organizing small groups, radical feminists made their debut on prime time and announced themselves to the world. This was the first militant demonstration by either branch of the movement, and it spawned many other "zap actions."

On Halloween a coven from WITCH surfaced on Wall Street "to pit their ancient magic against the evil powers of the Financial District—the center of the Imperialist Phallic Society."[40] After affixing WITCH stickers to George Washington's statue, the masked, wand-wielding witches danced around the big banks, chanting curses, and then invaded the Stock Exchange, where they formed a "sacred circle" to hex the money changers, who stood in awe. A leaflet they handed out expressed their attempt to reclaim the rich heritage of persecuted "wise women," the healers and heretics of past centuries—perhaps the first liberated women—many of whom were killed: "WITCH is an all-women Everything. It's theater, revolution, magic, terror, joy, garlic flowers, spells. It's an awareness that witches and gypsies were the original guerrillas and resistance fighters against oppression—particularly the oppression of women. . . . WITCH lives and laughs in every women. . . . If you are a women and dare to look within yourself, you are a Witch. You make your own rules."⁴¹

Thereafter, this coven and its offspring cast their spells at bridal fairs, AT&T, United Fruit Company, and other appropriate targets, the all-purpose acronym meaning different things to fit the occasion—for example, "Women Inspired To Commit Herstory." Among other imaginative actions by witches and nonwitches were protests at the New York Marriage License Bureau, a building takeover at the University of Chicago to resist the firing of a feminist sociologist, and the nonviolent storming of a Boston radio station by Bread and Roses women angered by an announcement that "chicks" were wanted as typists. They handed the manager eight baby chicks and were given airtime for a program on women's liberation.

As with the peace and freedom movements, the mass media had much to do with the success of feminism. Fame and its lures left their mark on this movement—but the media would never be the same. The latter "discovered" feminism in the "grand press blitz" of 1970.⁴² Though often portraying it in a mocking or trivializing fashion, or as a fad, coverage skyrocketed in major newspapers and magazines and on network TV. Having lost interest in the antiwar crusade and Black Power, they were looking for a glamorous new movement.

Yet radical feminists, knowing what they were up against, refused to be passive objects of the mass media's devouring appetite. The organizers of the first Miss America protest made a simple but momentous strategic decision that became a fundamental movement policy: speak only to female reporters. Not because "we were so naive as to think that women journalists would automatically give us more sympathetic coverage," Robin Morgan commented, "but rather because the stand made a political statement consistent with our beliefs."⁴³ As hoped, the policy had far-reaching ripple effects throughout the media industry. It not only generated more meaningful assignments for female journalists, freeing them from "the ghetto of the women's pages," and necessitated the hiring of more women, but it got them thinking about their second-class status in the media world.⁴⁴ Not surprisingly, many started organizing in their own workplaces for better opportunities and more coverage of feminist concerns. After months of agitation and a complaint to the EEOC, female employees at *Newsweek* reached an accord with management to accelerate the recruitment and promotion of women.

Some radicals engaged in militant direct action to stop the media's objectification of women: notably, an eleven-hour sit-in at *Ladies' Home Journal* to try to liberate it—they won a concession to produce a special supplement on feminism—and the seizing and barricading of the avant-garde Grove Press by employees protesting discrimination, the firing of women for organizing a union, and the publication of erotica that degraded women. The latter action was the movement's first skirmish against what it defined as pornography. Grove Press employees were also charged with resisting arrest when they demanded female cops.

Radical feminists had few illusions that they could upturn the communication industries, which by mass-producing sexist images of women had such an overwhelming impact on how women were perceived, and perceived themselves. Many figured that a more fruitful path was to create a network of alternative media run mainly by small collectives. The first feminist newspaper, *off our backs,* published in Washington (still alive two decades later), was followed by an effusion of journals and magazines, over 100 by 1971. Among the most influential were *Women: A Journal of Liberation, Quest, Feminist Studies, Signs,* and above all, the glossy popular magazine *Ms.,* which has reached a circulation of half a million since its founding in 1972. Closely linked to the alternative periodicals were feminist publishing collectives that churned out everything from literary and political anthologies to nonsexist, nonracist children's books.

As both a means and an end of social change, the movement's younger branch was determined to replace hierarchy, seen as a masculine principle, with the ideology and practice of "sisterhood." Less ambivalent than the New Left or SNCC, radical feminists by and large rejected leadership in any traditional sense—partly in reaction to the seeming hypocrisy of movement groups that kicked hierarchy out the front door only to bring it in the back. But it was chiefly because, if the feminist notion of power meant "possession of the self" rather than manipulation of other people, leadership by others had to be shunned in order for each woman to cultivate the strength to lead her own life. "Because so many of our struggles necessarily had to be carried on in isolation. . . ," wrote Leah Fritz, "it was imperative for women, as individuals, to gain the confidence to act autonomously"—which paralleled SNCC's response to the predicament of Southern blacks.[45] Thus, unlike NOW, for the most part radical feminist groups chose to do without leadership positions and vertical structures.

Yet as some began to realize, the absence of recognized leadership did not prevent the rise of leaders who had advantages in verbal ability or other skills, causing a good deal of internal tension. In a thoughtful critique of what she called the "tyranny of structurelessness," Joreen wrote that every group has a structure, and that covert structures generate covert elites. Lack of formal structure, then, becomes "a way of masking power," and when "informal elites are combined with a myth of 'structurelessness,' there can be no attempt to put limits on the use of power. It becomes capricious." Groups are unable to hold the de facto leaders accountable; not only are there no procedures to do so, but the elite's existence cannot easily be admitted. "If the movement continues to deliberately not select who shall exercise power, it does not thereby abolish power. All it does is abdicate the right to demand that those who do exercise power and influence be responsible for it."[46] The consequences, Joreen suggested, were the exclusion of women who had less time to give, diminished effectiveness, and difficulty charting a clear direction for individual groups and the whole movement. More and more activists shared these concerns as the "euphoric period of consciousness-raising" ebbed and they began to place a higher priority on direct institutional change to uproot sexism.[47]

Though one of the grievances that ushered in radical feminism was the male "star system" of the New Left, feminists were not immune to the "celebrity leadership syndrome" examined by Todd Gitlin in the context of SDS; indeed, the pervasive ideology of structurelessness, ironically, fostered it. Gitlin shows that although activists willingly contributed to the problem, the mass media was more to blame for undermining authentic movement leadership. When leaders of SDS and other radical groups veered away from face-to-face communitarian politics to work on a grander scale and reach a wider audience, first to end the war and then to make revolution, they "entered into an unequal contest with the media," which converted leaders like Mark Rudd, Tom Hayden, Jerry Rubin, and Abbie Hoffman into celebrities and cut them further adrift from any reciprocal democratic relationship with their constituents. The media, especially network TV, selected for celebrity those "who most closely matched prefabricated images of what an opposition leader should look and sound like. . . . Usually it was the flamboyant leader who seized media attention: a personality adept at manipulating symbolic devices like the inflammatory slogan." Not only was the media the only constituency that such "leaders" were accountable to, but by framing images and symbols, the media nullified real leadership, taking control of events and perceptions and entering the power vacuum as "unacknowledged arbiters, surrogate sources of legitimacy."[48]

Though less pronounced, the same dynamic operated in the younger branch of feminism. Because the radicals were unwilling to have recognized leaders or spokespersons, the news media appointed its own, whether or not they were truly representative. Not only did the grassroots collectives then have little control over feminist stars, even local ones, but resentments festered that erupted in open denunciation of the celebrities as elitists—which pushed them further away to the movement's outer edges. Kate Millett, author of the best-selling *Sexual Politics,* confided to a CR group about the anguish of feminist celebrity and its double bind: "All the while the movement is sending double signals: you absolutely must preach at our panel, star at our conference—implying, fink if you don't . . . and at the same time laying down a wonderfully uptight line about elitism." She said that she felt "a traitor to the movement, party to a shady deal, assenting while we cooperate with the System to create this fool of a leader we exploit full voltage while condemning the idea full volume. One is used and used up."[49] Millett was anointed to stardom by *Time* magazine, which put her on its cover in August 1970. When later she publicly declared her bisexuality at a feminist conference, *Time* dethroned her, claiming she had lost her credibility as the movement's "high priestess."[50]

Akin to the black freedom struggle—which was looked upon as a model—in analysis, aspirations, and organizing methods, the feminist movement was similar as well in offering two conflicting models of leadership. And just as SNCC's antileadership ethos was partly a response to the tight hierarchy of SCLC, the "leaderless" philosophy of the younger branch was seen as an alternative to NOW's top-down structure. While the pragmatic leadership style of the older branch allowed it to be surprisingly effective in challenging entrenched institutional sexism, the unbounded energy and creativity that flowed out of decentralized communities of sisterhood brought about changes in attitudes, language, and ways of life that permeated the whole society. Who could say which approach was more efficacious in the long run? Both were needed to move toward the equality and liberation of women. They complemented, corrected, and reinforced each other, and increasingly converged as the movement broadened in the early 1970s.

Our Bodies, Ourselves

An "important development in the women's movement over the past year," a radical feminist journal editorialized at the end of 1971, "has been the increased cross-fertilization between the so-called 'women's rights' sector and the 'women's liberation' sector. Feminists are discovering not only that moderate and radical feminists can be found in both camps . . . but also that they have a great deal more in common than was originally thought."[51] Pressure from within by radicals who joined NOW because it was the only national feminist outfit (and in some places the only group around) dovetailed with external pressure from radical groups to move NOW closer to the younger branch in structure, style, and goals. Not only did NOW chapters frequently adopt consensus decision-making and other staples of "feminist process," but they also used CR groups as an educational tool. Though NOW's chief aim was ratification of the Equal Rights Amendment by the states, it gave increasing priority to issues brought forward by the younger branch, especially abortion and violence against women. For NOW, too, the personal became political. In the mid-1970s festering conflicts between moderates and radicals, caused in part by the continuing emphasis on lobbying over movement-building, threatened to break NOW in two, but the rift was healed.

As centrifugal forces propelled the movement into an ever-widening arc of concerns and constituencies, some realized that "a diverse movement might be more valuable than a united one. The multitude of different groups reached out to different kinds of women, served different functions within the movement, and presented a wide variety of feminist ideas."[52] By 1972 the success of the feminist movement could be measured not only in impressive legal and legislative victories but by a sharp jump in the percentage of women who supported it, according to a Harris poll—notably, a large majority of those who were young, single, or black.

The movement's breadth of activism and accomplishment was staggering, leaving no area of American life untouched. To elect more women to public office, put feminist issues on the national agenda, and mobilize support for the ERA, Friedan, Congress members Bella Abzug and Shirley Chisholm, and other leaders of the older branch founded the National Women's Political Caucus in 1971. This multipartisan umbrella group eventually established hundreds of state and local units and had its first success in tripling the number of female delegates to the 1972 Democratic convention and winning approval of a solid women's plank.

Across the country women in organized labor fought an uphill battle to get male-dominated unions to pay more attention to working women's grievances about sexism and job discrimination and to get more women in union leadership. With NOW's help, they persuaded the AFL-CIO, formerly NOW's biggest foe, to back the ERA—arguing that protective laws for women were more discriminatory than helpful. (By the early

1970s most such legislation had been invalidated by the EEOC and federal courts, or extended to males.) In March 1974 over 3,000 women from fifty-eight unions gathered to establish the Coalition of Labor Union Women, which proved to be the most effective women's labor organization since the Women's Trade Union League in the early 1900s. Women started their own unions as well; probably the greatest gains were made organizing clerical workers, by groups like "9 to 5" in Boston. Professional women also organized, especially in the academic world, through autonomous caucuses and associations. Nowhere did feminists mount a more far-reaching assault on tradition than in the hallowed halls of churches and synagogues, fighting for the ordination of female clergy, the degendering of Scripture and even of God, and the creation of a nonpatriarchal feminist theology. Just one of the concerns of the National Coalition of American Nuns was domination by priests, "no matter what their hierarchical status."[53]

To find out more about the "second sex," a subject either ignored or warped by the academic mainstream, and to teach young women to reclaim their past and reshape their future, feminist scholars initiated women's studies courses and programs on hundreds of campuses, the first at San Diego State in 1970. At the other end of the educational spectrum, feminists from both branches successfully lobbied Congress to provide comprehensive child care services for working mothers—a prerequisite for equality both in the workplace and at home—though the bill died with President Nixon's veto. And they set up high-quality, low-cost day-care centers—often cooperatively run by parents—that countered early sex-role socialization.

Perhaps most path-breaking, radical feminists who felt demeaned or mistreated at the hands of the male medical establishment, particularly around birth control and pregnancy, organized self-help classes to enable women to know and care for their own bodies, including self-examinations. A group of Bread and Roses women in Boston taught a course on women's health that resulted in a collectively written handbook called *Our Bodies, Ourselves*. First published by the New England Free Press in 1971, it became the all-time feminist best-seller—and the bible of the women's health movement—growing thicker with each edition and being translated into eleven languages. Alternative clinics for women, specializing in abortion and pregnancy, sprouted up in many cities. Along with the resurgence of natural childbirth, home births, and midwifery, these innovations helped to empower women to take charge of their bodies and their lives.

The bible of the women's health movement.
Courtesy Boston Women's Health Book Collective

The aspiration to control one's own body emerged during the 1970s as the paramount theme for the younger branch, and to a lesser extent for the older branch. If sex roles—above all, society's primary definition of women as sex objects and mothers—constituted the main battleground for radical feminism, reproductive freedom would naturally sit high on the agenda, both the right to safe contraceptives and the right to end unwanted pregnancy. Abortion, self-induced or by someone else, had been a common though risky practice for centuries; it did not become generally illegal in the United States until the medical establishment campaigned against it in the mid-nineteenth century. During the 1960s coalitions of professional women and men succeeded in reforming antiabortion laws in some states: abortions, by a physician only, were permitted under certain conditions, still leaving the decision, however, to the physician, usually male. Then the new feminist movement arrived and turned the debate upside down, arguing firmly that abortion was a woman's basic right, that the decision was hers alone, and that abortion laws must be repealed, not reformed. They soon converted many women in the reform camp. One activist put it well:

When we talk about women's rights, we can get all the rights in the world—the right to vote, the right to go to school—and none of them means a doggone thing if we don't own the flesh we stand in, if we can't control what happens to us, if the whole course of our lives can be changed by somebody else that can get us pregnant by accident, or by deceit, or by force. So I consider the right to elective abortion, whether you dream of doing it or not, is the cornerstone of the women's movement . . . because without that right, we'd have about as many rights as the cow in the pasture that's taken to the bull once a year. You could give her all those rights, too, but they wouldn't mean anything; if you can't control your own body you can't control your future.[54]

And women would never be able to overcome job discrimination as long as involuntary pregnancy could upset their work lives, and as long as employers treated them as potential mothers more than as individuals.

Although initially even some feminists did not consider it a feminist issue, NOW leaders and others formed the National Abortion Rights Action League (NARAL) in 1969, which, along with other "pro-choice" groups, mobilized for legislative and judicial changes, such as pushing NAACP-type legal test cases through the courts. Radical feminists, who coupled their demand for free abortion with an end to coerced sterilization of poor, largely nonwhite women, joined with moderates to organize

Reproductive rights demonstration outside a Boston courthouse, 1975.
© *Ellen Shub*

abortion teach-ins and testify at legislative hearings. Characteristically, NOW activists gave formal testimony, while radicals talked graphically about their own abortions and sometimes disrupted the staid proceedings with speech-making and colorful guerrilla theater. Pro-choice groups also engaged in civil disobedience, referring women who wanted abortions to safe but illegal clinics.

All this agitation and litigation culminated in a monumental triumph for the feminist forces in January 1973, possibly their biggest ever. The Supreme Court struck down all state abortion laws, including more liberal ones, declaring that any restrictions on abortion during the first trimester of pregnancy violated a constitutional right to privacy; that abortion could be regulated in the second trimester only to protect a woman's well-being; and that abortion must be permitted even in the final three months if a woman's health or survival was at stake. Though *Roe v. Wade* did not grant women an unconditional right to abortion, it seemed to come close, since most abortions take place in the first trimester. Abortion was not only legal but soon a great deal safer.

While the historic decision temporarily quieted the crusade for choice, it sparked the rise of a passionate antiabortion movement instigated by Catholic clergy, fundamentalist preachers of the "electronic ministry," and organizers of the New Right. Eventually, the "right-to-lifers" succeeded in whittling down the ruling and barring public funds for abortions, which mainly affected poor women. As sociologist Kristin Luker points out, the fierce counterattack that made abortion the social issue of the 1970s was not about the rights of the fetus as much as it was about the proper role and responsibilities of women and "the place and meaning of motherhood." It was a backlash against feminism altogether and the feminist vision of empowerment, which was perceived as a serious threat by most men and by many women, especially those who were deeply religious and of lower-class backgrounds.[55]

The grass-roots right-to-life movement spilled over into a nationwide campaign to block ratification of the ERA, NOW's highest priority. Overwhelmingly approved by Congress, speedily ratified by all but three of the thirty-eight states needed for adoption, the ERA's passage seemed a sure thing. But momentum was stalled by the expertly organized and well-financed conservative opposition—in which many women, led by Phyllis Schlafly, played a prominent role. The amendment died when it did not win enough states by the 1982 extended deadline. One of the reasons for its defeat cited by political scientist Jane Mansbridge applies to the abortion controversy as well. These women's issues "not only gave a focus to the reaction against the changes in child rearing, sexual behavior, divorce, and the use of drugs that had taken place in the 1960s and 1970s, they also mobilized a group, traditional homemakers, that had lost status over the two previous decades and was feeling the psychological effects of the loss."[56]

Feminists lived out their vision of female empowerment most directly in the multifaceted campaign against rape and other violence against women that surged to the forefront during the mid-1970s once the abortion issue was no longer quite so pressing. Feminist thinkers like Susan Griffin and Susan Brownmiller developed a full-blown political analysis of rape: rather than seeing it as a deviation or a "crime of passion," they placed rape on a continuum of male aggression and power. They defined it as an act of violence, as a violation of sexual self-determination, and, in a social context that encouraged degradation of women and then blamed the victim, as mass terrorism to keep women down. "Rape," wrote Andra Medea and Kathleen Thompson, "is all the hatred, contempt, and oppression of women in this society concentrated in one act."[57] Brownmiller examined the "masculine ideology of rape" that made it the ultimate expression of male domination and the possession of women.[58]

"That women should *organize* to combat rape," noted Brownmiller, "was a women's movement invention."[59] With the incidence of rape rising sharply (reported rapes had doubled since the mid-1960s), the immediate priorities were to educate the public and aid the victims. In early 1971 New York Radical Feminists organized the first rape "speak-outs" where survivors told their traumatic stories in public; they demolished myths about rapists and condemned police and courts for not taking rape seriously and for treating them as though they were the offenders. Their intention was to make "rape a *speakable* crime, not a matter of shame."[60] Before long, concerned women all over the country set up hundreds of rape crisis centers offering emergency support services, especially phone "hot lines" staffed round-the-clock to counsel those in need. Motivated by the belief that there were no individual solutions to rape, that ending it required a larger social transformation, a crisis center could "reach a woman at a moment of profound rage and help her to channel it . . . toward the society which caused it."[61]

Feminists in NOW and other groups established local and national task forces to lobby for changes in rape laws and procedures—including prohibiting court testimony about a victim's sexual history and degree of resistance—and for new laws against marital rape. They succeeded also in getting Congress to fund a national center for prevention and control of rape. As usual, the younger branch took the lead in organizing creative direct action, from women's "anti-rape squads" that patrolled streets and pursued suspects to candlelit "Take Back the Night" marches (born in Italy and Germany), which dramatically protested all violence against women. Before long many radicals zeroed in on purveyors of pornography, who they accused of promoting a cultural climate of hostility toward and dehumanization of women. A vigorous intramovement debate on censorship versus sexual liberty soon followed. The growing public enlightenment about rape encouraged more and more women to break their silence about violence in the home, resulting in the formation of crisis centers and shelters for battered women.

Clearly one of the most effective and far-reaching remedies for what feminists considered a virtual epidemic of violence against women was to overcome socialization into passivity and learn skills of physical self-defense. Radical feminists started women's self-defense collectives that taught karate and other martial arts, offering women not only greater physical power but enhanced self-confidence, self-worth, and control of their lives. This training reaffirmed the counsel of Susan B. Anthony a century before that (in Brownmiller's paraphrase) "a strong mind in a strong body" was "a necessary step in the battle for equality."[62]

What is a lesbian? A lesbian is the rage of all women condensed to the point of explosion. She is the woman who, often beginning at an extremely early age, acts in accordance with her inner compulsion to be a more complete and freer human being than her society . . . cares to allow her. These needs and actions, over a period of years, bring her into painful conflict with people, situations, the accepted ways of thinking, feeling, and behaving, until she is in a state of continual war with everything around her, and usually with her self. She may not be fully conscious of the political implications of what for her began as personal necessity, but on some level she has not been able to accept the limitations and oppression laid on her by the most basic role of her society—the female role.[63]

So began a bold manifesto by the Radicalesbians, entitled "The Woman Identified Woman."

The biggest challenge to the bedrock feminist principles of sisterhood—the personal as political, and control of one's body—was the issue of lesbians in the movement. This arose as a vital, highly publicized conflict in both branches. Though a minority, from the start lesbians had made indispensable contributions in NOW, as well as in the radical

Battered women's "speak-out" against violence against women,
Boston City Hall Plaza, 1976. © *Ellen Shub*

groups—they had "carried the women's movement on their backs," said Millett—but had by and large kept their sexual identity hidden.[64]

The deep involvement of lesbians in feminist organizing coincided with the emergence of a strong gay liberation movement in the early 1970s, ignited by a June 1969 police raid on the Stonewall gay bar in Greenwich Village in New York. Four nights of violent resistance by gay men led to the formation of the Gay Liberation Front and other groups by activists who had been waiting for the right moment. The new movement, which "talked optimistically about new ideas like gay power and even gay revolution," Randy Shilts wrote, emboldened gays and lesbians to break through fear and publicly "come out."[65] Influenced by the black movement, particularly Black Power, and by radical feminism, it stressed that pride and dignity should be cultivated, that "gay is beautiful." Demanding fundamental change in order to eliminate what it called "heterosexism"— including heterosexual dominance and homosexual stigmas—the new gay movement moved far beyond the work of earlier groups such as the Mattachine Society and Daughters of Bilitis, which merely sought personal adjustment, public education, and eventual social acceptance and integration. During the next decade activists organized marches, nationwide "Gay Freedom Days," and many other activities to press their claims for civil and social rights. Some effectively organized the electoral clout of gay enclaves, notably in the homosexual "capital" of San Francisco. The movement would reach a historic breakthrough with the election of openly gay San Francisco supervisor Harvey Milk in 1977. (A year later Milk and Mayor George Moscone were shot dead in their Civic Center offices by young right-wing supervisor Dan White.)

Pushed from one side by the growing gay consciousness and from the other by discomfort and anger with a feminist movement that did not fully live out its commitment to sisterhood and personal freedom, lesbians could stay silent no longer. After all, they were oppressed on the basis of their sexuality more than heterosexual women—doubly oppressed and "doubly outcast"—yet acted as role models of what female liberation could mean, especially freedom from male supremacy.[66] They made it clear that being lesbian meant far more than sexual relationships with women. "It is a different way of life," explained Rita Mae Brown. "It is a life determined by a woman for her own benefit and the benefit of other women. It is a life that draws its strength, support, and direction from women."[67] The "lives of Lesbians provide an example of Feminist theory in action," wrote Sidney Abbott and Barbara Love with a dose of hyperbole to make their point. "The startling fact is that Lesbians already meet the criteria that Women's Liberation has set up to describe the liberated woman. . . . Lesbians have economic independence, sexual self-determination, that is, control over their own bodies and life-styles." They refused to be defined by male values, male concepts of femininity, or in relation to men. Thus, it was both fair and fitting, said Abbott and Love, that they be at the forefront of feminism, its "natural leaders."[68]

But many "straight" feminists in both branches, more vocally in the older, felt threatened by what Friedan called the "lavender menace" (the identifying color of the homosexual cause). Though deep-seated homophobia lay at the root of this, they argued privately and publicly that their enemies would pounce on the movement's "Achilles' heel" to undermine it—as indeed detractors did, equating "feminist" with "lesbian" and warning that the whole thing was a "lesbian plot," that lesbians were taking over the movement.[69] While Friedan and others worried about "sexual McCarthyism" from the outside, lesbian activists feared that this phenomenon could paralyze the movement from within and deny freedom to many of its own members.[70]

In the report of the 1969 Congress to Unite Women in New York, a NOW-sponsored effort to build a broad coalition on feminist issues, mention of participating lesbian groups and resolutions had been deleted. Infuriated, Rita Mae Brown and two other lesbians quit NOW, charging that "'lesbian' is the one word that causes the executive committee to have a collective heart attack" and calling a meeting of lesbians from both the feminist and gay movements.[71] They shared grievances, formed CR groups, wrote "The Woman Identified Woman" to explain the relationship between lesbians and feminism, named themselves the Lavender Menace (later Radicalesbians), and decided to present their manifesto at the next Congress to Unite Women in spring 1970. On the first night of the congress the lights in the meeting hall suddenly went out. Turned back on, a group of women in lavender T-shirts paraded in front, claimed the microphone, and denounced the feminist movement for its discrimination and prejudice. The response to this direct action was more favorable than they had expected; quite a few heterosexuals stood up to express support. The Menaces held jam-packed workshops over the weekend and won pro-lesbian resolutions.

The tide began to turn. At a second march for equality on a cold December day in Manhattan, the president of New York NOW herself handed out lavender armbands to the marchers—to Friedan's great consternation. The armbands symbolized backing for Kate Millett in her battle with *Time*. "It is not one woman's sexual preference that is under attack," their leaflet stated, "it is the freedom *of all women* to openly state values that fundamentally challenge the basic structure of patriarchy."[72] Persistent agitation by lesbians led to a marked change of atmosphere in feminist circles and eventually to acceptance of lesbians as equal participants with equally valid needs, first in the younger branch and then in the older. As if to ratify the new spirit of openness, the fall 1971 national NOW convention passed a strong resolution that unequivocally supported lesbians' right to define their own sexuality and life-style and that acknowledged "the oppression of lesbians as a legitimate concern of feminism."[73] This was followed up by lesbian workshops at NOW conferences, a national task force for lesbian issues, and lobbying for new laws banning discrimination against homosexuals.

Some lesbian activists had higher aspirations than mere acceptance. They wanted the movement to adopt "lesbian-feminism" as its political creed—defined by their new journal *The Furies* as a "critique of the institution and ideology of heterosexuality as a primary cornerstone of male supremacy"—and to take on an understanding of lesbianism as a political commitment. "Woman-identified lesbianism is, then, more than a sexual preference; it is a political choice. It is political because relationships between men and women are essentially political: they involve power and dominance. Since the lesbian actively rejects that relationship and chooses women, she defies the established political system."[74] They called for complete separatism from men, including personal relationships, and even from heterosexual feminists who were not "woman-identified." Charlotte Bunch wrote later in *Ms.* that separatism "was the only way we saw to create lesbian-feminist politics and build a community of our own in the hostile environment of the early seventies. Many lesbians chose a separatist strategy in order to build our own pride, strength, and unity as a people, to develop an analysis of our particular oppression, and to create a political ideology and strategy that would both force the movement's recognition of us and lead to the end of male supremacy."[75]

Their uncompromising stand brought criticisms of "vanguardism" and "lesbian supremacy" from other feminists; though less acute, the dogmatic moralism that plagued the New Left also seemed to hound the feminist movement. Yet as Robin Morgan discovered, most feminists continued to work together across the sexual divide. "Many lesbian women came to a more earnest feminism: a realization that we each need all women to survive—and that no woman's life-style . . . could be held in contempt for the sake of some abstract 'correct line.'"[76] After a period in which lesbian-feminists, like militant blacks, felt the necessity to create an independent identity and base of power, by the mid-1970s many were working on projects and coalitions with other feminists, including NOW. Acknowledging later that "separatism has its limits," Bunch noted that it "seemed to lead to isolation and powerlessness rather than to the politically engaged but independent stance we had envisioned."[77]

The preeminent contribution of lesbian-feminism was to actualize its compelling vision of an autonomous women's culture. This authentic movement culture—the movement and its culture being as closely meshed as in the Southern freedom struggle—was conveyed largely through self-supporting counterinstitutions, such as feminist bookstores, coffeehouses, small presses, and music cooperatives like Olivia Records. It flowered in many hues and its bountiful harvest included: the poetry of Adrienne Rich, Audre Lorde, and Judy Grahn; the dynamic "women's music" of Meg Christian, Margie Adam, Cris Williamson, and Holly Near; the artwork of Judy Chicago; and the outpouring of "free spaces," like women's music festivals, where independent and self-defining women could explore their commonality along with their differences.

Coming to grips with differences also involved defining the relationship of women of color, especially African-Americans, to the overwhelmingly white movement. Though they might not have called themselves feminists, numerous black activists—Sojourner Truth, Mary Church Terrell, Ida B. Wells, and Mary McLeod Bethune, to name a few—had battled for generations to better the lives of women both black and white. Like lesbians, black women were doubly oppressed, in "double jeopardy"— only worse.[78] As Pauli Murray commented, the black female "remains single more often, bears more children, is in the labor market longer and in greater proportion, has less education, earns less, is widowed earlier, and carries a relatively heavier economic responsibility as family head than her white counterpart."[79] Because sheer survival forced her to be strong and self-sufficient, a callous myth arose—abetted by a controversial study of the black family in his pre-Senate days by Harvard sociologist Daniel P. Moynihan—that "matriarchal" black women dominated their families and men, that indeed they were "already liberated."[80] But inner strength was a far cry from liberation, as Shirley Chisholm, the first black woman in Congress, pointed out.[81] And like their white sisters in the New Left, many young black women had not been treated as equals by their brothers in the black movement. According to a 1972 Harris poll, black females were markedly more supportive than white females of "efforts to strengthen and change women's status."[82]

Nevertheless, when the feminist movement came forth in the late 1960s, blacks did not join it in large numbers. Not only did many black women hold the perception that feminism divided and weakened the higher cause of black freedom, but many were also repelled by the unconscious racism of white feminists. Most importantly, white women, while bemoaning the absence of black women in the movement and welcoming them with open arms, did not make the sustained effort, including changes in politics and priorities, that was needed to reach prospective black feminists and make them feel more at home. The racism was by omission more than commission, manifested in ignorance of black women's reality, lack of attention to their special concerns (such as the plight of welfare mothers and domestic workers), and—"in their eagerness to promote the idea of sisterhood"—the myopic viewpoint that all women's experience being essentially the same, that of middle-class white women was universal.[83]

Still, a growing contingent of blacks were not willing, by default, to let the feminist cause be shaped solely by whites. They were determined to make it a movement for all women and to establish themselves as a visible presence in its midst. Moreover, because they had "an equal stake in women's liberation and black liberation," in Murray's words, they were "key figures at the juncture of these two movements."[84] Both to forge links between the movements and to "organize around those things which affect us most," black feminists formed their own groups, the most prominent being the National Black Feminist Organization (NBFO) founded in 1973 by a diverse assemblage: "We were married. We were on welfare. We were lesbians. We were students. We were hungry. We were well fed. We were single. We were old. We were young. Most of us were feminists. We were beautiful black women."[85] NBFO chair Margaret Sloan explained that "we needed a group of black women to come out and say 'We're here, we understand feminism—it's okay.'"[86] The statement of purpose proclaimed that "the distorted male-dominated media image of the Women's Liberation Movement has clouded the vital and revolutionary importance of this movement to Third World women, especially black women," who have "suffered cruelly in this society from living the phenomenon of being black and female, in a country that is *both* racist and sexist."[87]

On a smaller scale were groups like the Combahee River Collective in Boston, named after an 1863 guerrilla action in South Carolina led by Harriet Tubman that freed several hundred slaves during the Civil War. They were "committed to working on those struggles in which race, sex and class are simultaneous factors in oppression," such as forced sterilization, abortion, rape, domestic violence, and child care.[88] In fact, although priorities and approaches differed, it became clear that to one degree or another the core feminist issues affected almost all women.

Other women of color, particularly Latinas, also overcame cultural barriers and divided loyalties to participate in the feminist movement. Chicana and Puerto Rican women formed autonomous organizations, such as the Comission Femenil Mexicana National in the Southwest, the Mexican-American Women's Association, and the National Conference of Puerto Rican Women. Among other things, Chicana activists set up a service center for working women and a battered women's shelter, and were the backbone of the United Farm Workers' strikes and consumer boycotts.

The astonishing breadth and diversity of the feminist movement, its success in internal coalition-building, and the increasing centrality of minority women and lesbians all were vividly illustrated at the November 1977 National Women's Conference in Houston. Mandated and financed by legislation pushed by Congresswoman Bella Abzug, who chaired the International Women's Year Commission that coordinated it, the purpose of the conference was to propose to the government measures to achieve full equality. It was the culmination of public meetings in every state and territory, in which 130,000 women participated. The Houston delegates constituted a wide spectrum of women, including radical feminists on one end, progressive church women, trade unionists, and community activists in the middle, and at the other end a hard core of conservative "antis," sporting yellow "Majority" ribbons. With one-third of the body from racial minorities, disabled women highly visible, and middle-class whites actually underrepresented, it may well have been the most egalitarian political convention the nation had ever seen.

After cheering the arrival of a torch carried by multiracial relay runners all the way from Seneca Falls, New York, site of the first women's rights convention in 1848, the delegates hammered out a farsighted "national plan of action." During heated debate on the ERA a woman stood up at the rear and said slowly, "My name is Susan B. Anthony." At the close of her talk, the grandniece of the revered suffrage leader joined others in chanting "Failure is impossible!"—the elder Anthony's final public words. [89] The "antis" maneuvered in vain to block support of the ERA and abortion, as well as freedom of sexual preference, which was pushed by a well-organized lesbian caucus working in coalition with other groups. The climax of the gathering was the near-unanimous passage of the minority women's resolution drafted by a historic joint caucus of blacks, Latinas, Indians, Eskimos, Asians, and Pacific Islanders. Among many conservatives who voted for it were two white Mississippians who reached over to grasp each other's hands. The coliseum swayed with "We Shall Overcome."

One observer wrote of the feeling at Houston that "all of us were vital individual parts of an important collective, interconnected, whole."[90] A key black leader, Janice Kissner, commented that "a certain kinship, a certain closeness has evolved. I felt hostile before toward a lot of white women. After coming here . . . I have a feeling of sisterhood. . . . I think we have many more things in common than I thought we had."[91] Not only did she find mutual respect, community, and sisterhood, reported Minnesota delegate Anne Truax, but "there was a great sense of democracy in that meeting."[92]

Still growing in size and influence, the movement as it matured came to feel less like a nurturing family, or "a room of one's own," and more like what it really was—a massive and complex coalition of women with much in common but with many differences. Women of color vitally attuned to the "simultaneity of oppressions" affecting them felt the strongest need for linking issues and took the lead in building bridges of interdependence.[93] Yet although feminists of all persuasions made remarkable strides in including and joining with others, and learned that unity worth having is the offspring of great diversity, big obstacles to further coalescence remained—most glaringly in relation to the many women, like the Houston "antis," who did not trust feminism.

"We must recognize differences among women who are our equals," implored black lesbian feminist Audre Lorde, ". . . and devise ways to use each others' difference to enrich our visions and our joint struggles. The future of our earth may depend upon the ability of all women to identify and develop new definitions of power and new patterns of relating across difference. . . . Change means growth, and growth can be painful. But we sharpen self-definition by exposing the self in work and struggle together with those whom we define as different from ourselves, although sharing the same goals. For Black and white, old and young, lesbian and heterosexual women alike, this can mean new paths to our survival."[94] Lorde crystallized her thinking in a few lines of poetry:

> We have chosen each other
> and the edge of each others battles
> the war is the same
> if we lose
> someday women's blood will congeal
> upon a dead planet
> if we win
> there is no telling
> we seek beyond history
> for a new and more possible meeting.[95]

Chapter Four

Bearing Fruit

This chapter will evaluate the historical meaning and effectiveness of the social movements whose stories have been told in the prior chapters. It will look at both short-term accomplishments and, from the perspective of two decades later, long-term results. It will compare the effectiveness of the submovements coexisting within each larger crusade, and assess the collective social and political impact of all the movements taken together.

Effectiveness is a complicated matter when it comes to social movements, even if one has a clear definition in hand. The disruptive and cultural power generated by movements engaged in grass-roots democracy has been the primary agency of reform in the United States. For example, it has been the driving force behind abolishing slavery, enfranchising blacks and women, regulating capitalism, winning labor rights, and in the recent period, overthrowing white supremacy, ending the Vietnam War, and emancipating women. Yet this decisive impact on positive social change is easily hidden, since it is mainly indirect, one or more steps removed. In the first place, reforms are typically enacted and implemented by government as a result of pressure from movements, not by the movements or their leaders directly. To a significant degree (whether intended or not) movement activities affect intermediaries—such as the media, public opinion, politicians, even disaffected bureaucrats—who are then perceived as the pivotal actors in producing change. Second, a movement characteristically alters the moral, political, and cultural environment that in turn makes possible, and shapes, new policies and attitudes. Third, much of the impact on society involves various "ripple effects" that might appear disconnected from the movement that made the splash. Fourth, movement impact can be obscured by the frequent time lag between its plateaus of influence and the resulting changes. Finally, the potential impact of concrete reforms is lost if the reforms are not adequately implemented or enforced (partly the result of insufficient follow-through by activists). It is not surprising, then, that movement effectiveness is habitually undervalued, disparaged, or ignored.

The black freedom movement, the New Left, the antiwar movement, and feminism were remarkably effective in many respects. Much of their history-making, however, occurred in less visible ways beneath the surface of politics and policy formation, and in psychological and cultural domains as well as institutional ones.

Black Freedom?

To assess the effectiveness of the black freedom movement, in both the South and the North, is to face a troubling paradox. The Southern crusade proved highly successful in reaching its short-term goals of desegregation and voting rights, as well as in lifting black pride and self-esteem nationwide. Black Power produced immeasurable gains in psychic and cultural empowerment. Moreover, Southern and Northern activists laid the groundwork for later black electoral advances. Ending legal segregation was an unequivocal victory. But "integration" was a different story. It was a problematic goal to begin with, and only a minority of African-Americans have achieved the socioeconomic benefits of it. To the extent that it led to an exodus of newly middle-class blacks from the inner city, it exacerbated the poverty of the growing black underclass. Securing individual rights was a crucial step—but woefully inadequate to the task of grappling with the deepening economic powerlessness of urban blacks. The movement succeeded, and it failed. By raising expectations that could not be fulfilled, by overselling integration, and by minimizing economic solutions, its successes in some areas contributed to its failures in others.

In every Southern state nonviolent campaigns by SCLC, SNCC, CORE, and local activists (often aided by the NAACP) directly or indirectly desegregated thousands of public accommodations—bus lines, terminals, restaurants, stores, lodging, and so forth—and armed with the 1954 Supreme Court ruling, public schools and universities as well. The cumulative force of these protests achieved national legislation to outlaw segregation in 1964. Voter registration efforts that SNCC spearheaded in the Deep South initially brought only a small increase in voting, but drew national attention to black disfranchisement and built the foundation for the Selma campaign and the passage of the 1965 Voting Rights Act.

The 1964 Civil Rights Act established a national policy prohibiting racial segregation and discrimination, and in employment banned discrimination by gender as well. It provided limited judicial machinery to force compliance and excluded voting rights protection. The omnibus law was nowhere near as strong as activists had wanted, but was more stringent and broad-gauged than the original bill proposed by President Kennedy early in 1963. The result of its passage was that, in the words of historian C. Vann Woodward, "Jim Crow as a legal entity was dead."[1] The actual extent of Southern desegregation was mixed and directly proportional to the movement's priorities and the weight of social obstacles: most comprehensive in public accommodations—where it was nearly complete— significantly less in public education, and minimal in housing and occupation. Although slow progress in the latter two categories hindered school desegregation, a 1978 study claimed that by the early 1970s, "the great majority of southern black children no longer attended predominantly black schools."[2] But by 1980 the percentage of students attending integrated schools had apparently dropped. In the North, despite busing programs, de facto school segregation remains entrenched in most large cities.

Though restricted in scope and in enforcement mechanisms, the 1964 civil rights law would not have been proposed in its final version or passed by Congress without the popular power generated by the freedom movement. According to the firsthand account by Arthur Schlesinger, Jr., Kennedy believed that "the demonstrations in the streets had brought results; they had made the executive branch act faster and were now forcing Congress to entertain legislation which a few weeks before would have had no chance."[3] The 1963 Birmingham campaign in particular had quickened the pace and made the civil rights bill JFK's highest domestic priority. Aimed at its passage, the August March on Washington solidified support on Capitol Hill. Martin Luther King recalled that Kennedy, who two years before had decided not to pursue civil rights legislation for fear of antagonizing the Southern oligarchs who ruled key congressional committees, "frankly acknowledged that he was responding to mass demands."[4]

This was equally true for his successor. Lyndon Johnson opposed the bill as vice president. He joined the bandwagon upon inheriting the presidency, and his fabled skill at cajolery and arm-twisting played a big role in congressional passage. But it is not likely that he would have committed himself to it, or succeeded in swaying recalcitrant lawmakers, without the far-flung movement that transformed the moral and political environment. Massive, sustained protest, almost entirely nonviolent, compelled the government to act.

The other big legislative victory was the 1965 Voting Rights Act, which abolished literacy tests and other discriminatory hurdles and imposed federal registrars in counties where blacks were barred from voting. Prior to the Selma campaign President Johnson and the Justice Department had not intended to push a voting rights measure that year. LBJ personally made this clear to King in December 1964. "Martin," he reportedly told him, "we can't go for a voting rights bill in this session of Congress."[5] The three-month struggle led by SCLC—the culmination of the entire Southern movement, but especially of SNCC's four-year suffrage crusade—not only turned the administration around but accelerated the legislative process, strengthened the bill, and secured its passage.

Specifically, the nationally televised police brutality in Selma on "Bloody Sunday" and its aftermath sparked "the largest and most intense congressional and public reaction of any of the SCLC's southern campaigns," historian David Garrow notes. ". . . While the voting rights bill had been drafted prior to that now famous afternoon, there is little doubt that the attack of March 7 and the news coverage it received ensured that the bill would be enacted into law, and with only minimal delay and no weakening amendments."[6] New York Democrat Emanuel Celler, chair of the House judiciary subcommittee that worked on it, stated that the "climate of public opinion throughout the nation has so changed because of the Alabama outrages, as to make assured passage of this solid bill— a bill that would have been inconceivable a year ago."[7] As a result of Selma a half-hearted measure was sharpened into an uncharacteristically tough weapon to enforce voting rights—if the political will could be mustered to fully carry it out. Garrow, author of the most thorough analysis of Selma's political impact, concludes that the widespread public support for a strong law was primarily the result of SCLC's "very skillful actions" in Selma.[8]

The implementation of the Voting Rights Act in the eleven Southern states, particularly the use or threat of federal registrars, brought about a very substantial jump in black registration. From 1967 on, a growing majority of eligible blacks were registered to vote (61 percent by 1984).

Black elected officials increased markedly in absolute terms; for instance, Southern state legislatures had three blacks in 1968, ninety-nine in 1976. But their numbers did not rise proportionately with the black electorate, especially considering the level of office-holding. In 1984 blacks constituted about 20 percent of the South's registered voters, but held less than 5 percent of elected offices. Nearly all of these were local positions. As of 1988 none had yet been elected to a statewide office. Selma SCLC strategist Andrew Young and Texas state senator Barbara Jordan won congressional seats in 1972. A decade and a half later SNCC leader John Lewis defeated his former coworker Julian Bond to win the Atlanta seat held earlier by Young (currently mayor of Atlanta), and Mike Espy became the first black elected to Congress from Mississippi since Reconstruction. But many cities and counties with black majorities still had no black officials. Few like Atlanta (and recently Selma) were actually controlled by blacks. Mississippi NAACP leader Aaron Henry testified in 1975 that in his state, "little progress has been made in electing blacks to positions of real power and responsibilities in which we can affect state policy or exercise real political power on the county level."[9] He noted that only 2 percent of the state legislature was black.

What accounts for the South's "huge disproportion between registration and representation," which endured through the 1980s?[10] First, the Voting Rights Act was never strictly enforced even by the Johnson administration, and with obvious reluctance by his Republican successors. The extent and vigor of enforcement directly reflected the decline of the freedom movement, which in any case did not give much priority to this task, expecting the government to do its job. Second, an untold number of black citizens did not register and vote owing to fear of physical or economic reprisal. This fear persisted despite the fact that one incontrovertible effect of the 1965 law was a sharp reduction in overt terrorism as a primary weapon to preserve white supremacy (in part because the resulting prevalence of black jurors ended the custom of automatic acquittals). But that important advance made economic coercion (both individual and communitywide) the main recourse of reactionaries. Finally, through evasion of the law, obstacles to registration, removal of blacks from voting rolls, harassment, and the imposition of at-large elections, white power elites have continuously engaged in "massive, if covert, resistance to black political participation."[11]

Despite such limits, over the long term Southern black voters have gained significant political influence regionally and nationally, beyond the mere number of black elected officials. They made it possible for Jimmy

Carter to win the presidency in 1976, as he and others have confirmed. Their clout with moderate white senators was credited with blocking the Supreme Court nomination of Robert Bork in 1987. They were the backbone of the constituency that built the Rainbow Coalition in the 1980s and made Jesse Jackson a viable presidential candidate. The Southern black electorate allied with black strongholds in Northern cities—many of which are run by black mayors, partly a legacy of SNCC and Black Power—has unrealized potential for African-American electoral power on a national scale.

Ultimately, the achievement of full black political participation depends upon the economic empowerment of African-Americans, not only to preclude retaliation by employers but more generally because in an advanced capitalist society political expression is often ineffectual unless it is undergirded by economic resources of one kind or another. But the aspiration for collective economic power was never high on the agenda for either the Southern or Northern movement.

Although Black Power activists supported abolishing Jim Crow, they criticized the goal of integration, which its proponents did not clearly spell out or differentiate from desegregation. Ending segregation was the precondition for integration, but the latter was a much broader and more complex aim, especially in regard to Northern cities, and centered on economic advancement more than on civil rights. Black liberation groups challenged it for three reasons. First, it would interfere with the separatist strategy of unifying black communities into an independent political and cultural force. Second, they saw it as a "one-way street" if carried out on terms set mainly by white elites—for one thing, integration was likely to drown newfound black identity in a sea of white values.[12] Third, they did not think it was a realistic possibility for most blacks, because of economic and demographic barriers and white racist attitudes. (Some pointedly defined integration as the time between the first blacks moving in and the last whites moving out.) On balance the movement seems to have been only moderately successful in changing white attitudes: gains in this area were offset by reverses, that is, the white backlash against black progress heightened racist feeling in some sectors. History has so far proven the black liberation critique largely correct, though the separatist strategy turned out to be even less effective than the integrationist one—in part because its goals were more far-reaching.

Rhetoric aside, neither the Southern movement nor Black Power ever made group economic advancement a primary or immediate goal—though King and SCLC belatedly shifted in this direction with campaigns for "economic justice" in Chicago, Washington, and (fatefully) Memphis, and efforts were made to support black-owned businesses. Until 1966 Southern activists operated on the assumption that civil rights were the foundation of economic rights and that the latter would evolve out of the former. But civil rights alone "did not require much redistribution of material goods."[13] Black economic conditions in the South did improve slightly as a result of job upgrading, integrated schools that provided better training, and rising black influence in local governance—though cities and counties where blacks had power were among the poorest, with the least means to pay for better housing, schools, and services. Overall economic inequality actually grew worse (for example, the median income gap), in the North much more so than in the South.

To some extent socioeconomic integration took on a life of its own as a pathway for upwardly mobile blacks, aided not only by civil rights laws but by federal policies, such as affirmative action, that promoted equal opportunity on an individual basis. Roughly one-third of African-American families have made of their lives Horatio Alger tales, rising into the middle class and achieving some degree of economic parity. But over half have declined in well-being, and most of these have fallen into deepening urban poverty. As sociologist William J. Wilson has shown in *The Truly Disadvantaged*, integration has widened class divisions in the black populace.[14] Affirmative action has enormously favored blacks from more advantaged backgrounds at the expense of the rest. Professionals and other beneficiaries of integration have abandoned the inner cities, worsening the plight of the concentrated black underclass left behind. In these ghettos everyday life is dominated by drug wars and drug addiction. Joblessness, teenage births, fatherless families, welfare dependency, and violent crime are at record levels. At least half of all African-American children grow up in poverty. Harold Cruse suggests that for many, "the winning of civil rights legislation was similar to the legal release of a prisoner who has been pardoned, finally, after serving a life sentence for a crime he did not commit. But a long incarceration has left the unlucky prisoner bereft of the means of coping constructively with the social demands of his freedom."[15]

African-Americans at last won the rights of citizenship promised to them by the Fourteenth and Fifteenth amendments a century earlier, though these rights are still not always enforced. But as a group they did not make unequivocal progress in the other areas, especially in the economic realm, that fall outside the limited framework of the Constitution. Partly because of its orientation to constitutional guarantees—and later

to revolutionary ideals—the freedom movement failed to seriously challenge the fundamental problems of black poverty and unemployment, and
the resulting expansion of the black underclass. It faced here a tangle of
social ills rooted in interlocking oppression by race, class, and gender.
Yet it did substantially remove the other two layers of the "tripartite
system of domination," Aldon Morris concludes, "largely dismantling
those components which severely restricted the personal freedom of
blacks and disfranchised them in the formal political sense." Furthermore, the movement "altered and expanded American politics by providing other oppressed groups with organizational and tactical models,"
along with ideas, inspiration, and confidence—notably, women, gays and
lesbians, Hispanics, and American Indians.[16]

As chapter 1 tries to make clear, SCLC and SNCC pursued different
avenues to end segregation and transform the lives of Southern blacks.
What follows will compare the effectiveness of each approach. During
SNCC's first year (1960–61) its strategy and tactics were similar to those
of SCLC (which assisted SNCC's birth): nonviolent direct action to desegregate public accommodations and to pressure Washington to enact
strict civil rights laws. Only the targets and leadership/organizing styles
of the two organizations were different. Both aimed to appeal to the "liberal conscience" of the Northern white majority, the Eisenhower and
Kennedy administrations, and Congress to compel federal intervention.
From fall 1961 on, however, SNCC's chief strategy was voter registration, mainly in rural areas, to build local bases of black political power
and, by taking advantage of rural overrepresentation, to inflate black influence in legislatures and Congress. Direct action to desegregate non-
electoral institutions and put pressure on the government became
secondary for SNCC, though the need for federal action regained urgency by late 1963 because of the inability to register enough people and
the unrelieved vulnerability to harassment and terrorism.

SCLC's strategy of dramatic, short-term, media-centered campaigns
of civil disobedience in Southern cities was tremendously effective in securing important civil rights reforms. Because of the wise calculations of
its leadership, Washington's ascendant liberal politics, and the temper of
the times, the strategy was perfectly geared to this outcome. But the
new legislation on top of limited desegregation pacts in several cities
were all that SCLC achieved in concrete terms, though inestimable gains
were made in collective dignity and self-respect. The Civil Rights Act in
particular was roundly criticized by John Lewis, Malcolm X, and other

radical leaders for its inadequacies and for serving as a safety valve to vent explosive pressure while making hardly more than token changes. In his last book Martin Luther King made a searching analysis of SCLC and his own leadership, confirming much of the growing criticism from the left:

It was not necessary to build a widespread organization in order to win legislative victories. . . . As a consequence, permanent, seasoned and militant organizations did not arise out of compelling necessity.

But corrective legislation requires organization to bring it to life. Laws only declare rights; they do not deliver them. The oppressed must take hold of laws and transform them into effective mandates. Hence the absence of powerful organization has limited the degree of application and the extent of practical success.

We made easy gains and we built the kind of organizations that expect easy victories, and rest upon them. It may seem curious to speak of easy victories when some have suffered and sacrificed so much. Yet in candor and self-criticism it is necessary to acknowledge that the tortuous job of organizing solidly and simultaneously in thousands of places was not a feature of our work. . . .

Many civil rights organizations were born as specialists in agitation and dramatic projects; they attracted massive sympathy and support; but they did not assemble and unify the support for new stages of struggle. The effect on their allies reflected their basic practices. Support waxed and waned, and people became conditioned to action in crises but inaction from day to day. We unconsciously patterned a crisis policy and program, and summoned support not for daily commitment but for explosive events alone.

Recognizing that no army can mobilize and demobilize and remain a fighting unit, we will have to build far-flung, workmanlike and experienced organizations in the future if the legislation we create and the agreements we forge are to be ably and zealously superintended. Moreover, to move to higher levels of progress we will have to emerge from crises with more than agreements and laws. We shall have to have people tied together in a long-term relationship instead of evanescent enthusiasts who lose their experience, spirit and unity because they have no mechanism that directs them to new tasks.[17]

King had begun to chart a new strategy before he was killed. Whether he would have been able to unite progressive forces into a broad coalition for economic justice and peace is unanswerable, though probably unlikely.

It almost seems as if King were judging his own organization by the standards and strategic principles of SNCC. Unlike SCLC, SNCC could claim few short-run victories. Its small field staff registered only a fraction of those eligible to vote in selected communities, and though it made heroic efforts, it did not help establish independent enclaves of black political power in more than a handful of rural counties and in Atlanta. (A number of SNCC veterans later became successful liberal politicians, such as Julian Bond, John Lewis, and longtime Washington mayor Marion Barry, SNCC's first chair.) Nevertheless, the strategy of building autonomous electoral structures, local and statewide, was a sound long-run approach, not only to enforce rights laws but to empower black people to overcome racism and attack poverty. That the strategy was not as well implemented as it might have been, or that the mobilization of grassroots participation overwhelmed its ability to be institutionalized, does not vitiate the wisdom of the strategy. One reason for SNCC's failure to make more headway was the dearth of financial and human resources. SCLC consumed the lion's share of available funds, energy, and public attention for its more dramatic but less controversial activities.

SNCC proved to be most effective in less noticeable ways. SCLC and the mainstream movement would have had less impact, even in the short run, without pressure from SNCC (and CORE) to take stronger stands and be less compromising. Indeed, SCLC might never have gained its preeminent position in the Southern crusade without the catalytic force of the black student movement, the lunch counter sit-ins, the freedom rides, and (in regard to Selma) SNCC's voter registration work. On a deeper level, a "whole thought pattern, a whole culture has been influenced by SNCC," John Lewis asserted.[18] As previous chapters have shown, it had a substantial effect on other grass-roots struggles for change in the 1960s, and later.

In hindsight, both branches might have benefited by adopting a coordinated, two-pronged strategy that combined the approaches of SCLC and SNCC so that they would reinforce rather than detract from each other: dynamic mass direct action to win local agreements and national legislation, structured and timed to energize the patient, prosaic grassroots efforts to empower blacks over the long haul—which in turn would nourish the other. A movement just to make new laws was not sufficient. A direct action movement of comparable breadth and depth to enforce the laws, acting through new institutions built to last, was also crucial. Although the rhetoric on each side made it seem so, there was no irreconcilable conflict between desegregation and black empowerment, as Malcolm X pointed out, or between centralized and decentralized modes of activism. Cooperation and coordination that went beyond temporary ad hoc coalitions—above all, closer cooperation at the grass roots—

would have furthered the goals of each organization and enhanced the long-run effectiveness of the whole movement.

War and Peace

Though its actual participants constituted a small minority of the population, the American anti–Vietnam War movement was arguably the largest and strongest peace mobilization in world history. Through education and direct action it generated, and dramatically focused, the majority public opposition that brought an end to the nation's longest war. By themselves the Vietnamese adversaries could not do more than maintain the military stalemate—still a phenomenal accomplishment; they could not expel American forces, nor stop the bombing. Without the movement the war most likely would have continued indefinitely, or until North Vietnam was literally destroyed. Moreover, the success of the ten-year peace campaign led to a long period free of major American warfare, though covert interventions did not cease and world peace remained a dream.

In spring 1968, after three years of seeming to have no effect on the Vietnam War's relentless escalation, antiwar activists suddenly saw their protests bearing fruit. President Johnson put a limit on U.S. troops, cut back the bombing of North Vietnam, called for peace talks, and withdrew from reelection. His startling March announcement convinced many New Leftists that the war was waning and that racism was now the main issue, a conclusion underscored by Martin Luther King's killing four days later. Unlike legislative gains that the Southern freedom movement could rightly claim credit for, the shift in Vietnam policy resulted from two other factors besides the growing antiwar crusade: the military strength of the Vietnamese Communists, as illustrated by the Tet offensive; and the impact on the public and policymakers of the black ghetto uprisings (especially in Newark and Detroit the previous summer), and of the black movement North and South.

Memos to Defense Secretary Clark Clifford from high Pentagon officials lobbying for de-escalation indicated that these men worried about the reaction of "civil rights groups" to enlarging the war and the likelihood of "widespread unrest in the cities," as well as increased draft resistance and war protests.[19] The urban revolts, and their political articulation by Black Power leaders, had a multilevel effect on the Vietnam arena: First, they expanded opposition to the war among blacks (and white liberals) who saw it as wrecking the already inadequate "war on poverty" and as using young black males disproportionately as cannon fodder—black voters being a key segment of the Democratic electorate. Second, the revolts generated anxiety among policymakers that the nation could not afford both guns and butter and that the administration could not afford a combined coalition for peace and economic justice. Third, the fear of bigger "riots" that summer was a major factor pushing Johnson to leave office, which in itself helped to slow down the war.

Nevertheless, the antiwar movement, supported by many blacks, had at least as great an impact as the urban violence. By late 1967 the cumulation of mass demonstrations, campus protests, and mounting draft resistance had catalyzed accelerating opposition to the war by liberal intellectuals, journalists, and politicians, and soon by much of the middle class. Since the Johnson administration had been unable to persuade most of the informed public of the morality of the war effort, it was particularly vulnerable to attack on moral grounds. Thus, it was the movement's strong moral critique and contagious moral fervor, combined with the fear of induction, that motivated masses of students to speak out (possibly the former being a greater pull on women, the latter on men). Both the critique and its dynamic expression galvanized dissent inside the Democratic party and enabled Eugene McCarthy and then Robert Kennedy to oppose the president for renomination. These challenges, especially Kennedy's, were the crucial direct influences on White House decision-making in early 1968, but they would not have materialized without the movement and its rising public pressure. Thus, although the movement, especially demonstrations and draft resistance, had considerable direct effect on LBJ and his inner circle, its primary impact was to mobilize intermediaries—most importantly, civilian Pentagon bureaucrats and Senators McCarthy and Kennedy—to move against the war.

The peace crusade had a larger impact on the Nixon administration, partly because it broadened significantly after 1968, and partly because it emerged as the main threat. For various reasons urban revolts diminished, and the NLF lost ground in Vietnam after the Tet offensive. Campus-based activism, violent and nonviolent, white and black, eclipsed the ghetto in media and governmental attention. And the movement now had a more unmediated influence on the administration and Congress because by fall 1969 it had gained majority support for U.S. withdrawal (according to polls). The president and lawmakers of both parties were positioning themselves for the 1970 and 1972 elections.

It is a bittersweet tale of defeat pulled out of the jaws of victory, which nevertheless prevailed in the end. No doubt the movement, spearheaded by draft resistance (along with overt and covert revolt by combat soldiers), was the impetus behind Nixon's decision to gradually withdraw troops—replacing them with an expanded air war, since pilots and technology were more dependable than a conscripted army. In a well-documented cause and effect, the nationwide October 1969 Moratorium, bringing to a focus all prior protest, directly blocked Nixon and Kissinger from substantially escalating the war, very likely with the use of tactical nuclear weapons. Not knowing this, activists believed once again that the unprecedented protests had had no effect. Subsequently, Nixon and Kissinger stepped up the secret bombing of Cambodia and Laos as they crafted a new policy aimed at deferring further escalation until they had weakened the movement and made the war less visible.

Judging that he had regained public support, Nixon invaded Cambodia six months later. But the majority of Americans would not countenance enlarging the ground war, particularly into an officially neutral country. The national student strike and the Kent State killings prodded Congress to terminate the "incursion," but by then it was over. A resurgence of protest in 1972 kept the electorate sufficiently volatile that the president was forced to agree to a preelection settlement permitting North Vietnam's troops to remain in the South, its key demand all along. After Nixon won reelection by the largest margin ever, he retracted the agreement and tried to get better terms by brutalizing Hanoi during the thirteen-day "Christmas bombing," but North Vietnam's leaders were not swayed. The final settlement, essentially the same as the prior version, was the fruition of eight years of sustained protest.

Although U.S. troops withdrew and POWs came home, the conflict did not end until the Watergate drama emboldened Congress to cut off funds for the continued bombing and eventually made Nixon resign. In a sense, Watergate can be interpreted as the final stage of the movement, on three levels: First, the main motivation of the cover-up was to conceal Nixon's own illegal actions to suppress antiwar activism (above all, the Ellsberg break-in). Second, both the surge of public distrust toward the president and the media's vigorous offensive against him resulted in part from his handling of the war and dissent; the climate of hostility was deepened by the movement's unceasing attacks on him and by the media's anger about its manipulation by the White House. Third, the war would not have ended in spring 1975 had Nixon stayed in office. He had little to lose by sending back the B-52s—an option too risky for his chosen successor. The Watergate crisis was not only caused indirectly by the movement but the campaign of exposure was an extension of the movement by other means. Moreover, Watergate would have had a very different course without the breakdown of public authority brought on by all the movements of the era.

To sum up, the antiwar movement broadly defined had a decisive cumulative impact on ending the war, first of all by making that objective legitimate and popular. Its specific achievements were restraining or stopping escalations (especially all-out bombing), forcing the withdrawal of ground troops, attaining a tenuous but irreversible peace settlement, and barring the use of nuclear weapons. The movement blocked the military from getting what it needed, or thought it needed, in order to "win" and, directly or indirectly, brought down both the administrations that waged full-scale war in Indochina. The movement was the perennial leaven and focal point of widespread public opposition, which by 1969 constituted a clear majority and finally ended direct intervention four years later. Most important from a larger historical perspective, the movement forced the U.S. government to abandon its long-held goal of preserving a non-Communist South Vietnam and prompted cuts in the defense budget, restrictions on covert action by intelligence agencies, and limitations (de jure and de facto) on the president's war powers. All of this contributed to the decline of American global power after a generation of predominance.

The pervasive consciousness-raising accomplished by the New Left and the antiwar movement helped to put a lasting imprint on U.S. foreign policy that, a bit faded, even survived the "Reagan revolution." A strong majority consensus against the use of American troops in foreign wars, and against any military involvement that does not bring quick success (Grenada, for example), still persists. This so-called Vietnam syndrome—an unhealthy tendency from its critics' point of view—blocked direct military action in Angola and Iran in the 1970s, and in El Salvador and Nicaragua in the next decade. But it led to a new doctrine of "low-intensity conflict" that drove intervention underground, where it was conducted mainly by secret CIA-related networks, as in Central America. Nonetheless, an anti-interventionist spirit stalks the land that, due to the threat of thermonuclear weapons, the decline of American hegemony, changes in the Soviet Union, and other altered conditions, may be long-lasting. It is not isolationism, but rather a sense that global peace is better realized through peaceful and constructive means than by armed force.

Returning to the home front, what was the movement's impact on the Selective Service System? Overall, about 10 percent of those called refused induction (or failed to report). A larger number, perhaps half a million, never registered. Though impressive by any standard, defiance of the draft never reached sufficient proportions to interfere with the supply of manpower to the battlefield. Yet the Pentagon memos are replete with alarm that bigger draft calls would provoke unmanageable resistance. It was probably the credible threat that noncooperation and evasion, already increasing geometrically, would spread with alacrity among youth subcultures, white, black, and brown, that most troubled policymakers. The well-publicized noncooperation campaign combined with the draft's glaring inequities compelled Nixon to reduce draft calls, institute a lottery process, and eventually phase out induction completely. Moreover, the end of classification and deferments meant the shutdown of the "channeling" system, whose "pressurized guidance" had manipulated the life choices of millions of young men (and women). From one angle, draft resistance may have been almost too effective, since Nixon defused much of the fury behind the antiwar crusade by removing the draft as an issue, the war effort's weakest link. However limited its effect on stopping the war, abolishing conscription was an important victory for human rights.

Apart from their impact on foreign and defense policy, the antiwar movement and the New Left had a significant effect on enlarging freedom of expression. Along with the black movement, feminism, and the counterculture, they put to rest the last vestiges of McCarthyism and made nonconformity, active dissent, and questioning of authority more legitimate than ever before in American life. New Left, feminist, and black scholars expanded intellectual freedom by widening the bounds of acceptable inquiry and debate. "Ideas and outlooks forcibly eliminated from academic discourse in the McCarthy period became available again," comments historian Richard Ohmann, "to the great enrichment of scholarship and teaching."[20] Higher education has become much more inclusive of diverse perspectives and population groups.

Tolerance for unconventional values and life-styles has grown markedly in many social sectors. Holding off strong political and cultural currents pushing in the opposite direction, many Americans now "have an unparalleled range of alternatives for identity," writes Richard Flacks, "an unprecedented richness of resources for self-development, and a degree of freedom for self-expression that brings us closer to the ideal of liberty than we, or anyone else, have ever been. This more open and pluralistic cultural situation was one of the main historical effects of the New Left and movements of the sixties."[21] Such advances in personal freedom and social openness have been battered by the New Right and its allies but thus far have proven remarkably durable. On numerous fronts, including fights for reproductive choice and lesbian and gay rights and against governmental and corporate surveillance, activists influenced by the earlier struggles (many of them movement veterans) have mounted a diffuse but effective countervailing power to resist the totalitarian tendencies of our times.

What about the comparative effectiveness of different branches and strategies of the antiwar movement and the New Left? The nonviolent strategy of draft resistance had a telling effect on the media, Congress, and policymakers. The draft's moral and structural vulnerability made it a very appropriate target; as noted above, national security bureaucrats feared that noncooperation would become popular. But after 1969 the draft was no longer at the center of concern. Each of the other main protest strategies—campus disruption and large-scale, legal marches—exerted great influence as well, the former by mobilizing a mighty surge of student opposition that ricocheted throughout society, the latter by showing the media and government that the movement spoke for many nonstudent constituencies. The October 1967 Pentagon siege proved that the movement had potential to confront the war machine directly—and that "Johnson's war" had become so unpopular that troops were needed to put down dissent. What seems evident in hindsight is that all three strategies complemented each other in significant ways. A fourth strategy, the national Moratoriums, had an extraordinary immediate impact on halting a planned escalation, but it faded fast—partly because its participants had no idea how powerful they had been.

Until August 1968 antiwar activism was predominantly nonviolent—that is, it involved an implicit or explicit commitment to refrain from injuring or dehumanizing another person. For most, nonviolence was an accepted tactic, not a basic principle. After 1968 there was considerably less intentional violence than is generally believed. Most prevalent was a range of in-between actions that might be called "unviolent," including peaceful protest that turned violent only in self-defense, or for lack of nonviolent training. Because of the mixed message conveyed, these actions were not as effective as demonstrations that stayed nonviolent despite unprovoked police attack. David Garrow's conclusion about Selma, that public backing was gained particularly by the sharp contrast between the behavior of the two sides, also rings true for the antiwar crusade. The more clearly this contrast was communicated, the more efficacious the action seemed to be (for example, the Pentagon confrontation, and Columbia's "big bust"). Conversely, the more the media could spotlight inflammatory language or provocative moves by activists (Chicago 1968), the more public hostility would outweigh support.

The message was completely distorted by deliberate violent tactics such as preplanned street battles, arson, or bombing—indeed, this became the message. Such actions by the Weather Underground and other groups (never more than a small fraction) discredited the entire movement and provided the Nixon administration with ample justification to intensify its war against dissent. It may never be known which damaged the movement more, the systematic repression or the ugly sectarian infighting and its offspring, self-destructive terrorism. Unquestionably, the strategy of "armed struggle" had a negative impact on ending the war; in fact, it helped to prolong the war. Rather, it was the continuum of activity up to the dividing line of premeditated violence that eventually halted the war and changed foreign policy for a generation.

Though for principled reasons neither chose to become centralized antiwar organizations, SDS and the Resistance succeeded admirably in mobilizing grass-roots opposition to the war and the draft, mainly among white youth. Despite the fact that this work consumed most of their energy and resources, it was never their exclusive goal. Like SNCC, most New Leftists had their eyes on more fundamental change and knew this might take a long time. Deferring to realism many did not think that they could generate power soon enough to end the current war; they hoped to be able to stop future ones. For most of its seven-year life span, SDS was committed to strategies of long-term local organizing—efforts to either build a campus-based foundation of a broad American left, or to forge an "interracial alliance of the poor." They rejected a single-issue approach (and dramatic media spectacles), no matter how urgent the issue, holding consistently that racism was as great an enemy as imperialism and that both were inextricably tied to their common source in corporate capitalism. The white New Left was even less successful than SNCC in pursuing its long-run strategy that looked beyond the war—partly because the war overwhelmed all other priorities. As in SNCC's case, this may still have been the wisest path to meaningful change; but the journey was cut short.

Women: The Changer and the Changed

The feminist crusade very likely had the most far-reaching historical impact of all these movements, but because so much of its success has been intangible and "personal," its impact is more difficult to measure. Each branch of feminism deserves credit for positive social change: the older branch for public policy changes that materially improved many women's lives, especially in education and employment; the younger branch for altering gender roles and expectations and enhancing women's self-worth and self-confidence. As the two branches converged more and more during the 1970s, their impacts intertwined. Under the radicals' influence, the National Organization for Women came to adopt personal autonomy as a central focus and put major resources into issues like abortion and violence against women. The younger branch was eventually able to combine sex-role and sexuality issues with economic ones. Still, each branch was primarily responsible for those changes that reflected its own priorities; they will be examined in turn.

NOW and its allies had remarkable success in winning legislative and legal reforms at the national level. In a few years they gained official commitments to civil and limited economic rights that took the black movement much more time and strife to achieve, though they built upon that movement's victories. (Of course, like African-Americans, women had been fighting for individual rights for well over a century.) By 1973 most of NOW's 1968 "Bill of Rights for Women" had been attained at least in part. The older branch not only constructed a permanent "policy system" dedicated to women's issues—a formidable "iron triangle" of Washington lobbyists, congressional offices, and bureaucrats—but a "federal policy of equal opportunity, if not total equality, was clearly emerging in piecemeal fashion," Jo Freeman noted in 1975, "and the legal and administrative tools were being forged with which feminist groups could viably work toward equal opportunity."[22]

The older branch made the biggest gains in attacking discrimination in higher education, efforts led by the Women's Equity Action League (WEAL). Path-breaking reforms in this area included Executive Order 11375 (1967) barring gender discrimination in federal contracts, and the 1972 Education Amendments Act, part of the flood of women's legislation enacted in the first half of the 1970s. Indicative of the shift in educational opportunity is the fact that between 1970 and 1980 the percentage of females in medical school tripled, and in law school quintupled. In the late 1980s one-quarter of all new graduates of law, medical, and business schools were women, compared to 5 percent two decades earlier. A 1986 national survey on education reported that "the most dramatic finding is the extent to which the women's movement of the late 1960s has affected American higher education in the 1980s."[23] Though women are becoming physicians, lawyers, scientists, and managers in much greater numbers, like people of color they have not advanced as much in academic professions, especially as tenured scholars—a remaining white male bastion.

Though the Equal Employment Opportunity Commission set up by the 1964 Civil Rights Act never adequately enforced equal job opportunity for women or minorities, it was the first in a series of policy tools, including affirmative action, that substantially improved the hiring and promotion of women in many areas, even in the building trades. But while work opportunities have expanded, the aggregate "earnings gap" has only slightly narrowed—females earn one-third less than males. Lack of improvement in this area is largely the result of continued occupational segregation and gender stereotyping. Feminists won equal pay for the same work, but this did not make much difference. They moved on to demand equal pay for jobs of "comparable worth," which is still unrealized for the most part. In general these gains in education and employment have disproportionately favored white middle-class women.

On another front, lobbying and litigation by NOW and the National Abortion Rights Action League, bolstered by grass-roots organizing, led to the momentous 1973 Supreme Court decision legalizing abortion, which made abortion much safer and more accessible. Yet the ruling triggered a vigorous "right-to-life" backlash that succeeded in cutting off public funds for abortions, which adversely affects poor women and teenagers; antiabortionists may even push the Supreme Court to overturn *Roe v. Wade*. (The July 1989 *Webster* decision weakened it.) This is despite the fact that, partly due to feminism, a majority of the public has (since the early 1970s) steadily supported a woman's right to choose an abortion.

NOW and related groups failed to achieve comprehensive national child care legislation or any sort of feminist family policy. Ellen Boneparth writes that, "while women's roles as workers have received increasing governmental attention over the last two decades, their roles as mothers, as childbearers and childrearers, have either been ignored or misrepresented in the public policy arena."[24] Freeman suggests that these failures "point out the biggest challenge to developing future public policy affecting women: breaking the tradition that a woman's obligations and opportunities are largely defined by her family circumstances." What is most needed, she says, are further reforms to promote the abolition of the sexual division of labor and its ideology that women are a dependent class.[25] Granting this, one should not disregard the extent to which public policies generated by the older branch have facilitated changes in gender roles, particularly among the middle class.

Though radical feminists aided all these efforts—for example, by set-ting higher standards for change, which made "moderate" demands more achievable, and by pushing the older branch to address underlying is-sues—their effectiveness tended to be of a qualitatively different and deeper nature. The younger branch generated changes in consciousness and attitude, in self-image and self-assertion, that touched the lives of most women (and men) to a greater or lesser degree, especially their personal and institutional relationships with men and, more importantly, with other women. Whereas the older branch shook the system of gen-der roles from the outside in, so to speak, radical feminists hammered away at it from the inside out. The former operated on the assumption that structural reforms would in turn alter attitude and behavior; the lat-ter believed that personal transformation was the vehicle of institutional change. In fact, each approach reinforced the other, making their impact integrated and multidimensional. The radicals were most effective, notes theorist Charlotte Bunch, when they raised questions and challenged conventional values in ways that persuaded many women, and some men, to open themselves to new ideas, look at things in new ways, and act accordingly.[26]

In concrete terms the most profound impact of the younger branch was in confronting the whole gamut of sexuality issues, which were pre-viously taboo, and in empowering women to take control of their bodies, in every sense. Radical feminists initiated and led the crusade against all forms of violence against women. Sexual assault in particular may not have decreased—in part because its definition has expanded to include marital and "acquaintance" rape. Statistics do show that more women are choosing to report rape. What clearly changed was that many women now had tools and resources to prevent it, resist it, and recover from it. Activists "transformed the issue of rape from a private matter to one of major public policy concern. Services to rape victims ranging from crisis counseling to self-defense training have supported by public funds. Legal reforms have occurred both in the prosecution of rape cases and in the criminal penalties for rapists. New police procedures and training programs have been instituted to move the criminal justice system to-ward aiding rather than punishing the victim."[27] Direct outgrowths of the politicization of rape were the emergence of domestic violence as a public concern, the creation of battered women's shelters throughout the coun-try, and eventually, public attention to physical and sexual abuse of chil-dren. Radical feminists were responsible as well for a veritable revolution in women's health care and childbearing, heralded by *Our Bodies, Our-selves,* the most influential of all feminist writings.

The accent of the younger branch on the power of ideas, language, and images as levers of change fostered a politically conscious outpouring of feminist literature, poetry, music, visual art, and drama that has re-shaped American culture. It also spawned scholarship and a profusion of women's studies programs that have pushed beyond traditional bounda-ries and opened new paths of intellectual discovery. A growing body of multidisciplinary feminist theory on the "nature" and oppression of women may have far-reaching consequences for how women are viewed and how they see themselves. Though mainly symbolic, the expurgation of sexist language (male as generic) is probably the most pervasive change. The values and the vision of women's empowerment articulated by radicals have undermined the *ideological* dominance of male and het-erosexual supremacy, while the older branch did more to challenge the *institutional* props of male dominance. Furthermore, as black feminist scholar Bell Hooks observes, radical feminist thinkers have decon-structed the larger "ideology of domination that permeates Western cul-ture on various levels," including gender, race, class, and sexuality, with long-term effects too early to gauge.[28] And "feminist process" as a method of cooperative decision-making has given democracy a new dimension.

As with the black movement, feminism as a whole was least effective in uplifting women economically as a group, beyond offering a degree of equal opportunity to fortunate individuals. Many women independently advanced in economic status, but the "feminization of poverty" forced many others to decline, especially those without employed spouses. Though liberal and socialist feminists stressed socioeconomic issues more than did either black activists or the New Left, they failed to make significant changes in the structural subordination of women in the econ-omy and the generally low status of the female work force. Even less did they alleviate the economic disadvantages of women that are inherent in traditional modes of motherhood, or the financial perils of divorce and single parenting.

Still, the life situation of many younger women in the 1990s is markedly different from the social reality their mothers and aunts faced a genera-tion ago, and not just in the middle class. Largely because of the feminist movement, Ferree and Hess suggest, "few young women expect to spend their lives as full-time housewives; few accept discrimination against women as justified and inevitable; few consider battering and sex-ual assault something women want or deserve. Most are aware that op-portunities for women in politics and the professions have increased substantially over the past decade; most expect their husbands to share housework and child care. . . . The sense of changeless repression, of constant pressure for women to become kitchen-bound domestic servants that animated young feminists in the late 1960s, is not reflected in the experience of younger women today."[29] The movement has transformed American society so deeply that changes are often taken for granted by those who did not have to fight for them.

Though the two strands of feminism overlapped, they pursued distinct missions. Liberal feminists strove for legal and institutional equality, radicals for personal and group empowerment and variously defined forms of liberation. The older branch engaged primarily in legislative and administrative lobbying, usually in a centralized fashion. Younger feminists did not abstain from ad hoc, locally based lobbying when appropriate, but they concentrated on consciousness-raising, creating counterinstitutions (rape crisis centers, women's health clinics, publishing collectives, and so forth), and cultivating an autonomous women's culture. These were efforts not only to fulfill women's immediate needs and aspirations and to change their lives, but to prefigure a feminist society. Socialist feminists in this camp served as a bridge between the branches and organized chiefly around economic concerns at the workplace, in social service agencies, and at home.

Few if any intended it, but these different strategies strengthened each other in ways that contributed greatly to the overall success of the movement. First, the two branches sometimes attacked the same issue from opposite directions—for example, radicals would challenge the domestic servant role while NOW opened up job opportunities. Second, the younger branch stimulated grass-roots awareness and pressure and fought ideological battles on issues such as reproductive freedom and violence against women, while the older branch mobilized national campaigns to win specific legal reforms in these areas. Third, the uncompromising moral fervor and integrity of the younger branch on the one hand motivated many moderate women to become feminists, and on the other hand made groups like NOW seem legitimate and respectable in comparison, thus giving them more credibility and leverage in the policymaking process. (The same conclusion can be made about the two branches of the Southern freedom movement.) Moreover, by setting forth visionary and seemingly utopian goals, radical feminists raised the level of expectations and of actual social change. Finally, the coexistence of the two branches expanded the range of issues tackled by feminism and, correspondingly, the breadth of constituencies drawn into the struggle. The

younger branch attracted those who for reasons of age, style, or perspective were not likely to be energized by NOW, WEAL, or the National
Women's Political Caucus; these groups recruited instead professional
and older women who in most cases would not have been open to more
radical ideas.

The interdependence of the branches helped to produce a movement
of unprecedented scope, diversity, and accomplishment. Like the struggles for peace and racial justice, the feminist movement has diminished
since the 1970s, but as with the others, it lives on in a less visible fashion—still making history from the margins if not at center stage.

A Crisis of Democracy?

This study emphasizes the fact that these social movements were not
separate entities but were interconnected in various ways. One common
thread was that all were powerful expressions of grass-roots democracy
during the same historical period. As such, they had an unintentionally
combined impact on social change that went beyond particular issues. In
what sense? First, each movement (or a branch of it) had visionary goals
that would have required fundamental restructuring of the society; to the
extent that these long-term goals vaguely converged, the movements
were headed in similar directions. Although these goals were not realized, the shared values that animated them—such as the right to personal
autonomy—spread far and wide.

But the combined impact resulted more from an affinity of means than
of ends—the cumulation of diverse activities that disrupted institutions
and everyday routines, challenged old values, and offered new perspectives. These activities not only convulsed the power structure but in the
long run reshaped the political and cultural landscape. The ideas and social critiques that accompanied direct action permeated the intellectual
world and rippled throughout society. Many people gained a greater
voice in the decisions affecting their lives, at home, at work, in the neigh-
borhood. A democratic ethos found expression in many realms.

The movements were so effective in confronting the American system
and its basic assumptions that certain elites grew very alarmed. The
Trilateral Commission was founded in 1973 by corporate and political
leaders in North America, Western Europe, and Japan to foster multinational cooperation among the higher circles of leadership. One of its
first missions was to investigate the "crisis of democracy" precipitated
by turbulent movements in all three regions. Harvard political scientist

and State Department adviser Samuel Huntington, architect of the "forced urbanization" policy of the Vietnam War, wrote the report on what was perceived as the most severe crisis, in the United States.

"The essence of the democratic surge of the 1960s," Huntington discovered,

> was a general challenge to existing systems of authority, public and private. In one form or another, this challenge manifested itself in the family, the university, business, public and private associations, politics, the governmental bureaucracy, and the military services. People no longer felt the same compulsion to obey those whom they had previously considered superior to themselves in age, rank, status, expertise, character, or talents. Within most organizations, discipline eased and differences in status became blurred. Each group claimed its right to participate equally—and perhaps more than equally—in the decisions which affected itself. . . . Authority based on hierarchy, expertise, and wealth all, obviously, ran counter to the democratic and egalitarian temper of the times, and during the 1960s, all three came under heavy attack.

In short, he rued, "the questioning of authority pervaded society."[30]

According to Huntington and other commentators, the delegitimation and breakdown of authority structures, from the White House and the military to the male-dominated nuclear family, had made liberal democratic institutions nearly ungovernable. Government at all levels had lost public consent. Most disturbing, the Vietnam War and the crusade against it fractured the political establishment that had been relatively united on foreign and military policy since World War II. It was not mere hyperbole when President Nixon warned of revolution, or Henry Kissinger looked back upon a "near civil war." The postwar system was shaken to its foundations, and the men in power felt the tremors. Those who had been excluded from the system's benefits, or alienated from its moral and cultural poverty, appeared to be pulling it apart.

Though two presidents were forced out and major reforms were adopted, the structures of power did not, of course, collapse. But a subtle transformation occurred below the commanding heights. Frozen social veins began to melt. A general fluidity opened new channels of possibility in politics, culture, and everyday life. Contrary to myths about the "me decade," grass-roots political participation actually broadened in the 1970s and was more effectively expressed inside formal institutions: local government, education, the media, and the workplace. At the national level ex–movement leaders even held influential positions in the

Carter administration. Words that C. Vann Woodward penned about the postwar South a century before could well apply to the 1970s: "It was a time of experiment, testing, and uncertainty. . . . Alternatives were still open and real choices had to be made."[31] Things were unsettled and in flux; to some degree the future was up for grabs.

But most activists, weary and disillusioned, did not realize the historic opportunity that they had created to chart a new social path. With help from the war and the ghettos, they had succeeded in undermining the prevailing ideology of liberalism and the elites who championed it. But in the fluid situation that resulted—more favorable than they imagined— they were not prepared to offer a new public philosophy, new program- matic solutions, and a new social charter to replace the old discredited ones, all of which could have percolated upward from the grass roots. Instead, the political and ideological power vacuum was soon appropri- ated from top to bottom by the New Right and neo-conservatives, who had been methodically gaining ground since Goldwater's big defeat in 1964. The conservatives rose to power partly by relentless repudiation of the New Left, the black movement, and feminism. The conclusion to draw, however, is not that these movements' alleged "excess of democ- racy" seeded the right-wing ascendance of the 1980s, but that they failed to provide a coherent alternative to it when the terrain was still contested.

Chapter Five

Readiness Is All

There's a special providence
in the fall of a sparrow . . .
the readiness is all.

—Hamlet

Historians will long debate the effectiveness of these movements. Most would probably concur that they succeeded more than they failed. The effort to evaluate them provokes perplexing questions about whether, and how, they could have done better, how they could have left legacies less equivocal. Why were they not *more* successful? Why did they stop growing? Why did they decline? Although each movement had problems specific to its own development, these were less determinative than more general factors applying (more or less) to all of them, enumerated below in descending order of importance:

1. Success itself. Sooner or later, the movements achieved many of the immediate goals that had initially motivated activists—notably, civil rights laws, withdrawal from Vietnam, and reforms banning gender discrimination and legalizing abortion. Enough goals were reached, partway at least, to deflate the various crusades. This is not to deny that partial victories also spurred movement growth, bringing in more participants, funds, and media attention. In some cases (for example, ending conscription), concessions had the effect of co-optation, of serving the interests of the authorities more than those of social change. The movements crested during an era when, domestically, liberalism was at its peak and in a strong position (politically and fiscally) to grant certain demands.

2. Internal divisions took a heavy toll—the divisive spirit as much, perhaps, as the actual splits. Divisiveness resulted from an inability to accept differences and to engage in constructive conflict.

177

3. Many participants abandoned their movement after becoming demoralized or disillusioned. This was caused largely by emotionally wrenching divisiveness and by believing that they had failed—either they did not know how effective they had been, or success came too late. Locked in an all-or-nothing mind-set, countless women and men were painfully disillusioned when their dreams of fundamentally re-creating society could not be realized.

4. The inexorable human life cycle could be stretched, but not stalled. The vast majority of activists were young people in their teens and twenties. The stage of youth could not be prolonged indefinitely. At a certain juncture, particularly when goals had been partly attained, individuals decided to put a higher priority on personal life—finishing school, starting careers, raising families. It is much easier to be a dedicated activist without a full-time job or a family to support. None of the movements figured out how people could participate on a regular basis without disrupting everyday lives and commitments. Regardless of life-cycle pulls, the inherent difficulty of activist organizing, and the energy required, made it psychologically and physically hard to sustain. Activists tired of living "on the edge." These reasons also help to explain why more people did not join up, especially those who were older and already more "settled."

5. The aging factor coincided with another insurmountable reality: dramatic economic decline in the 1970s partly caused by war-induced inflation and the erosion of American global power. Young people who had grown up in relative abundance—or in the case of blacks, with expectations of it—suddenly faced increasing scarcity. It was no longer so feasible to live on subsistence in the margins; being able to get a good job when it was needed could not be assumed. Anxiety about economic security diverted the energy of many activists into earning a living.

6. Repression, legal and extralegal. In the early stages of the freedom movement and the New Left, overzealous law enforcement helped to expand the movements and mobilize public support—for example, the brutality of Southern police, and prosecutions for draft violations. No doubt the New Left got a publicity boost from the Chicago Eight conspiracy trial, and the Black Panthers would not have become so famous without the "Free Huey" campaign. But beyond a certain point the repression was debilitating, most of all for black liberation groups. Arrests and prosecutions were less harmful than covert activities (especially the FBI Cointelpro operations) that exacerbated internal divisions and made them unmanageable.

Consider the proposition that activists had some control over, or ability to affect, the three most important factors suggested above: success, divisiveness, and despair. These problems were more subjective than objective. For instance, "success" could have been redefined, or priority could have been placed upon internal conflict resolution instead of group dissolution. The other factors were largely beyond their control: life-cycle imperatives, the declining economy, and repression. (Still, it was not inconceivable for movements to find creative ways to make do with reduced commitment and numbers; and repression would have been less easily justified if all activists had spurned violence.) Though the distinction can never be neatly drawn, so-called objective conditions are much less open to modification by human actors than subjective factors, which are more amenable to will and choice.

In any event, different and more positive outcomes were not foreclosed or beyond possibility. Within certain overall constraints, leeway existed for other choices to be made, other priorities set, other strategies pursued. The rest of this chapter will briefly look at a number of problems and defects shared by these movements that, in hindsight, might have been handled with greater wisdom. Although most are relevant to one or more of the broad factors mentioned above, each had an independent impact as well. In each area, alternative courses might have enhanced the effectiveness, longevity, and historical meaning of the movements of the 1960s.

Organizational Structure

Expressed in myriad forms—even taking hold at lower echelons of centralized organizations—participatory democracy was an essential and exemplary feature of the 1960s' movements; it also raised problems that contributed to their demise. It worked remarkably well at the local level, especially in small groups, but was never extended further or institutionalized at higher levels. Tensions arose between national leaders and grass-roots activists over clashing agendas and assertions of local autonomy. Rapid growth in the number of members overwhelmed fragile democratic forms. There seemed to be an inverse proportion, at times, between internal democracy and effectiveness in making change. Relative structurelessness facilitated participation but also allowed dominant individuals and determined minorities to take control; the outer openness sometimes concealed an inner oligarchy. Mistakenly seen as synonymous, participation and democracy came unhinged. The decline of genuine democracy—for example, in SDS and SNCC—ultimately led to a decline in participation. Furthermore, the passion for autonomy, combined with political and stylistic differences, made it problematic for the radical groups to coordinate efforts with more moderate and hierarchical groups (such as SCLC and NOW) around shared issues and goals. For these reasons, and others suggested below, decentralized movement organizations ceased growing and could not sustain themselves. Partial remedies might have been for all players to respect the need for a diversity of organizational structures and styles—both internally and movementwide—which might have improved cooperation, and to put priority on intermediate regional structures (and regionalism generally) as a balance wheel between local initiative and national coordination.

Leadership

One of the virtues of participatory democracy was that it encouraged leadership to emerge from the grass roots. Ella Baker's comment about the preeminent leader of the 1960s could have applied to all those in the higher circles of protest: "The movement made Martin rather than Martin making the movement."[1] Yet while creatively displaying leadership in every sense of the word, young activists by and large felt ambivalent about it—questioning its validity, downplaying its value, and confusing it with the authoritarianism that they challenged on all fronts. Participants in the radical branches of each movement rejected hierarchical structures and invented alternative forms animated by an ideal of shared, collective leadership dispersed as widely as possible.

Trapped in a false dichotomy, SNCC activists, New Leftists, and radical feminists assumed that strong leaders would inevitably undermine "group-centered leadership" (factions in SNCC and SDS later turned away from this orientation). They tried to suppress forceful individual leadership by refusing to acknowledge or institutionalize it, but this only made it invisible. Covert leadership could be as elitist as a formal hierarchy. As a result, dynamic and charismatic leaders exercised varying degrees of unaccountable power. This default by both leaders and followers contributed to the "celebrity leadership syndrome": the mass media *independently* selected or certified leaders, regardless of whether they were legitimate representatives, and pulled them away from their constituents into a rarefied orbit of stardom. Gitlin notes that "a movement that could agree on goals and positions would permit its leaders less discretion to create policy in front of the cameras. . . . The issue, at bottom, is whether a movement can develop clear standards for what it expects from leaders . . . and whether leaders can avert celebrity's traps without abandoning leadership altogether."[2] The key question was not whether to allow strong leaders to arise, but how to implement some measure of control and restraint and to formalize accountability. Leadership ought to have been treated as a vital resource and nurtured at every level (including more attention to leadership training). Leadership from the top did not have to stifle that at the bottom; different strata of leadership needed to be structurally interwoven so that each would at once empower, and limit, the others.

Nonviolent Direct Action

Though not as widespread as is commonly thought, violent rhetoric and tactics became prominent in the late 1960s for several reasons, among them the frustrations of the war and racism, the attractions of Third World revolutions, media responsiveness, intensifying repression, and illusions of greater effectiveness. Another reason was that the militant nonviolent alternative did not fulfill its promise, in part because it was misunderstood and underestimated on all sides. Starting with the Montgomery bus boycott, ban-the-bomb protests, and the student lunch counter sit-ins, nonviolent civil disobedience was used widely (though minimally by feminists) and played a crucial role in achieving movement goals. But it was conducted without much grounding in the history of this Gandhian method, resulting in a lack of thoroughness and rigor. Even in the South, where Gandhian tactics were emulated by SCLC, SNCC, and CORE, they could have been applied more consciously, with better attention paid to different conditions and contexts, as well as to the limitations of such tactics. In the New Left and the peace movement, typically, civil disobedience was not carefully organized, guided by clear principles, or adequately prepared for by nonviolent training; it was frequently spontaneous. Nor was it geared to concrete strategies, which were often nonexistent. The Southern freedom movement proved exemplary in these respects, but SCLC's crusades had a shortsighted emphasis on appealing to conscience and rationality and petitioning the federal government; SCLC did not stay around for local implementation and follow-through. Except for SNCC, none of the movements linked nonviolent protest with ongoing community organizing or with programs for fundamental change. Disciplined nonviolent action was rarely bold or forceful enough to correct the general belief that equated "militant" with "violent," and "nonviolent" with "passive." In short, neither those who practiced it nor those who dismissed it gave civil disobedience a fair test of its potency and potentiality.

Redefining Difference

The wrecking of SDS in a frenzy of name-calling and recrimination at its last convention in June 1969 was an extreme manifestation of the moral absolutism that plagued all the movements to various degrees. Moral passion, based on an "ethic of absolute ends," is the lifeblood of social movements and a healthy force for change.[3] But it can easily produce dogmatism, intolerance, and an inability to respect differences, which can tear movements apart. Why was self-righteous moralism so pronounced during the 1960s?

First of all, it was a time not only of dizzying change but of relentless uncertainty. Everything else being unstable, both politically and personally, activists insisted upon ideological certainty—the one variable they had control over. Marxism-Leninism and its equivalents satisfied this need better than less dogmatic perspectives with more room for contingency; the historical inadequacies of Marxism-Leninism were largely ignored. Entwined with the commitment to revolution—socialist, nationalist, or feminist—was the spread of "guilty Third Worldism": the compulsion to obey or mirror the moral certitude of heroes from the oppressed.[4] Secondly, moral absolutism was a convenient vehicle for the public acting out of emotional distress. Little attention was paid to the distortion of political thought and action caused by unacknowledged "emotionalism," nor to developing processes for healing personal pain and reversing the flight from reality. Thirdly, self-destructive moralism filled the void created by the lack of coherent political strategies, which resulted in part from the increasing frustration of activists who lost touch with the texture of American conditions and possibilities and took refuge in the fantasyland of instant revolution.

Ends and Means

Though limited in scope, the explicit strategy formulated by the older branches of these movements was second nature to them; strategizing was a task facilitated by hierarchical structures. In the radical submovements—although less so in SNCC—serious strategic planning was inhibited by the urgency of immediate action, the obsession with imminent revolution, and with theories to guide it, and the determination of movement members to live their political vision in the here and now. All three factors were expressions of the prefigurative ethic of immediacy that was a defining characteristic of the age. Rather than linking ends and means (understood as distinct categories), younger activists tended to fuse or conflate the two. This resulted in an overreliance on tactics, and on direct action as an implicit strategy in itself. Both temperamentally and intellectually, activists resisted leaping out of the present moment to set intermediate objectives and plans to achieve them. Radical feminists replaced strategy—a patriarchal concept?—with notions of open-ended process. Furthermore, radicals with broad agendas and visionary goals had problems with the specific content of strategy. The New Left, for example, faced two overriding issues simultaneously—the war and racism—and despite its multi-issue orientation, resolved at critical junctures to place one over the other, instead of focusing on their interconnections. Moreover, much of the New Left seemed averse to organizing among the white middle class that they had left behind; they were searching for new identities. Along with the prefigurative ethic of immediacy, these factors help to explain why the New Left never fashioned a clear-cut, long-term strategy to end the war.

Coalition-building

Everyone agreed that coalitions were necessary—to generate the widest support for single issues, to link up with other pressing concerns, to unite diverse constituencies behind common goals, and (for some) to win electoral power. Why then was coalition-building not a bigger priority in movement work? Beneath the positive rhetoric, coalitions within and between movements (locally and nationally) were seen by many as a threat to internal cohesion, to political clarity and integrity, and to the realization of both immediate and long-term ends. The collapse of the Big Six civil rights coalition after Atlantic City and the escalation of the Vietnam War—both seeming to confirm the bankruptcy of liberalism—taught black and white radicals to keep their distance from liberals and to chart an independent course. For this and other reasons, the national antiwar coalitions did not succeed in solidifying the progressive constituency. Moreover, traditional "coalition politics," identified with narrow self-interest and expedient compromise, fell short of the high political standards of 1960s' activism; it needed to be redefined and refashioned to express new values. Coalitions were also threatening because they meant working with people of different backgrounds, styles, and perspectives. "Coalition work is not work done in your home," explains singer/historian Bernice Reagon, a veteran of the Southern freedom movement. ". . . You shouldn't look for comfort."[5] A coalition rarely felt like a community, a place of nurturing. People had to give more than they got.

Feminists forging alliances among women proved to be the most creative coalition-builders. As each branch reached out in its own ways to relevant constituencies, and to the other branch, the movement became in effect one big coalition composed of many smaller ones. Radical feminists moved beyond the dogmatic exclusivity of the early years and led the whole movement toward making diversity a guiding value. They learned over time that if groups seeking to work together could honestly face their differences, they would have less trouble embracing what they had in common, that acknowledging and validating differences could foster trusting cooperation and a genuine unity that might last.

Language and Communication

Many activists assumed that politically and morally correct positions would speak for themselves, thus, that it mattered little *how* their views were expressed to the larger public. Some believed that certain groups (wage workers, racial minorities, the poor) would respond to the class appeals of a Marxist perspective imported from Europe, where class conflict has not been as hidden. The Southern freedom movement, on the other hand, proved exemplary in its public discourse—though it can be faulted for the limitations of its "noneconomic liberalism." SCLC, SNCC, and CORE spoke in a double language, each in its own way, that resonated deeply among blacks yet summoned up latent principles of liberty, justice, and democracy most Americans could identify with. Perhaps they were making the best of what Du Bois called the "double-consciousness" of a people striving to reconcile the divided identity of being African-American.[6] This contrasted sharply with the alienating "un-American" rhetorics of late SDS, Yippies, Black Panthers, and early radical feminists, who did not convey their messages in language the majority could hear. From the abolitionists, Knights of Labor, and Farmers Alliances of the nineteenth century to the Rainbow Coalition today, mainstream Americans have shown they can accept radical ideas that are articulated in ways that make sense in the context of their own lives, especially if such ideas draw upon familiar American themes. Many movement people did not heed the failures in this regard of the Old Left, which was undermined in part by inappropriate discourse.

If political language became a barrier, so did the process of communicating it. More may have been lost than gained in shifting from the "personal, deep communication type of politics" fostered by each movement to the imperatives of mass media abstraction when the crusades became famous, participation soared, and war, racism, and sexism appeared intractable.[7] The movements' human triumphs, their moments of authenticity, and a large measure of their effectiveness resulted from the vast cumulation of face-to-face connections between activists and other citizens. It was the courage and caring of SNCC workers who showed up at their rickety homes that emboldened black Mississippi sharecroppers to register to vote. It was the stories that Resistance organizers told of their own lives and choices that persuaded draft-age peers to join them in the shared risk of prison. It was the personal relationships he made with draft resisters and pacifists and his immersion in the antiwar community that compelled Daniel Ellsberg to release the Pentagon Papers. It was the intimate baring of souls and secrets between women that built the feminist movement. Social change that requires individuals to transform their own lives cannot be mass-produced by means of high-tech communication, especially if guiding values are violated in the process.

Paths in Utopia

Though movement people of the 1960s and 1970s struggled to right tangible wrongs, most were buoyed by imaginings of social rebirth, of a future-society-in-the-making. Southern activists, for instance, called it the "beloved community" (derived from the Kingdom of God of Social Gospel theology), depicted in song as well as speech. What seems unique is the extent to which these visions, usually quite vague, were inextricably personal and social; they were dreams of a new self, in a new society. No matter how hard activists labored for the liberation of others, most aspired to remake their own lives as well, according to ideals that permeated their newfound identities. These visions—shaped by leaders and cultural figures—conveyed fundamental movement values, focusing on freedom, community, and increasingly, empowerment. They played a vital role in motivating activists to take risks, sustain commitment, make leaps of faith toward higher goals, push change to its furthest limits, and deepen the personal meaning of participation. At least in the radical branches activists strove to live their visions, to embody ideals in immediate relationships and activities, to deny the chasm between present and future. Conflicts arose, often in the same group, between those committed to modeling values in the here and now and others more concerned with pragmatic efficiency. Tensions emerged within groups, and within individuals, between dreams of personal fulfillment and dreams of community as they tried to actualize both—reproducing the old antinomy in American culture between the dominant "first language" of individualism and the "second language" of communitarian responsibility.[8] They yearned for community yet found in it impediments to self-development. When the two seemed to clash, individualism generally won.

The movement visions rejuvenated a long tradition of radical imagination that has coexisted uneasily with the Lockean "liberal tradition" overshadowing it. Two related tendencies parched this flowering of authentic radicalism in the 1960s. One was lack of understanding that the most compelling transformative visions of the past did not perpetuate a false dichotomy between individuality and the demands of community, small or large, but tried to imagine, as King put it, a "socially conscious democracy which reconciles the truths of individualism and collectivism."[9] Too often activists (white more than black, men more than women) sought to blot out individuality with artificial community or rigid conformity—or to make community a vehicle for untrammeled self-expression. Rarely did they think about how the "two languages" of American political culture could speak to each other, how society could be reorganized so that individuality and community could nourish rather than deplete each other.

Secondly, in trying to transcend the inheritance of liberalism, they failed to see that an honest radicalism cannot fully disentangle itself from the pervasive liberal tradition; inescapably, it aims at realizing, and reshaping, liberal values (such as rights). The most honorable and effective American radicals of the 1960s and prior times accepted the fact that they had to plow the soil of change with available tools. For one thing, they perceived that a European-style revolution, whether class or racially based, was virtually impossible here, even if desirable. This knowledge did not, however, lead them to conclude that the only alternative was liberal reformism. The more the self-proclaimed revolutionaries of the 1960s espoused armed struggle, the more they abandoned the radical ground some of them had earlier trod. Many leapt from unacknowledged liberalism to simple-minded revolutionism, never considering a third path less traveled. To a large extent, relevant radical politics—often confused with militant *tactics*—was overridden in the fateful stampede toward ideological certainty. This interpretation disagrees with a view put forth by antiwar leader Frank Bardacke that the big mistake was that "we misjudged the period," believing "we were living in truly revolutionary times."[10] The reality that revolution was not a viable option (and never has been) does not necessarily mean the period was closed to fundamental change in less cataclysmic forms—which indeed might have been more thoroughgoing than the results gained by violently seizing state power, as well as more consistent with movement values.

Democracy

The heart of authentic radicalism is the expansion of democracy. During the 1960s activists lived out democratic ideals in every form imaginable, and without any form at all. For the most part it was the raw experience of democracy without institutionalization or, more important, theoretical articulation. Lenin once stated that a revolutionary movement needs a revolutionary theory; it is no less true that democratic movements need democratic theories. The democratic advances might have been deepened and better defended with clearer theoretical guidance. Instead, the intellectual labor of these movements drifted elsewhere, analyzing problems not solutions, or adapting ill-fitting theories from distant struggles that actually diminished democratic practice. Serious thinking about democracy would have been useful in several areas, among them: the democratizing of everyday life, including interpersonal relations, which the New Left put on the agenda and radical feminists fervently fought for; the extension of participatory democracy to broader spheres of self-governance, especially national organizations and public bureaucracies, linking lower and upper levels of decision-making; the integration of movement-based, grass-roots democracy with electoral-representative democracy (initially in local politics) without sacrificing the former's principles and purposes; as an intermediate objective, the pursuit of "nonreformist reforms" to create new centers of democratic power and further democratize the government; finally—the fruit of all this "practical theory"—the exploration of the contours of a full-fledged democratic society in which centralization and decentralism can come to terms.[11]

Although half the American public does not even vote, and most of the rest have experienced only a semblance of democracy, the language of democratic ideals can still inspire people because it taps into core principles of the American creed—the only real commonality that citizens of this land share. Explicit democratic visions that spelled out concrete change might have opened doors to Americans alienated from the democracy of smoke and mirrors, of forms with little substance, that was unable to resolve the pressing problems of the era. They might have provided a language to help activists with clashing goals and priorities bridge their differences, and help them connect diverse issues and constituencies behind broader aims of democratization.

With so much begun, and so much left unfinished, the collective aspiration to see democracy live up to its root meaning—people empowered—is an enduring legacy of these movements to those citizens who make history today and tomorrow.

Notes and References

Introduction

1. Michel J. Crozier, Samuel P. Huntington, and Joji Watanuki, *The Crisis of Democracy: Report on the Governability of Democracies to the Trilateral Commission* (New York: New York University Press, 1975), 113.

2. Richard Flacks, *Making History: The American Left and the American Mind* (New York: Columbia University Press, 1988), 62; on the postwar charter: ibid., 53–67.

3. See Samuel P. Huntington, *American Politics: The Promise of Disharmony* (Cambridge, Mass.: Belknap Press of Harvard University Press, 1981), chaps. 1–5.

4. Daniel Bell, *The Cultural Contradictions of Capitalism* (New York: Basic Books, 1976), 84.

Chapter One

1. Quoted in Stephen B. Oates, *Let the Trumpet Sound: The Life of Martin Luther King, Jr.* (New York: New American Library/Mentor, 1982), 58.

2. Frances Fox Piven and Richard A. Cloward, *Poor People's Movements: Why They Succeed, How They Fail* (New York: Random House/Vintage, 1979), 192.

3. Quoted in Frank Adams, *Unearthing Seeds of Fire: The Idea of Highlander* (Winston-Salem, N.C.: John F. Blair, 1975), 122.

4. Quoted in Howell Raines, *My Soul is Rested: Movement Days in the Deep South Remembered* (Harmondsworth, U.K.: Penguin Books, 1983), 44; Rosa Parks radio interview by Sidney Roger, Montgomery, Ala., 1956 (cassette recording from Pacifica Radio Archive, Los Angeles).

5. Quoted in Oates, *Let the Trumpet Sound*, 60.

6. Quoted in "Eyes on the Prize: America's Civil Rights Years," PBS television series (1987), segment 1, "Awakenings (1954–1956)."

7. Quoted in Raines, *My Soul Is Rested*, 44.

8. Martin Luther King, Jr., *Stride Toward Freedom: The Montgomery Story* (New York: Harper Brothers, 1958), 74.

9. Quoted in Raines, *My Soul Is Rested*, 45.

10. Quoted in Oates, *Let the Trumpet Sound*, 6, 10.

11. King, *Stride Toward Freedom*, 59.

12. Quoted in Juan Williams, *Eyes on the Prize: America's Civil Rights Years* (New York: Viking Press, 1987), 74.

13. Quoted in King, *Stride Toward Freedom*, 62–63.

14. Ibid., 64.

15. Quoted in ibid., 77.

16. Quoted in ibid., 78; quoted in Raines, *My Soul Is Rested*, 61.

17. King, *Stride Toward Freedom*, 85.

18. On *satyagraha*, see Joan V. Bondurant, *Conquest of Violence: The Gandhian Philosophy of Conflict* (Berkeley and Los Angeles: University of California Press, 1971).

19. Aldon D. Morris, *The Origins of the Civil Rights Movement: Black Communities Organizing for Change* (New York: Free Press, 1984), 62.

20. James H. Cone, *Black Theology and Black Power* (New York: Seabury Press, 1969), 94, 103.

21. Quoted in Morris, *The Origins of the Civil Rights Movement*, 60.

22. Ibid., 11.

23. Ibid., 46, 89.

24. Quoted in ibid., 94.

25. Quoted in ibid., 92.

26. Quoted in Raines, *My Soul Is Rested*, 76.

27. Quoted in ibid., 75.

28. Quoted in Clayborne Carson, *In Struggle: SNCC and the Black Awakening of the 1960s* (Cambridge: Harvard University Press, 1981), 12.

29. Ibid., 12.

30. Quoted in Morris, *The Origins of the Civil Rights Movement*, 201.

31. Quoted in ibid., 115.

32. Ella Baker interview by Clayborne Carson, New York, New York, 5 May 1972 (unpublished document).

33. "SNCC: Founding Statement," in Judith C. Albert and Stewart E. Albert, *The Sixties Papers: Documents of a Rebellious Decade* (New York: Praeger, 1984), 113.

34. Ella Baker, *Southern Patriot*, May 1960, quoted in James Forman, *The Making of Black Revolutionaries* (Washington, D.C.: Open Hand Publishing, 1985), 218; Ella Baker, "Developing Community Leadership," in Gerda Lerner, ed., *Black Women in White America: A Documentary History* (New York: Pantheon, 1972), 352.

35. Quoted in Morris, *The Origins of the Civil Rights Movement*, 231.

36. Quoted in Raines, *My Soul Is Rested*, 110.

37. James Peck, *Freedom Ride* (New York: Simon & Schuster, 1962), 128.

38. Quoted in Carson, *In Struggle*, 34.

39. Quoted in Howard Zinn, *SNCC: The New Abolitionists* (Boston: Beacon Press, 1965), 46.

40. Quoted in James Farmer, *Lay Bare the Heart: An Autobiography of the Civil Rights Movement* (New York: Arbor House, 1985), 205–06.

41. Robert Kennedy, *In His Own Words: The Unpublished Recollections of the Kennedy Years* (New York: Bantam, 1988), 89.

42. Quoted in Farmer, *Lay Bare the Heart*, 206–07.

43. Carson, *In Struggle*, 37.

44. Quoted in David L. Lewis, *King: A Biography*, 2d ed. (Urbana: University of Illinois Press, 1978), 163.

45. Quoted in David J. Garrow, *Bearing the Cross: Martin Luther King, Jr., and the Southern Christian Leadership Conference* (New York: Random House/Vintage, 1988), 217.

46. Bernice Reagon, "In Our Hands: Thoughts on Black Music," *Sing Out!* 24 (January/February 1976): 1; ibid., 1; quoted in Williams, *Eyes on the Prize*, 177.

47. Quoted in Reagon, "In Our Hands", 2; quoted in Forman, 247; on Albany freedom songs and "We Shall Overcome" see Bernice Johnson Reagon, "Songs of the Civil Rights Movement 1955–1965: A Study in Culture History" (Ph.D. diss., Howard University, 1975), chapters 2, 3, 5.

48. Quoted in Morris, *The Origins of the Civil Rights Movement*, 251.

49. Ibid., 260; quoted in ibid., 253.

50. Martin Luther King, Jr., *Why We Can't Wait* (New York: New American Library/Mentor, 1964), 61.

51. Ibid., 81, 86.

52. Quoted in Morris, *The Origins of the Civil Rights Movement*, 254.

53. Quoted in Lewis, *King*, 194.

54. King, *Why We Can't Wait*, 101.

55. Quoted in Oates, *Let the Trumpet Sound*, 229.

56. Quoted in Raines, *My Soul Is Rested*, 158.

57. Garrow, *Bearing the Cross*, 351.

58. Farmer, *Lay Bare the Heart*, 215.

59. Forman, *The Making of Black Revolutionaries*, 370.

60. King, *Why We Can't Wait*, 122.

61. Quoted in Forman, *The Making of Black Revolutionaries*, 336.

62. Quoted in Carson, *In Struggle*, 94.

63. Anne Moody, *Coming of Age in Mississippi* (New York: Dell, 1968), 307.

64. Fannie Lou Hamer, *To Praise Our Bridges: An Autobiography* (Jackson, Miss.: KIPCO, 1967), 12.

65. Quoted in Raines, *My Soul Is Rested*, 249.

66. Quoted in ibid., 250; Hamer, *To Praise Our Bridges*, 12; quoted in Zinn, *SNCC*, 94; Hamer, *To Praise Our Bridges*, 13.

67. Quoted in Raines, *My Soul Is Rested*, 233.

68. Quoted in Carson, *In Struggle,* 171.

69. Quoted in Raines, *My Soul Is Rested,* 240; on SNCC organizing in Mississippi, see Bob Moses, "Mississippi: 1961–1962," *Liberation* (January 1970): 7–17.

70. Quoted in Zinn, *SNCC,* 80.

71. Quoted in Raines, 253; Hamer, *To Praise Our Bridges,* 14.

72. Sally Belfrage, *Freedom Summer* (Greenwich, Conn.: Fawcett, 1966), 92.

73. Quoted in ibid., 65.

74. Ibid., 186.

75. Ibid., 209–10.

76. Zinn, *SNCC,* 252.

77. Belfrage, *Freedom Summer,* 250.

78. Forman, *The Making of Black Revolutionaries,* 387.

79. Quoted in Raines, *My Soul Is Rested,* 254; "The Life of Fannie Lou Hamer," Pacifica radio program, 1983 (cassette recording from Pacifica Radio Archive, Los Angeles).

80. Quoted in Carson, *In Struggle,* 127.

81. Quoted in Forman, *The Making of Black Revolutionaries,* 395.

82. Quoted in Garrow, *Bearing the Cross,* 347.

83. George Breitman, ed., *Malcolm X Speaks: Selected Speeches and Statements* (New York: Grove Press, 1965), 150.

84. Ibid., 142–43.

85. Ibid., 34.

86. Ibid., 111.

87. Quoted in Charles E. Fager, *Selma, 1965: The March That Changed the South,* 2d ed. (Boston: Beacon Press, 1985), 135–36.

88. Ibid., 158.

89. Quoted in ibid., 162.

90. Stokely Carmichael and Charles V. Hamilton, *Black Power: The Politics of Liberation in America* (New York: Vintage Books, 1967), 100.

91. Quoted in Carson, *In Struggle,* 166.

92. Cleveland Sellers, *The River of No Return: The Autobiography of a Black Militant and the Life and Death of SNCC* (New York: William Morrow, 1973), 151.

93. Quoted in ibid., 153.

94. Quoted in Carmichael and Hamilton, *Black Power,* 115.

95. Quoted in Forman, *The Making of Black Revolutionaries,* 446.

96. Quoted in Sellers, *The River of No Return,* 166.

97. Quoted in Martin Luther King, Jr., *Where Do We Go from Here: Chaos or Community?* (Boston: Beacon Press, 1968), 30–31.

98. Sellers, *The River of No Return,* 164, 169.

99. Quoted in Oates, *Let the Trumpet Sound,* 305.

100. Quoted in ibid., 417–19; quoted in ibid., 422–23.

101. Quoted in ibid., 426; King, *Where Do We Go from Here,* 187.

102. *Report of the National Advisory Commission on Civil Disorders* (Kerner Commission) (New York: E. P. Dutton, 1968), 10.

103. Ibid., 38.

104. Quoted in ibid., 85.

105. Quoted in ibid., 91.

106. Quoted in ibid., 92.

107. Ibid., 107, 1–2.

108. Quoted in Clayborne Carson, et al., eds., *Eyes on the Prize: America's Civil Rights Years, A Reader and Guide* (New York: Penguin Books, 1987), 220.

109. Carson, *In Struggle,* 282.

110. Angela Davis, *With My Mind on Freedom: An Autobiography* (New York: Bantam, 1975), 318.

111. John Lee Norris, "Just Another Page (September 13–72)," in Celes Tisdale, ed., *Betcha Ain't: Poems from Attica* (Detroit: Broadside Press, 1974), 30.

112. Quoted in Carson, *In Struggle,* 301.

Chapter Two

1. Earle Reynolds, *The Forbidden Voyage* (New York: David McKay, 1961), 36.

2. Quoted in ibid., 61.

3. Lawrence S. Wittner, *Rebels Against War: The American Peace Movement, 1933–1983* (Philadelphia: Temple University Press, 1984), 251.

4. Quoted in Robert Cooney and Helen Michalowski, eds., *The Power of the People: Active Nonviolence in the United States* (Los Angeles: Peace Press, 1977), 139.

5. Quoted in Barbara Deming, *Revolution and Equilibrium* (New York: Grossman Publishers, 1971), 69.

6. Quoted in Kirkpatrick Sale, *SDS* (New York: Random House/Vintage, 1974), 47.

7. Quoted in ibid., 49.

8. SDS, "The Port Huron Statement," in Judith C. Albert and Stewart E. Albert, eds., *The Sixties Papers: Documents of a Rebellious Decade* (New York: Praeger, 1984), 181.

9. Wini Breines, *Community and Organization in the New Left: 1962–1968* (New York: Praeger, 1982), 57.

10. SDS, "The Port Huron Statement," 194–95.

11. Quoted in Sale, *SDS,* 59.

12. Carl Oglesby, *The New Left Reader* (New York: Grove Press, 1969), 13.

13. C. Wright Mills, "Letter to the New Left," in ibid., 26.

14. Quoted in Breines, *Community and Organization in the New Left*, 9.

15. Tom Hayden, *Reunion: A Memoir* (New York: Random House, 1988), 81.

16. Paul Goodman, *Growing Up Absurd: Problems of Youth in the Organized System* (New York: Random House, 1960), 12.

17. Mills, "Letter to the New Left," 26.

18. Bettina Aptheker interview by author, Santa Cruz, Calif., 18 February 1986.

19. Mario Savio, "An End to History," reprinted in Loren Baritz, ed., *The American Left: Radical Political Thought in the Twentieth Century* (New York: Basic Books, 1971), 449.

20. Quoted in Robby Cohen, "Pre-FSM Activism," *Daily Californian*, 1 October 1984, 18.

21. Mario Savio lecture at University of California at Berkeley, 2 October 1984 (cassette recording from University of California Language Laboratory, Berkeley).

22. Quoted in Hal Draper, *Berkeley: The New Student Revolt* (New York: Grove Press, 1965), 98.

23. Bettina Aptheker lecture at University of California at Berkeley, 2 October 1984 (cassette recording from University of California Language Laboratory, Berkeley).

24. Sheldon S. Wolin and John H. Schaar, "The Abuses of the Multiversity," in Seymour Martin Lipset and Sheldon S. Wolin, eds., *The Berkeley Student Revolt: Facts and Interpretations* (Garden City, N.Y.: Doubleday/Anchor Books, 1965), 360.

25. Aptheker lecture at University of California at Berkeley, 2 October 1984.

26. Quoted in Doris Kearns, *Lyndon Johnson and the American Dream* (New York: Harper & Row, 1976), 198.

27. John T. McNaughton, "Annex—Plan for Action for South Vietnam" (24 March 1965), in Neil Sheehan et al., *The Pentagon Papers* (New York: Bantam, 1971), 432.

28. Quoted in Stanley Karnow, *Vietnam: A History* (New York: Viking Press, 1983), 414.

29. Michael Maclear, *The Ten Thousand Day War, Vietnam: 1945–1975* (New York: St. Martin's Press, 1981), 126.

30. Quoted in Karnow, *Vietnam*, 414.

31. Paul Potter, "Speech to the April 17, 1965 March on Washington," in Albert and Albert, *The Sixties Papers*, 224.

32. Quoted in Sale, *SDS*, 190.

33. Todd Gitlin, *The Whole World Is Watching: Mass Media in the Making and Unmaking of the New Left* (Berkeley and Los Angeles: University of California Press, 1980), 27.

34. Sale, *SDS*, 215.

35. Quoted in ibid., 242–44.

36. Quoted in Nancy Zaroulis and Gerald Sullivan, *Who Spoke Up?: American Protest against the War in Vietnam 1963–1975* (New York: Holt, Rinehart & Winston, 1985), 3.

37. Quoted in Alice Lynd, ed., *We Won't Go: Personal Accounts of War Objectors* (Boston: Beacon Press, 1968), 186.

38. Quoted in David Halberstam, *The Best and the Brightest* (Greenwich, Conn.: Fawcett/Crest, 1973), 779.

39. Daniel Ellsberg, *Papers on the War* (New York: Simon & Schuster, 1972), 42.

40. Quoted in Zaroulis and Sullivan, *Who Spoke Up?*, 103.

41. Quoted in ibid., 112.

42. Quoted in Sale, *SDS*, 281.

43. Greg Calvert interview by author, Menlo Park, Calif., 5 December 1985.

44. Selective Service System, "Channeling," Washington, D.C., July 1965, memorandum reprinted by the Resistance, Palo Alto, Calif., n.d.

45. David Harris, "On the Resistance," pamphlet published by the Resistance, Palo Alto, Calif., n.d.

46. Greg Calvert, "In White America: Radical Consciousness and Social Change," *National Guardian* (25 March 1967), reprinted by Radical Education Project, Ann Arbor, Mich., 1967; on "new working class" strategy and SDS history 1966–68, Calvert interview by author, 5 December 1985; see also, Greg Calvert and Carol Neiman, *A Disrupted History: The New Left and the New Capitalism* (New York: Random House, 1971).

47. Quoted in Michael Ferber and Staughton Lynd, *The Resistance* (Boston: Beacon Press, 1971), 81.

48. Staughton Lynd, "The Movement: A New Beginning," *Liberation* (May 1969).

49. Quoted in Alice Lynd, *We Won't Go*, 206.

50. Paul Rupert interview by author, San Francisco, 5 January 1975.

51. Quoted in Ferber and Lynd, *The Resistance*, 91.

52. Joreen, "The Tyranny of Structurelessness," in Anne Koedt, et al., eds., *Radical Feminism* (New York: Quadrangle/New York Times Book Co., 1973), 285.

53. Stuart McRae, "Oakland Week," *Resist* (December 1967).

54. Dave Dellinger, *Revolutionary Nonviolence* (Garden City, N.Y.: Doubleday/Anchor Books, 1971), 362.

55. *East Village Other,* New York (1 November 1967), quoted in Sale, *SDS,* 384.

56. Quoted in Norman Mailer, *The Armies of the Night* (New York: Signet Books, 1968), 141.

57. Quoted in Dave Dellinger, *More Power Than We Know: The People's Movement Toward Democracy* (Garden City, N.Y.: Doubleday/Anchor Books, 1975), 126.

58. Quoted in Ferber and Lynd, *The Resistance,* 136; quoted in Zaroulis and Sullivan, *Who Spoke Up?,* 141.

59. Quoted in Maclear, *The Ten Thousand Day War,* 195.

60. Quoted in Neil Sheehan et al., *The Pentagon Papers,* 592.

61. Quoted in Karnow, *Vietnam,* 534.

62. Quoted in Townsend Hoopes, *The Limits of Intervention* (New York: David McKay, 1969), 179–80.

63. Quoted in ibid., 192.

64. Quoted in ibid., 216.

65. Quoted in Kearns, *Lyndon Johnson and the American Dream,* 343.

66. Quoted in Sale, *SDS,* 419.

67. Quoted in Jerry L. Avorn, et al., *Up Against the Ivy Wall: A History of the Columbia Crisis* (New York: Atheneum, 1968), 61.

68. Ibid., 22.

69. Sara Evans, *Personal Politics: The Roots of Women's Liberation in the Civil Rights Movement and the New Left* (New York: Random House/Vintage, 1980), 201.

70. Sale, *SDS,* 438.

71. Oglesby, *The New Left Reader,* 290.

72. Jann Wenner, "The *Rolling Stone* Interview: Dan Ellsberg," reprint (San Francisco: Straight Arrow Publishers, 1973), 37.

73. Quoted in Dellinger, *Revolutionary Nonviolence,* 384.

74. Quoted in Zaroulis and Sullivan, *Who Spoke Up?,* 179.

75. Quoted in James Miller, *"Democracy Is in the Streets": From Port Huron to the Siege of Chicago* (New York: Simon & Schuster, 1987), 295.

76. Dellinger, *More Power Than We Know,* 125.

77. William Styron, "Eyewitness," in Donald Myrus, ed., *Law and Disorder: The Chicago Convention and Its Aftermath* (Donald Myrus and Burton Joseph, 1968).

78. Quoted in Zaroulis and Sullivan, *Who Spoke Up?,* 194.

79. Quoted in ibid., 194–95.

80. Quoted in Lewis Chester, et al., *An American Melodrama: The Presidential Campaign of 1968* (New York: Viking Press, 1969), 582.

81. Quoted in ibid., 584.

82. Quoted in Daniel Walker, *Rights in Conflict: Chicago's 7 Brutal Days* (New York: Grosset & Dunlap, 1968), vii.

83. Quoted in Gitlin, *The Whole World is Watching,* 189.

84. Quoted in David Farber, *Chicago '68* (Chicago: University of Chicago Press, 1988), 207.

85. Dellinger, *More Power Than We Know,* 126.

86. Quoted in Farber, *Chicago '68,* 17.

87. Quoted in ibid., 177–79.

88. Michael Rossman lecture at University of California at Berkeley, 18 November 1987 (author's cassette recording).

89. Norman Mailer, *The White Negro* (San Francisco: City Lights Books, n.d., unpaginated).

90. Rossman lecture at University of California at Berkeley, 18 November 1987.

91. Ibid.

92. Theodore Roszak, *The Making of a Counter Culture* (Garden City, N.Y.: Doubleday, 1968, 1969), 265.

93. Ibid., 50–51, 5.

94. Quoted in Ferber and Lynd, *The Resistance,* 88, 91.

95. Albert and Albert, *The Sixties Papers,* 40.

96. Stew Albert, "People's Park: Free for All," in ibid., 436, 435.

97. Todd Gitlin, *The Sixties: Years of Hope, Days of Rage* (New York: Bantam, 1987), 355.

98. Ibid., 361.

99. Rossman lecture at University of California at Berkeley, 18 November 1987.

100. Robert A. Rosenstone, " 'The Times They Are A-Changin' ": The Music of Protest," *Annals of the American Academy of Political and Social Science* 382 (March 1969): 143.

101. Lyrics reprinted in Peter Blood-Patterson, ed., *Rise Up Singing* (Bethlehem, Pa.: Sing Out Corporation, 1988), 240.

102. Andrew Kopkind, "A New Culture of Opposition," *Current* (October 1969), 59.

103. Quoted in Gitlin, *The Sixties,* 222–24.

104. Abbie Hoffman, *Revolution for the Hell of It* (New York: Dial Press, 1968), 102.

105. *New York Times,* 20 January 1969, sec. 1, p. 21.

106. Quoted in *New York Times,* 21 January 1969, sec. 1, p. 24.

107. Quoted in H. R. Haldeman, *The Ends of Power* (New York: Times Books, 1978), 83.

108. Quoted in U.S. Senate, Armed Services Committee, *Bombing in Cambodia,* S. Rept., 93rd Cong., 1st sess. (Washington: Government Printing Office, 1973), 417.

109. Quoted in Ferber and Lynd, *The Resistance,* 208.

110. Quoted in ibid., 209.

111. Carl Oglesby, "Notes on a Decade Ready for the Dustbin," *Liberation* (August-September 1969): 6.

112. Sale, *SDS*, 562.

113. Richard Flacks, *Youth and Social Change* (Chicago: Rand McNally/Markham, 1971), 101.

114. Richard Nixon, *The Memoirs of Richard Nixon* (New York: Grosset & Dunlap, 1978), 393; quoted in ibid., 396; ibid., 397.

115. Quoted in Tad Szulc, *The Illusion of Peace: Foreign Policy in the Nixon Years* (New York: Viking Press, 1978), 150–51.

116. On Duck Hook plan and nuclear targets, see Seymour M. Hersh, *The Price of Power: Kissinger in the Nixon White House* (New York: Summit Books, 1983), 120, 126; see also, Roger Morris, *Uncertain Greatness: Henry Kissinger and American Foreign Policy* (New York: Harper & Row, 1977), 164.

117. David Broder, column, *Washington Post*, 7 October 1969.

118. Quoted in "Oct. 15: A Day to Remember," *Newsweek* (27 October 1969): 32.

119. Quoted in Morris, *Uncertain Greatness*, 165.

120. Quoted in *New York Times*, 4 November 1969, sec. 1.

121. Dwight Chapin memo to H. R. Haldeman, 16 October 1969, quoted in Jeb Stuart Magruder, *An American Life: One Man's Road to Watergate* (New York: Atheneum, 1974), 81–83.

122. Quoted in Garry Wills, *Nixon Agonistes: The Crisis of the Self-Made Man* (New York: New American Library/Mentor, 1971), 366.

123. Quoted in Barbara Deming, *We Cannot Live Without Our Lives* (New York: Grossman Publishers, 1974), 30.

124. Quoted in Zaroulis and Sullivan, *Who Spoke Up?*, 346.

125. Deming, *We Cannot Live Without Our Lives*, 33.

126. Daniel Ellsberg lecture, Isla Vista, Calif., 13 May 1975 (author's cassette recording).

127. "An Interview with Daniel Ellsberg," *WIN* (1 November 1972): 7; ibid., 8.

128. Randy Kehler talk reprinted in *Liberation & Revolution: Gandhi's Challenge*, Report of the Thirteenth Triennial Conference of the War Resisters International (London: War Resisters International, 1969), 106–07.

129. Quoted in J. Anthony Lukas, "After the Pentagon Papers—A Month in the New Life of Daniel Ellsberg," *New York Times Magazine* (12 December 1971): 106; on Ellsberg and Pentagon Papers: Daniel Ellsberg interviews by author, San Francisco, 29 October 1976; Kensington, Calif., 16 December 1977, 5 October 1978; Randy Kehler interview by author, Whately, Mass., August 1976.

130. Robert Ellsberg, "On Daniel Ellsberg: Remembering the Pentagon Papers," *1976 Peace Calendar* (New York: War Resisters League, 1975).

131. Quoted in Lukas, "After the Pentagon Papers," 104.

132. Quoted in Marvin and Bernard Kalb, *Kissinger* (Boston: Little, Brown, 1974), 383.

133. Quoted in Frank Snepp, *Decent Interval* (New York: Random House/Vintage, 1978), 557.

Chapter Three

1. "SNCC Position Paper, November 1964," in Mary King, *Freedom Song: A Personal Story of the 1960s Civil Rights Movement* (New York: William Morrow/Quill, 1987), 568, 569.
2. "A Kind of Memo from Casey Hayden and Mary King to a Number of Other Women in the Peace and Freedom Movements," in ibid., 573.
3. Quoted in Sale, *SDS,* 526.
4. Sara Evans, *Personal Politics: The Roots of Women's Liberation in the Civil Rights Movement and the New Left* (New York: Random House/Vintage, 1980), 108.
5. Women's Liberation Workshop, "Liberation of Women," *New Left Notes,* 10 July 1967, reprinted in ibid., 240–42.
6. Quoted in ibid., 192.
7. Betty Friedan, *The Feminine Mystique* (New York: W. W. Norton, 1963, 1983), 383.
8. Quoted in Jo Freeman, *The Politics of Women's Liberation* (New York: Longman, 1975), 54; quoted in Donald Allen Robinson, "Two Movements in Pursuit of Equal Employment Opportunity," *Signs* 4 (Spring 1979): 423.
9. Friedan, *The Feminine Mystique,* 125.
10. Ibid., 77, 102.
11. Ibid., 15.
12. Quoted in Betty Friedan, *"It Changed My Life": Writings on the Women's Movement* (New York: W. W. Norton, 1985), 77.
13. Ibid., 83.
14. "NOW Statement of Purpose," in ibid., 87, 88, 90.
15. Ibid., 95.
16. Maren Lockwood Carden, *The New Feminist Movement* (New York: Russell Sage, 1974), 125–26; quoted in ibid., 120.
17. Freeman, *The Politics of Women's Liberation,* 56.
18. Quoted in ibid., 189.
19. Jo Freeman, "Women and Public Policy: An Overview," in Ellen Boneparth, ed., *Women, Power and Policy* (Pergamon Press, 1982), 56.
20. Friedan, *"It Changed My Life,"* 104.
21. Ibid., 141.
22. Quoted in *New York Times,* 27 August 1970, sec. 1.
23. Evans, *Personal Politics,* 218.
24. Charlotte Bunch, *Passionate Politics: Feminist Theory in Action* (New York: St. Martin's Press, 1987), 4.
25. Ibid., 6.

26. Ti-Grace Atkinson, *Amazon Odyssey* (New York: Links Books, 1974), 10–11.

27. Evans, *Personal Politics*, 211.

28. Quoted in ibid., 211.

29. Simone de Beauvoir, *The Second Sex* (New York: Bantam, 1961), xvi; quoted in Gayle Graham Yates, *What Women Want: The Ideas of the Movement* (Cambridge, Mass.: Harvard University Press, 1975), 93.

30. "Redstockings Manifesto," in Robin Morgan, eds., *Sisterhood Is Powerful: An Anthology of Writings from the Women's Liberation Movement* (New York: Random House/Vintage, 1970), 533–34.

31. Kate Millett, *Sexual Politics* (Garden City, N.Y.: Doubleday, 1970), 363.

32. Bunch, *Passionate Politics*, 43.

33. Shulamith Firestone, *The Dialectic of Sex: The Case for Feminist Revolution* (New York: Bantam, 1971), 11–12.

34. Vivian Gornick, *Essays in Feminism* (New York: Harper & Row, 1978), 71.

35. Bunch, *Passionate Politics*, 30.

36. Pamela Allen, *Free Space: A Perspective on the Small Group in Women's Liberation*, 2d ed. (Washington, N.J.: Times Change Press, 1970), 6–7.

37. Robin Morgan, "Women Disrupt the Miss America Pageant," in Robin Morgan, *Going Too Far: The Personal Chronicle of a Feminist* (New York: Random House, 1977), 64.

38. Quoted in Ann Popkin, "The Personal Is Political: The Women's Liberation Movement," in Dick Cluster, ed., *They Should Have Served That Cup of Coffee: Seven Radicals Remember the 60s* (Boston: South End Press, 1979), 190.

39. Morgan, *Going Too Far*, 65.

40. "WITCH Hexes Wall Street," reprinted in ibid., 75.

41. WITCH leaflet, in Morgan, *Sisterhood Is Powerful*, 539–40.

42. Quoted in Freeman, *The Politics of Women's Liberation*, 148.

43. Morgan, *Going Too Far*, 63.

44. Ibid., 63.

45. Gornick, *Essays in Feminism*, 169; Leah Fritz, *Dreamers and Dealers: An Intimate Appraisal of the Women's Movement* (Boston: Beacon Press, 1980), 16–17.

46. Joreen, "The Tyranny of Structurelessness," in Anne Koedt, Ellen Levine, and Anita Rapone, eds., *Radical Feminism* (New York: Quadrangle/New York Times Book Co., 1973), 286, 291, 297.

47. "Editorial: *Notes from the Third Year*", in ibid., 300.

48. Todd Gitlin, *The Whole World Is Watching: Mass Media in the Making and Unmaking of the New Left* (Berkeley and Los Angeles: University of California Press, 1980), 128, 154, 144.

49. In Kate Millett, *Flying* (New York: Alfred A. Knopf, 1974), 92–94.

50. "Women's Lib: A Second Look," *Time* (14 December 1970): 50.

51. "Editorial: *Notes from the Third Year,*" 301.

52. Freeman, *The Politics of Women's Liberation,* 83.

53. Quoted in ibid., 163.

54. Quoted in Kristin Luker, *Abortion and the Politics of Motherhood* (Berkeley and Los Angeles: University of California Press, 1984), 97.

55. Ibid., 193–94.

56. Jane J. Mansbridge, *Why We Lost the ERA* (Chicago: University of Chicago Press, 1986), 5–6.

57. Andra Medea and Kathleen Thompson, *Against Rape* (New York: Farrar, Straus & Giroux, 1974), 11.

58. Susan Brownmiller, *Against Our Will: Men, Women and Rape* (New York: Bantam, 1976), 445; see also, Susan Griffin, *Rape: The Power of Consciousness* (New York: Harper & Row, 1979), especially pp. 16–22.

59. Brownmiller, *Against Our Will,* 447.

60. Ibid., 445.

61. Medea and Thompson, *Against Rape,* 127.

62. Brownmiller, *Against Our Will,* 451.

63. "The Woman Identified Woman," in Koedt, Levine, and Rapone, *Radical Feminism,* 240.

64. Quoted in Sidney Abbott and Barbara Love, *Sappho Was a Right-on Woman: A Liberated View of Lesbianism* (New York: Stein & Day, 1973), 146.

65. Randy Shilts, *The Mayor of Castro Street: The Life and Times of Harvey Milk* (New York: St. Martin's Press, 1982), 42.

66. Sidney Abbott and Barbara Love, "Is Women's Liberation a Lesbian Plot?" in Vivian Gornick and Barbara K. Moran, eds., *Woman in Sexist Society* (New York: New American Library/Signet, 1972), 610.

67. Quoted in Bunch, *Passionate Politics,* 186.

68. Abbott and Love, *Sappho Was a Right-on Woman,* 136–37.

69. Quoted in Abbott and Love, "Is Women's Liberation a Lesbian Plot?," 614.

70. Quoted in Abbott and Love, *Sappho Was a Right-on Woman,* 124.

71. Quoted in Abbott and Love, "Is Women's Liberation a Lesbian Plot?," 614.

72. Quoted in Abbott and Love, *Sappho Was a Right-on Woman,* 122.

73. Quoted in ibid., 134.

74. Nancy Myron and Charlotte Bunch, eds., *Lesbianism and the Women's Movement* (Baltimore: Diana Press, 1975), 10; Charlotte Bunch, "Lesbians in Revolt," *The Furies* 1 (January 1972), reprinted in Bunch, *Passionate Politics,* 162.

75. Charlotte Bunch, "Learning from Lesbian Separatism," *Ms.* (November 1976), reprinted in Bunch, *Passionate Politics,* 184–85.

76. Quoted in Freeman, *The Politics of Women's Liberation,* 138; quoted in Gornick, *Essays in Feminism,* 165; Morgan, *Going Too Far,* 7.

77. Charlotte Bunch, "Beyond Either/Or: Nonaligned Feminism," *Quest: A Feminist Quarterly* 3 (Summer 1976), reprinted in Bunch, *Passionate Politics*, 53.

78. Frances M. Beal, "Double Jeopardy: To Be Black and Female," in Morgan, *Sisterhood Is Powerful*, 340.

79. Pauli Murray, "The Liberation of Black Women," in Mary Lou Thompson, ed., *Voices of the New Feminism* (Boston: Beacon Press, 1975), 99.

80. Quoted in Bell Hooks, *Ain't I a Woman: Black Women and Feminism* (Boston: South End Press, 1981), 187.

81. "Feminism: 'The Black Nuance,'" *Newsweek* (17 December 1973): 89.

82. Louis Harris, *The Anguish of Change* (New York: W. W. Norton, 1973), 95.

83. Hooks, *Ain't I a Woman*, 190.

84. Murray, "The Liberation of Black Women," 101.

85. Quoted in "Black Feminism: A New Mandate," *Ms.* (May 1974): 97, 98.

86. Quoted in "Feminism: 'The Black Nuance,'" *Newsweek* (17 December 1973): 89.

87. Quoted in "Black Feminism: A New Mandate," 99.

88. "The Combahee River Collective Statement," in Barbara Smith, ed., *Home Girls: A Black Feminist Anthology* (New York: Kitchen Table: Women of Color Press, 1983), 280–81.

89. Quoted in Lindsy Van Gelder, "Four Days That Changed the World," *Ms.* (March 1978): 90.

90. Ibid., 89.

91. Quoted in Lucy Komisar, "Feminism as National Politics," *Nation* (10 December 1977): 625.

92. Quoted in Evans, *Personal Politics*, 232.

93. Barbara Smith, "Introduction," in Smith, *Home Girls*, xxxiii.

94. Audre Lorde, *Sister Outsider* (Trumansburg, N.Y.: Crossing Press, 1984), 122–23.

95. Ibid., 123.

Chapter Four

1. C. Vann Woodward, *The Strange Career of Jim Crow,* 3d ed., rev. (New York: Oxford University Press, 1974), 186.

2. Elliot Zashin, "The Progress of Black Americans in Civil Rights: The Past Two Decades Assessed," *Daedalus* 107 (Winter 1978): 242.

3. Arthur Schlesinger, Jr., *A Thousand Days: John F. Kennedy in the White House* (Boston: Houghton Mifflin, 1965), 969–70.

4. Quoted in ibid., 976.

5. Quoted in David J. Garrow, *Bearing the Cross: Martin Luther King,*

Jr., and the Southern Christian Leadership Conference (New York: Random House/Vintage, 1988), 598.

6. David J. Garrow, *Protest at Selma: Martin Luther King, Jr., and the Voting Rights Act of 1965* (New Haven, Conn.: Yale University Press, 1978), 134.

7. Quoted in ibid., 113.

8. Ibid., 235.

9. Quoted in Garrow, *Protest at Selma,* 210.

10. Charles E. Fager, *Selma, 1965: The March That Changed the South,* 2d ed. (Boston: Beacon Press, 1985), 221.

11. Ibid., 222.

12. Stokely Carmichael and Charles V. Hamilton, *Black Power: The Politics of Liberation in America* (New York: Vintage Books, 1967), 55.

13. Zashin, "The Progress of Black Americans in Civil Rights," 239.

14. William J. Wilson, *The Truly Disadvantaged: The Inner City, the Underclass, and Public Policy* (Chicago: University of Chicago Press, 1987).

15. Harold Cruse, *Plural but Equal: A Critical Study of Blacks and Minorities and America's Plural Society* (New York: William Morrow, 1987), 267–68.

16. Aldon D. Morris, *The Origins of the Civil Rights Movement: Black Communities Organizing for Change* (New York: Free Press, 1984), 286–87.

17. Martin Luther King, Jr., *Where Do We Go from Here: Chaos or Community?* (Boston: Beacon Press, 1968), 158–59.

18. Quoted in Clayborne Carson, *In Struggle: SNCC and the Black Awakening of the 1960s* (Cambridge, Mass.: Harvard University Press, 1981), 302.

19. Quoted in Townsend Hoopes, *The Limits of Intervention* (New York: David McKay, 1969), 179–80, 192; see also, Lyndon B. Johnson, *The Vantage Point: Perspectives of the Presidency 1963–1969* (New York: Holt, Rinehart & Winston, 1971), 426.

20. Richard Ohmann, letter to editor, *New York Review of Books* (4 December 1986): 60.

21. Richard Flacks, *Making History: The American Left and the American Mind* (New York: Columbia University Press, 1988), 186.

22. Jo Freeman, *The Politics of Women's Liberation* (New York: Longman, 1975), 171.

23. "College Freshmen Still Reveal Liberal Streak," *San Francisco Chronicle,* 31 October 1986.

24. Ellen Boneparth, in Ellen Boneparth, ed., *Women, Power and Policy* (New York: Pergamon Press, 1982), 121.

25. Jo Freeman, "Women and Public Policy: An Overview," in ibid., 62, 63, 65.

26. Charlotte Bunch interview, "Women's Magazine," KPFA-FM, Berkeley, Calif., 22 November 1986.

27. Boneparth, *Women, Power and Policy,* 165.

28. Bell Hooks, *Ain't I a Woman: Black Women and Feminism* (Boston: South End Press, 1981), 194.

29. Myra Marx Ferree and Beth B. Hess, *Controversy and Coalition: The New Feminist Movement* (Boston: G. K. Hall, 1985), 181–82.

30. Michael J. Crozier, Samuel P. Huntington, and Joji Watanuki, *The Crisis of Democracy: Report on the Governability of Democracies to the Trilateral Commission* (New York: New York University Press, 1975), 74–76.

31. Woodward, *The Strange Career of Jim Crow*, 33.

Chapter Five

1. Quoted in David J. Garrow, *Bearing the Cross: Martin Luther King, Jr., and the Southern Christian Leadership Conference* (New York: Random House/Vintage, 1988), 625.

2. Todd Gitlin, *The Whole World Is Watching: Mass Media in the Making and Unmaking of the New Left* (Berkeley and Los Angeles: University of California Press, 1980), 178–79.

3. Max Weber's term, quoted in Wini Breines, *Community and Organization in the New Left: 1962–1968* (New York: Praeger 1982), 1.

4. Todd Gitlin, *The Sixties: Years of Hope, Days of Rage* (New York: Bantam, 1987), 397.

5. Bernice Johnson Reagon, "Coalition Politics: Turning the Century," in Barbara Smith, ed., *Home Girls: A Black Feminist Anthology* (New York: Kitchen Table: Women of Color Press, 1983), 359.

6. W. E. B. Du Bois, *The Souls of Black Folk* (1903; New York: Dodd, Mead, 1979), 3.

7. Quoted in Alice Lynd, ed., *We Won't Go* (Boston: Beacon Press, 1968), 206.

8. Robert N. Bellah, et al., *Habits of the Heart: Individualism and Commitment in American Life* (New York: Harper & Row/Perennial Library, 1986), 20.

9. Martin Luther King, Jr., *Where Do We Go From Here: Chaos or Community?* (Boston: Beacon Press, 1968), 187.

10. Frank Bardacke, letter to editor, *Zeta* (September 1988): 3.

11. Charlotte Bunch, *Passionate Politics: Feminist Theory in Action* (New York: St. Martin's Press, 1987), 11.

Selected Bibliography

Albert, Judith C., and Albert, Stewart E. *The Sixties Papers: Documents of a Rebellious Decade.* New York: Praeger, 1984. A comprehensive, well-annotated documentary history that covers all the major movements as well as the counterculture.

Boneparth, Ellen, ed. *Women, Power and Policy.* New York: Pergamon Press, 1982. A wide-ranging collection of essays on public policy issues affecting women and how the feminist movement engaged these issues.

Branch, Taylor. *Parting the Waters: America in the King Years 1954–1963.* New York: Simon & Schuster, 1988. The first volume of a two-volume biographical history of Martin Luther King, Jr., grounding King's leadership in the history and dynamics of the Southern black church. Though the subtitle is slightly misleading, it places King in the larger political and social context of the era and emphasizes his relationship with other movement leaders and organizations. An abundance of fresh information and an exceptionally well-crafted narrative.

Carden, Maren Lockwood. *The New Feminist Movement.* New York: Russell Sage, 1974. An early account of the feminist movement that explores the two branches and how they were interrelated and looks carefully at issues causing tension and division within the movement, such as hierarchy versus decentralism.

Carson, Clayborne. *In Struggle: SNCC and the Black Awakening of the 1960s.* Cambridge, Mass.: Harvard University Press, 1981. Definitive history of the Student Nonviolent Coordinating Committee, written from a sympathetic yet constructively critical perspective. Concentrates on SNCC's political and ideological development and internal conflicts, especially the creative tension between individual autonomy and community on the one hand, and pressures for political effectiveness on the other.

Evans, Sara. *Personal Politics: The Roots of Women's Liberation in the Civil Rights Movement and the New Left.* New York: Random House/Vintage, 1980. This study examines how women who questioned their second-class status in the Southern freedom movement and New Left moved toward the creation of an independent women's movement. It includes an original interpretation of the role of Southern white women and the influence of liberal Protestantism in the South. Solidly researched, with skillful use of oral history.

Fager, Charles E. *Selma, 1965: The March That Changed the South.* 2d ed. Boston: Beacon Press, 1985. A vivid account of the Selma voting rights campaign, including its long-term effectiveness in enfranchising Southern black people, by a journalist who participated in it.

Ferber, Michael, and Lynd, Staughton. *The Resistance.* Boston: Beacon Press, 1971. A sympathetic history of the national group that organized noncooperation with the draft in the late 1960s, by two of its key leaders. Extensive use of oral history.

Flacks, Richard. *Making History: The American Left and the American Mind.* New York: Columbia University Press, 1988. Essential reading to understand the broader "left tradition" in which the movements of the 1960s took place, the extent of continuity and change from prior movements, and lessons for the future. Flacks analyzes the historical tensions between "making history" and "commitment to everyday life" that undermine movement-building and suggests ways to overcome this false dichotomy.

Freeman, Jo. *The Politics of Women's Liberation.* New York: Longman, 1975. Supportive but critical political-sociological study of both branches of the feminist movement. Freeman was a founder and theoretician of the radical branch, but her account stresses NOW's contributions and downplays the differences between the two branches. Insightful analysis of structure and organization, especially of what she calls elsewhere "the tyranny of structurelessness" in radical feminist groups.

Friedan, Betty. *The Feminine Mystique.* New York: W. W. Norton, 1963, 1983. Despite its white middle-class orientation, Friedan's famous exposition on 1950s' domesticity is a compelling examination of the various social and cultural forces that pressured women to accept domestic roles and to suppress aspirations beyond home and family.

Garrow, David J. *Bearing the Cross: Martin Luther King, Jr., and the Southern Christian Leadership Conference.* New York: Random House/Vintage, 1988. Exhaustively researched, detailed biography of King and history of SCLC that relies heavily on oral history and FBI transcripts of wiretapped conversations.

———. *Protest at Selma: Martin Luther King, Jr., and the Voting Rights Act of 1965.* New Haven, Conn.: Yale University Press, 1978. The most thorough study of the Selma voting rights campaign and its immediate impact on the drafting and passage of the 1965 Voting Rights Act.

Gitlin, Todd. *The Whole World Is Watching: Mass Media in the Making and Unmaking of the New Left.* Berkeley and Los Angeles: University of California Press, 1980. Incisive historical analysis by a former SDS leader of the unfolding relationship between the New Left and the mass media, concentrating on SDS. Gitlin shows how activists influenced media coverage and how the media shaped the course of the movement, particularly the process by which the media converted leaders into celebrities and uprooted them from accountability.

————. *The Sixties: Years of Hope, Days of Rage.* New York: Bantam, 1987. A combination history and memoir, gracefully written, that explores the growth and development of the New Left, with secondary consideration of the black freedom movement and the origins of radical feminism. Most valuable is the interpretation of the symbiotic relationship between the New Left and the counterculture.

King, Mary. *Freedom Song: A Personal Story of the 1960s Civil Rights Movement.* New York: William Morrow/Quill, 1987. King was a key leader of SNCC whose critiques of "male supremacy" in the movement had a catalytic influence on the birth of radical feminism. Her memoir sheds light on the internal dynamics of SNCC; particularly informative is the inside account of Mississippi organizing, Freedom Summer, and the Freedom Democratic Party.

Koedt, Anne; Levine, Ellen; and Rapone, Anita. *Radical Feminism.* New York: Quadrangle/New York Times Book Co., 1973. An early anthology of radical feminist writings, both experiential and theoretical, that contains some of the most widely discussed feminist essays of the period.

Miller, James. *"Democracy Is in the Streets": From Port Huron to the Siege of Chicago.* New York: Simon & Schuster, 1987. A history of the New Left that focuses on the lives and contributions of several early leaders of SDS. Miller's critical analysis of participatory democracy as an emerging political theory is unequaled. The book goes downhill toward the end when it abandons its grounding in SDS history and, in a celebratory fashion, chronicles the political adventures of Tom Hayden as a seemingly one-man movement.

Morgan, Robin. *Sisterhood Is Powerful: An Anthology of Writings from the Women's Liberation Movement.* New York: Random House/Vintage, 1970. The first collection of radical feminist writings to reach a large audience, Morgan's fine anthology served as a bible for the younger branch of feminism.

Morris, Aldon D. *The Origins of the Civil Rights Movement: Black Communities Organizing for Change.* New York: Free Press, 1984. Morris examines the roots of the freedom movement in earlier organizing efforts and preexisting leadership networks and emphasizes the crucial role of local organizations and especially the black "church culture."

Sale, Kirkpatrick. *SDS.* New York: Random House/Vintage, 1974. The most comprehensive history yet written about SDS, thoroughly researched, with cogent analysis of ideological developments and internal conflicts. Its main limitation is an overemphasis on the national leadership, and lack of close attention to the diversity of local chapters.

Smith, Barbara, ed. *Home Girls: A Black Feminist Anthology*. New York: Kitchen Table: Women of Color Press, 1983. A wide-ranging collection that presents the rich cultural and political diversity of black feminist experience and ideas.

Zaroulis, Nancy, and Sullivan, Gerald. *Who Spoke Up?: American Protest against the War in Vietnam 1963–1975*. New York: Holt, Rinehart & Winston, 1985. To date the only complete history of the antiwar movement; detailed and anecdotal, good use of oral history, with solid accounts of the national antiwar coalitions and internal divisions. It lacks depth of analysis, however, and is unduly critical of the more radical tendencies.

Index